Cultural Sociology

Cultural sociology is widely acknowledged as one of the most vibrant areas of inquiry in the social sciences across the world today. The Palgrave Macmillan Series in Cultural Sociology is dedicated to the proposition that deep meanings make a profound difference in social life. Culture is not simply the glue that holds society together, a crutch for the weak, or a mystifying ideology that conceals power. Nor is it just practical knowledge, dry schemas, or know how. The series demonstrates how shared and circulating patterns of meaning actively and inescapably penetrate the social. Through codes and myths, narratives and icons, rituals and representations, these culture structures drive human action, inspire social movements, direct and build institutions, and so come to shape history. The series takes its lead from the cultural turn in the humanities, but insists on rigorous social science methods and aims at empirical explanations. Contributions engage in thick interpretations but also account for behavioral outcomes. They develop cultural theory but also deploy middle-range tools to challenge reductionist understandings of how the world actually works. In so doing, the books in this series embody the spirit of cultural sociology as an intellectual enterprise.

More information about this series at
http://www.palgrave.com/gp/series/14945

Ron Eyerman

Memory, Trauma, and Identity

palgrave
macmillan

Ron Eyerman
Yale University
New Haven, CT, USA

Cultural Sociology
ISBN 978-3-030-13506-5 ISBN 978-3-030-13507-2 (eBook)
https://doi.org/10.1007/978-3-030-13507-2

Library of Congress Control Number: 2019933319

This Palgrave Macmillan imprint is published by the registered company Springer Nature Switzerland AG
The registered company address is: Gewerbestrasse 11, 6330 Cham, Switzerland

Series Editor's Foreword

Ron Eyerman is a *compleat* intellectual whose extraordinary theoretical breadth, empirical curiosity, and narrative subtlety have played a central role in transforming cultural trauma from a social theory into a research paradigm. Early in Eyerman's career, the Vietnam War veteran turned Swedish self-exile walked the hallways of high theory and philosophy, influenced by Hegel, challenging structural Marxism with notions of reification and subjectivity. Later, bringing his abstract theorizing closer to the earth, Eyerman published studies of new social movements; influenced by Alain Touraine, he developed a new understanding of social movements as culturally engaged and propelled by "movement intellectuals." In the late 1990s, Eyerman leapt from these earlier intellectual involvements into the newly emerging world of cultural sociology, becoming a key player in the international group of social theorists who developed the theory of cultural trauma.

In the two decades since he made that leap, Eyerman has elaborated, revised, developed, and applied cultural trauma theory to an extraordinary wide range of social situations, events, heartfelt sufferings, political tragedies and moral triumphs. What gradually became apparent was that Eyerman had found his America. In one sense, his lifelong voyage of intellectual discovery was over: he had discovered the big problem. In another sense, however, his journey had just begun.

As one deeply researched and theoretically innovative monograph followed upon another, Eyerman showed what cultural trauma could really do. It was not "just a theory," but an enormously productive empirical tool. Eyerman deftly deployed it to wedge open one black box after another: paradoxical responses to centuries of racial oppression; paroxysms triggered by political assassinations; moral, social, and decidedly unnatural responses to natural disasters; enduring wounds from the Soviet massacre of 1,500 Polish military officers and explosive reactions to revelations of its cover-up; how the Holocaust tore at the hearts of Jewish social theorists who did not believe in the Jewish religion; how the searing responsibilities of perpetrator trauma are avoided, as illustrated by the social responses to the My Lai massacre; and America's debilitating, severely polarizing constructed memories of the Vietnam war.

Eyerman is a sophisticated social theorist, but he is also, thankfully, a fact-monger and a story teller, for which his many devoted readers are eternally grateful. In case after case, book after book, article after article, he ingests an enormous amount of empirical detail and proceeds to reconstruct old and new social crises in narrative forms that demonstrate counter-intuitive conceptual arguments in such an accessible manner that they go down like sweet syrup. The insistence that social facts become collectively mediated representations; that social narration is omnipresent; that social conflicts are social dramas; that social suffering and collective memory are inseparable; that affect is central to social conflict; that painful and unexpected events are always transformed into tests for that ephemeral but all-important thing theorists call collective identity and everybody else calls "society"—Eyerman makes all this seem like social life, not social theory. That is his skillful craft.

New Haven, CT, USA Jeffrey C. Alexander

Acknowledgements

This book is truly a collective effort. This is so in the literal sense, as several of these chapters are co-authored, and I thank my collaborators for our discussions and their insights. There are many others to thank as well, such as the shifting members of that movable intellectual feast known as the Center for Cultural Sociology at Yale. Many of the ideas in these essays were formed and tested in the stimulating environment of our Friday Workshops. Nothing written here would have seen the light of day without those discussions. My co-directors, Philip Smith and Jeffrey Alexander, deserve much of the credit, but the real source of all that creative energy are those who over the last 15 years gave so much of their spirit to our collective endeavor. You are too many to name, but you know who you are. I would like to mention Todd Madigan though, who not only co-authored one of the chapters and was a participant at these workshops, but also edited and compiled the index for this volume. Eric Woods agreed to write an afterword that was such a pleasure to read that it helped convince me to carry on. Johanna Esseveld was the first to suggest this project and saw to it that I contacted the editors at Palgrave, first Mireille Yannow and then Mary Al-Sayed. Both were enthusiastic and thus helped make this all possible. Johanna also read every word of every essay and she is my first and best critic!

For Permission to republish these essays, I acknowledge Sage Publications, Fordham University Press, Paradigm Publishers and the editors at the *Croatian Political Science Review*.

Contents

CHAPTER 1

Introduction: Identity, Memory, and Trauma

This book is a collection of essays that develops and applies the theory of cultural trauma. My introduction will outline that theory and describe how it emerged as a fruitful tool for comparative analysis of historical events. The outline is simple: I begin with the origins of the theory, then continue through a series of applications that have turned an concept into a research framework, one that has now reached the level of a paradigm in comparative historical analysis. Finally, I will conclude with a synopsis of the chapters contained in this volume.

As a conceptual framework for analyzing historical events, cultural trauma has its origins in the meeting of a group of sociologists at Stanford University's Center for the Advanced Study in the Behavioral Sciences (CASBS). The group was organized by Neil Smelser, director of the CASBS, and Jeffrey Alexander, then professor of sociology at UCLA, and together we spent the academic year spanning 1999–2000 in the center's bucolic setting. Other members included me (I was associated with Sweden's Uppsala University at that time), Bjorn Wittrock (also of Uppsala), Bernhard Giesen (of Konstanz, Germany), and Piotr Sztompka (of Krakow, Poland). We were brought together to reflect on and develop theories of social integration/polarization, not trauma; however, we soon found that we had nothing very interesting to say about the former, but much to say about the latter. This realization emerged as much from internal group tensions as from a common theoretical understanding or research interest. These tensions were more historical than personal, for once we decided that a sociological conception of

R. Eyerman, *Memory, Trauma, and Identity*, Cultural Sociology,
https://doi.org/10.1007/978-3-030-13507-2_1

"trauma" would be an interesting topic for discussion, an emotional confrontation broke out between Sztompka and Giesen concerning events in Poland and Germany in the aftermath of the Second World War. Giesen (the German) suggested that German refugees forced out of Poland and other parts of Europe suffered from collective trauma. That German suffering could be placed within the same conceptual framework as that suffered by Poles enraged Sztompka (the Pole) and led to a very heated and almost physical confrontation. With the distance of time, I can see now that this incident and the powerful emotions it evoked among serious scholars revealed that we were on to something, that a social concept of trauma connected to collective memory might be an entrée into a fertile field of research. In this way, developing a sociological theory of trauma became our focus. We began to organize our sessions around a new set of readings, which individual members of our group suggested and then took responsibility for presenting. This continued over the course of the year and eventually included invited speakers, such as the Stanford historian Norman Neimark, an expert on genocide, and Kenneth Thompson of the Open University, a leading scholar on the subject of moral panics.

In addition to reading the classical psychological theories suggested and presented by Neil Smelser (a practicing psychoanalyst as well as a sociologist), we read and discussed the more recently developed literary approaches to trauma by Cathy Caruth (1996) and others, including the sociologist Kai Erikson (1994) and the historian Arthur Neal (1998). All this was facilitated by the helpful and accommodating research librarians at Stanford University. In the collective volume we later published (Alexander et al. 2004), Smelser authored a chapter contrasting psychological and cultural trauma. As for myself, I came to the center with a long interest in African American culture, and I used the group as a sounding board for developing a theory about collective identity, collective memory, and the origins of the term *African American*. The theory of cultural trauma that we were developing provided me with a conceptual framework to bring together the various strands of my research into coherent form. This became the basis for my chapter in our collective volume, "Cultural Trauma: Slavery and the Formation of African American Identity" and for the book of the same title I wrote concurrently. Because history intervened, my own book was published in 2001—before our collective volume, *Cultural Trauma and Collective Identity* (2004)—creating a small controversy about the first usage of the term "cultural trauma," as well as my having to reply to many quires concerning my citation of an as-then nonexistent book on cultural trauma as a resource. It was an unforeseen incident that was the cause. As our collectively edited volume was in press, two high jacked airliners crashed into the World Trade Center towers in New York City, and our publisher, the University of California Press, decided that in the wake of that event no book bearing the phrase "cultural trauma" could appear in print without some mention of it. The book was thus delayed so that Neil Smelser could write what is now the epilogue, "September 11, 2001 As Cultural Trauma" (2004b) and a new cover depicting the burning Twin Towers could be created.

The notion of cultural trauma that emerged out of our discussions—and later crafted into a coherent theory by Jeffrey Alexander (2004a) and Neil Smelser (2004a)—provided the framework with which to present the results of our year together. In our co-edited book, Alexander and Smelser offered formalized definitions of cultural trauma that were then followed by case studies applying the concept. Alexander, who in the book's preface offers a slightly different history of our meetings, writes, "Cultural trauma occurs when members of a collectivity feel they have been subjected to a horrendous event that leaves indelible marks upon their group consciousness, making their memories forever and changing their future identities in fundamental and irrevocable ways" (2004a: 1). By placing emphasis on "feeling" and "group consciousness," Alexander laid out a meaning-centered, constructivist path to trauma, as feelings require interpretation and consciousness calls for articulation and representation. After distinguishing psychological- from cultural trauma, Smelser further distinguished social- from cultural trauma, where the latter is defined as a "memory accepted and publicly given credence by a relevant membership group and evoking an event or situation which is (a) laden with negative affect, (b) represented as indelible, and (c) regarded as threatening a society's existence or violating one or more of its fundamental cultural presuppositions" (2004a: 44). Both Smelser and Alexander link cultural trauma to articulation and the social processes that lead to its representation and acceptance. Continuing Alexander's criticism of a "naturalistic" approach to trauma, Smelser argues, traumas are "made not born" (2004a: 37); this was another marker of a constructivist approach to trauma. Thus there were two distinct "others" that a cultural conception of trauma defined itself against. The first was the pathological and individual-oriented notion of trauma that Freud and others had developed. The second concerned the debate within the philosophy of social science between constructivism and realism. In declaring, traumas are "made, not born," Smelser made his position clear: collective trauma required interpretation. Nothing—no matter how powerful or hurtful—was culturally "traumatic" in itself. Interpretation and acceptance are meaning-centered cultural processes that require communication and communicators, what Alexander had identified as "carrier groups." What these groups "carried" was at the time still unclear, but their necessity as agents in the process of trauma articulation and transmission was deemed essential. With this initial presentation of a nonpathological and constructivist notion of cultural trauma, the remaining chapters in the book apply the framework across a range of cases: mine focuses on African American identity formation and stresses collective memory and its narration; Giesen's "Trauma of the Perpetrators" (2004) focuses on the construction of post-Second World War German national identity; Sztompka's "Trauma of Social Change" (2004) develops a model of postcommunist transition with Poland as the example; Alexander's "On the Social Construction of Moral Universals" (2004b) presents a case for historicizing the "Holocaust"; and Smelser's epilogue explores the unfolding trauma processed related to the events of 9/11.

The careful reader of *Cultural Trauma and Collective Identity* will note that the line between constructivist and realist or naturalistic notions of trauma was not easily maintained. The same may be said of the intention to offer an alternative to the pathological notion of trauma of psychoanalysis. In his powerful essay on perpetrator trauma, Giesen uses Freudian terminology to describe the time lag between incident and articulation in the "trauma process," invoking a period of "latency," while Sztompka offers a model for studying societal transition in his examination of Poland's post-communist phase, a model that fits comfortably within the realist traditions of social science. My own chapter on African American identity formation attempts to tread the line running between all these positions. I stress the powerful emotions that the slave condition engendered, while at the same time highlighting the narratives—tragic and progressive—that were constructed by succeeding generations of African Americans as a means to understand and channel those emotions. Such initial lack of consistency and coherence was no hindrance to the innovative discussions that led to the articulation of this framework or to its growing popularity. Sociology, after all, is known for its being multilayered and rife with internal tension. Over the many years of emergence as an academic discipline, the various attempts to impose either conceptual or methodological hegemony have been short-lived.

In spite of—or because of—the innovative tensions built into its original formulation, the theory of cultural trauma has further evolved through an increasing number of applications. After studying African American identity formation, I applied the theory first to political assassination and then to a national catastrophe. In a 2008 book about the assassination of the Dutch filmmaker and political provocateur Theo van Gogh (2008), I operationalize cultural trauma as a public discourse in which the foundations of an established collective identity are brought up for debate. In my book, the identity in question concerned what it meant to be Dutch in the wake of the murder of two highly visible public figures: the charismatic sociologist-turned-politician Pim Fortuyn and his friend and equally provocative van Gogh. In formulating my analysis I combine the theory of cultural trauma with Victor Turner's theory of social drama in order to produce a "performative" account of the van Gogh assassination and its impact on Dutch society. There I define two different senses of cultural trauma. First, referring to Alexander's interpretivist take on cultural trauma, I assert that such a trauma can be thought of as a "tear in the social fabric, which requires interpretation and repair" (Eyerman 2008: 22), to which I add my own perspective, one that runs slightly orthogonal to Alexander's, by claiming that the concept of cultural trauma is also a heuristic that "permits us to set boarders around an occurrence that reaches back into the past and forward into the future" (Eyerman 2008: 164). My claim is not only that such an occurrence "tears the social fabric," but also that this tear must be (1) articulated and represented, (2) "laden with negative affect," and (3) accepted by a group (as Smelser points out).

As in my earlier work on African American identity formation, the role of narration and mediated representation remains crucial to my conceptualization of cultural trauma. My subsequent scholarship turns to the role of the mass media in the emergence of an incident—the "breach" (Turner 1980) or "tear" (Alexander 2004a) that rends the social fabric.[1] This emergence sets in motion a meaning struggle, a process involving competing interpretations of what precisely has occurred, who was responsible, and what should be done to repair the tear. Here one can see the realist (tear in the social fabric) and constructivist (interpreting what the tear means) perspectives combine to produce a "trauma drama" as competing interpretations are aired through various media and social forums. This is the process that the theory of cultural trauma frames and analyzes. It is a process through which collective identity (i.e., who we are) is debated and reformulated and where collective memory (i.e., who we were) is called upon and reformulated.

I followed the book on the assassination of Theo van Gogh with *The Cultural Sociology of Political Assassination* (2011), a book in which cultural trauma provides the framework for a comparative study of six political assassinations. In this book the central question concerns identifying the catalyst to trauma processes, and through the exploration of this question, I show cultural trauma to be a contingent outcome of a powerful and potentially shattering incident (e.g., a political assassination). I researched six assassinations in three different countries where the assassinations had occurred in relative proximity: in Sweden (Prime Minister Olof Palme in 1986 and Foreign Minister Anna Lindh in 2003), the Netherlands (Pim Fortuyn in 2002 and Theo van Gogh in 2004), and the U.S. (Martin Luther King, Jr. and Robert Kennedy, both in 1968). The guiding question in this comparative analysis is this: Under what conditions does political assassination catalyze cultural trauma?[2] I conclude that these assassinations resulted in cultural trauma in the Netherlands and the U.S., but not in Sweden. In my analysis, I isolate several factors whose interplay conditioned this result. These factors are (1) timing, (2) the political context, (3) how authority is performed, (4) the content of mass-mediated representations, and (5) the presence and performance of carrier groups, which include journalists but goes beyond the mass media. For example, the fact that Sweden had not had a political assassination for centuries prior to 1986 and that a second assassination occurred more than a decade later were important factors in explaining why cultural trauma did not occur. Assassination and political violence generally were seen as anomalous and Sweden as exceptional. This is not so in my two other cases. Although the Netherlands shared with Sweden a long history free from political assassination, the critical difference between these two cases is the relatively short period between the assassinations in the Netherlands (only two years compared to 17 years in the Swedish case). Also important was the quick political succession and the symbolic role played by the Swedish and Dutch monarchies in this process. In both cases this proved significant. The U.S., of course, has no such symbolic figure of national unity, but the performance of other public representatives, such as that of Robert Kennedy after King's assassination, still had an impact on the public mood.

In each of the six assassinations I analyze, the mass media was important in either calming or exciting public reaction, and managing this reaction was seen as a central task for those representing the nation. Furthermore, mass media also served as a vehicle for transmitting this symbolic performance of authority, and these representations were key to shaping the meaning of these assassinations, most importantly in addressing the issue of who was responsible and what should be done in response. In the management of public reaction, which was highly emotional and volatile in each of the cases, it was significant that a perpetrator be quickly identified and in the best case be described as either mentally ill or a "lone wolf" (preferably both). This sort of interpretation was thought to have the capacity to minimize public anxiety and check the emergence of the sorts of conspiracy theories that could rile the public. The role of mass media was crucial in the wake of these assassinations, for the various outlets had instant access to a large audience who themselves drew their understanding largely from the mass media they consumed. This analysis—a decade old as of this writing—would probably have to be amended today, as the role of cable television and most especially social media has expanded enormously and could provide the means for alternative explanations.

The next iteration of cultural trauma as a framework for comparative research began with the idea of organizing a two-stage workshop to publish a follow-up to *Cultural Trauma and Collective Identity*. The plan was to broaden the range of cases to show the versatility of the framework, and the result was *Narrating Trauma* (Eyerman et al. 2013). As the title indicates, highlighting the role of narration and the construction of "trauma narratives" reflected a renewed and strengthened constructivist positioning within the theory of cultural trauma. As Alexander and Breese write in their introduction, "Collective traumas are reflections neither of individual sufferings or actual events, but symbolic renderings that reconstruct and imagine them in a relatively independent way" (Alexander and Breese 2013: xxvii). They go on to highlight the role of cultural creators, those who construct the "trauma" in the form of narratives that address the questions, What happened? Who were the victims? Who were the perpetrators? and What can be done? The role of narration and cultural agents—either individuals or carrier groups—had been emphasized from the inception of cultural trauma theory, but in this book the role was highlighted through the exploration of an ever-broadening applicability of our framework. This turn to narrative also focused attention on the means through which these narratives were transmitted. While not all the articles collected in *Narrating Trauma* systematically followed this prescription, the fact that this aspect of the "trauma drama" was more clearly formulated helped redirect, as well as broaden, empirical analysis.

In my own contribution to *Narrating Trauma* (written with Dominick Bartmanski and included in the present volume), "The Worst Was the Silence: The Unfinished Drama of the Katyn Massacre" (Bartmanski and Eyerman 2013) we studied the suppression of narration and its subsequent emergence as a powerful force in social change and the reconstruction of national identity. "Katyn" refers to an infamous site of mass execution where in 1940 more than 15,000 members of the Polish elite were summarily shot then buried in mass graves under the direction of the Soviet secret police. This crime was part of a long-term Soviet strategy to deny postwar Poland qualified leadership. At the time of the killings, the Soviet government had recently concluded a secret agreement with Nazi Germany dividing the projected spoils of Europe at the end of the war. For decades the Soviet leadership denied responsibility for these killings, blaming the Germans when the bodies were uncovered and maintaining that lie for decades. To make this denial possible, public silence had to be ensured, and the few who knew the truth or even suspected it were threatened or killed. Those who carried knowledge of the massacre, the counter-narrative to the government's official position, did so at their peril all through the postwar Soviet occupation. Trauma was thus individualized and privatized, contained within the realm of individual and family memory, yet at the same time kept alive. This trauma only became public—and thus collective—with the emergence of popular movements against the Soviet-supported regime in the late 1970s. "Avenge Katyn" became a powerful slogan in the rising resistance that would eventually put an end to Soviet domination in the 1980s.

I employ a similar focus on narrative and those who create and carry it to study Hurricane Katrina in *Is This America?* which I published in 2015. In this reconstruction of the debate over the "meaning" of what was first described as a "natural disaster," I use newspaper, television, and other journalistic accounts along with artistic and musical representations to reveal a narrative shift to social, rather than natural causes for what had occurred. In the process, I uncover many twists and turns in the narratives about Katrina as a prescripted "severe weather story" that transformed into one of human tragedy and victimhood as media accounts revealed the suffering of those left behind in flooded areas without electricity or adequate food and water. The search for perpetrators began as the "natural disaster" was redefined as ultimately social. The issue of race and poverty was highlighted in the images and stories that emerged, especially from a devastated New Orleans. Media accounts moved from typical, scripted descriptions of suffering to impassioned advocacy as onsite reporters found it increasingly difficult to remain within their professional role as neutral observer; many became rescuer and defender as they covered the plight of a stranded population. With electricity scarce and normal cell phone networks inoperative, the satellite phones and portable generators carried by journalists became the main source of information, even for public officials.

Using the cultural trauma framework to analyze this process of meaning making in the face of great suffering, I raise the question "Trauma for whom?" In addressing the question of whether the hurricane and its disastrous aftermath was cause for cultural trauma (and if so, for whom?), I conclude that the catastrophe called Katrina tested or burst the boundaries of established roles and modes of understanding in several discourses. Mass media coverage of disasters was significantly altered as journalists cast aside their scripts and moved from neutral reportage to advocating for those whose shattered lives they witnessed: "Journalists became public intellectuals, emotionally and politically engaged in what they were meant to report" (Eyerman 2015: 145). Katrina also revealed basic cleavages in American society, bringing racial and class inequality to the public eye. The response to Katrina by public officials—all the way from the police to the president—was cause for great public debate as media accounts of the rescue efforts and "blame game" that followed were filled with the negative attributes that Smelser had pointed to as a necessary aspect of cultural trauma. Katrina was called a "national tragedy" and "national shame" in bold headlines for weeks on end. While this might not have shaken the foundations of national identity, it did raise the question with which I titled my book, "Is this America?" Many wondered how a wealthy and powerful nation could betray so many of its citizens. If not a cultural trauma at the national level, Katrina was surely a blow to the fragile collective identity of African Americans, one more indication of their precarious standing in American society. If this *is* America, what is their place in it? While Katrina will remain a negative sign etched into American collective memory, a symbol of shame and political incompetence, for African Americans it is something more: an indication that the heralded gains of the civil rights movement are more myth than reality. If not at the national level, Katrina was cause for cultural trauma for this group, another powerful reminder of their vulnerability and status in American society. This line of thought, that one could speak of a distinctive "racial memory" in the U.S., along with the idea of a continuous process of cultural trauma among African Americans, was subsequently pursued by Angela Onwuachi-Willig (2016), as I discuss below.

To both highlight and comment on the focus on narration in the understanding of cultural trauma, I wrote "Cultural Trauma: Emotion and Narration" for the *Oxford Handbook of Cultural Sociology* (2012). The aim in this piece is to draw attention to the importance of the individual- and collective emotional reaction to a horrific incident that usually precipitates its narration. This is meant to recall the "realist" aspects of cultural trauma and act as a corrective to the constructivist focus on narrative. Using the example of my studies of political assassination, including an article on Harvey Milk (Chapter 4 in the present volume), I note that all references to "trauma" entail a strong emotional affect; in effect, I am asking, Why employ the term if one seeks to avoid this connotation? I argue that the idea of a specifically "cultural" trauma should embrace rather than abandon this emotional dimension, regardless of whether the root cause of the emotion is "real," (i.e., stemming from something that has actually occurred), or imagined. Of course, such reactions *are* real for those who believe an incident to be real. Citing Smelser once again, cultural trauma is conditioned by "an invasive and overwhelming event that is believed to undermine or overwhelm one or several essential ingredients of a culture or the culture as a whole" (2004a). It is not necessary that such an event actually occurred so long as it "is believed to undermine" a culture or a collective identity. The powerful emotions this belief evokes are real in either case; the emotional response is the basis of any cultural trauma that may follow. To account for this, I refine the understanding of cultural trauma in the following way:

> Cultural traumas reflect deeply felt emotions and identities that are publicly expressed and represented in … discursive process[es], implying an expressive and communicative dimension that makes claims to authenticity and sincerity. The veracity of such claims must be addressed; something which points beyond traditional discourse analysis. More than that, as discursive process, resulting from extreme violence and exposing the deep emotional base that grounds individual and collective identity, cultural trauma is both an articulation/representation of this emotional grounding and at the same time a working-through, a searching attempt at collective repair. (Eyerman 2012: 579)

Invoking the phrase "working through" might seem to rely on psychoanalytic approaches to trauma, but this is not my intention. Rather, the phrase is meant to point to the collective attempts at repairing the torn social fabric and return to some semblance of normalcy in order to carry on. There is nothing necessarily pathological about this, but since this is a process laden with emotion, expressions of individual and collective anger, even violence, are likely to occur. However, there are usually institutionalized processes to call upon in this process, with legal and political procedures coming immediately to mind. Through such processes, emotions can be vented and relieved (the trials that followed some of the political assassinations I study are but one example). Fundamentally, the point of the *Oxford Handbook* article is to remind us of the place of affect and strong emotional response in the development and application of the theory of cultural trauma.

Outside of my own reflections on cultural trauma as a framework for historical and comparative research, others have provided insightful overviews. In the *Routledge Handbook of Cultural Sociology*, Giuseppe Sciortino writes, "the core of the CTP [cultural trauma process] is the analysis of the symbolic processes through which suffering—real or perceived—is inscribed with compelling meaning" (Sciortino 2018). After this concise description, Sciortino goes on to outline several ways in which the "model" has been expended and refined. The first expansion of cultural trauma theory he points to is the incorporation of social performance through the concept "trauma drama." "Traumas have been investigated as intended to achieve effective re-fusion of representation, affect, and widely shared cultural scripts" (Sciortino 2018). As examples he offers Bartmanski's and my study of Katyn (mentioned above) and

Akiko Hashimoto's (2015) examination of the struggle to re-narrate Japanese national identity after their defeat in the Second World War (a piece that is included in the same volume as another by Onwuachi-Willig (2016) who applies cultural trauma in an analysis of the murder of Emmett Till. I will return to this below). With regard to a second way cultural trauma theory has been elaborated, Sciortino identifies those who have "revised the list of potential actors performing the drama" (2018). As examples, he offers Degloma's (2009) study of the rhetorical strategies of "trauma carrier groups," Zhukova's (2016a, b) comparative study of "trauma management" after Chernobyl in the Ukraine and Belarus, and Gao's (2015) study of Mao's China through the lens of cultural trauma and collective identity formation.

I can further elaborate on these new directions. Angela Onwuachi-Willig (2016) not only expands the boundaries in the application of the cultural trauma framework, she, along with Inge Schmidt (2013) and Mira Debs (2013) investigates the more everyday, routine aspects of cultural trauma. Rather than looking at discrete shocking incidents, such as a political assassination or a natural catastrophe, or even a complex "event" like a war or revolution, these authors reveal how the everyday lives of individuals and groups can be usefully analyzed with the aid of cultural trauma. Schmidt develops the idea of "perpetual trauma" to account for the activities and worldview of Mother's Against Drunk Driving (MADD). After an introduction to cultural trauma, Schmidt writes,

> existing theory only addresses trauma in which the trauma process take place after the trauma event occurs. MADD and drunk driving provide an example of a trauma process that is not retrospective but occur in real time. The trauma claim is not in the past tense but instead in present and future tense. (2013: 241)

She then goes on to distinguish "retrospective" from "perpetual" trauma, where the latter are "ongoing, random, tragic events that plague everyday life—such as drunk driving, incurable diseases, or global terrorism" (2013: 243). In addition to "trauma narratives," Schmitt also introduces the idea of "trauma organizations," which expands carrier groups to include formal organizations, like MADD. This work has the effect of linking the study of cultural trauma to social movement studies, another innovation.

Onwuachi-Willig (2016) includes Schmitt in her review of the cultural trauma literature and compares her own extension of the theory to Schmitt's:

> I, like Schmidt, hope to add and enrich the already powerful and resonant body of literature on cultural trauma theory. Unlike Schmidt, however, I do not contest the notions of temporality underlying the theory. Instead I focus solely on past events and their impact, and I seek to extend cultural trauma theory by rethinking the notion that collective and cultural traumas based on past events occur only when cultural expectations are shattered… I reveal how one's position and status in a society, and thus how one experiences certain routine occurrences, can shape the emergence of the cultural trauma process…I argue that the accumulation of routine harms and any corresponding publicity, rather than the disruption of the routine itself, are what enable dialogue about the meaning of the injury and thus the narration of a cultural trauma. (2016: 340)

The harm Onwuachi-Willig refers to above is that inflicted upon African Americans routinely in American society; she argues that this harm is institutionalized and continuous and that specific traumatic incidents, like the notorious murder of Emmett Till in 1955, only reinforce that routinized and cumulative process of collective trauma.

Mira Debs (2012) extends the framework of cultural trauma to include material objects in her study of how the destruction of symbolically charged objects—in this case the Giotto frescoes that were badly damaged during an earthquake in 1977—"created a cultural trauma of objects: the comparable loss of human life, the object's totemic significance to the collective, and the time-frame until the object can be repaired" (2012: 479). Debs focuses on the Umbria-Marche earthquake and the impact on Italian national identity of the damage to the Basilica of St. Francis of Assisi that contained the frescoes. In the process, Debs constructs a model that can be more generally applied, and she thoughtfully provides a list of ten potential cases.

Together with Eric Woods, Debs edited a volume of the journal *Nations and Nationalism* (2013) that contains a section devoted to cultural trauma theory. The two articles that most directly address cultural trauma are Debs's own "Using cultural trauma: Gandhi's assassination, partition and secular nationalism in post-independence India" and Gulay Turkmen-Dervisoglu's "Coming to terms with a difficult past:

the trauma of the assassination of Hrant Dink and its repercussions on Turkish national identity" (2013). In these articles, both Debs and Turkmen-Dervisoglu apply the framework of cultural trauma, especially as regards shocking incidents like political assassinations. Both are concerned with the impact of such incidents on national identity and thus include theories of nationalism in their accounts and highlight the construction of trauma narratives. As Debs explains, "I suggest that the success of these trauma narratives depends on several criteria: the ease of narrating the event, how it is linked to underlying cultural meanings/frames and how the event interacts with historical contingencies" (2013: 635). Revealing how events (in this case political assassinations) become "successful trauma narratives" is the goal of the chapter, and the aforementioned variables are used to show the relative contingency of this "success." Turkmen-Dervisoglu also begins with an assassination—that of the Turkish-Armenian journalist Hrant Dink in 2007—with the aim of addressing the broader question, "Why [are] some nations ... less willing to acknowledge past atrocities [?]" (2013: 674). The past atrocity in this case is the mass killing of Armenians in 1917, sometimes referred to as the "Armenian genocide." In the process, Turkmen-Dervisoglu reveals how collective forgetting is as important to national identity formation as collective remembering. Turkmen-Dervisoglu also extends the notion of cultural trauma into the realm of the perpetrator and collective guilt, a path initially opened by Giesen (2004). The idea of individual and collective forgetting, and perpetrator and collective guilt, is also central to the analysis of the 1963 Birmingham school de-segregation violence by Sandra Gill (2017). Gill uses the cultural trauma framework to reveal how memory and forgetting are intertwined as she analyzes the interviews she carried out with her white high school classmates in one of the schools most affected by the violence.

Ekatherina Zhukova (2016a, b) applies the cultural trauma framework to analyze and compare the attempts to manage affect in the aftermath of the 1986 Chernobyl[3] nuclear catastrophe. As previously noted she expands the dimensions of the theory in the process. One clear innovation is the inclusion of "ontological security" into the cultural trauma lexicon. Zhukova (2016a) argues that the breakdown of the "taken-for-granted" during the meltdown at the nuclear plant included the very ground people walked on. As their natural habitat was contaminated, security quickly turned to insecurity, initiating a process of cultural trauma. In a related article Zhukova (2016b) compares the performance of the responsible political authorities in their attempt to manage the trauma process.

Since its first formulation at the CASBS, the theory of cultural trauma has been applied, expanded, and revised. The seven essays collected here are part of that wider process. They are ordered chronologically from "The Past in the Present: Culture and the Transmission of Memory," first published in *Acta Sociologica* in 2004. Using my work on the construction of African American identity as a basis, the article focuses on the uses of the past for present understanding and action. I show how the memory of past enslavement has been a continuous thread in the attempts to mobilize collective projects at the same time it has been used by others to stigmatize them. Regarding the former I point to the role of black intellectuals in the formation of a positive and self-affirming collective identity under the rubric "African American":

> Slavery is a cultural marker, a primal scene and site of memory in the formation of African American identity. Succeeding generations of African American intellectuals have formed their own sense of identity and mission as they have reflected upon and interpreted its meaning. In the process, they articulated and reconstructed the collective narrative. (Eyerman 2004: 163)

The role of intellectuals in articulating collective identification and representing collective identity is the focus of the article, "Intellectuals and Cultural Trauma" (2011), first published in the *European Journal of Social Theory*. Here I show that the role of intellectuals, broadly understood as those who articulate and represent ideas and opinions to the public, is crucial to the construction and presentation of trauma narratives. Using political assassination as an example, I describe how intellectuals act as a carrier group in facilitating the process of cultural trauma. I then analyze the evolution of the idea and social role of the intellectual.

"Harvey Milk and the Trauma of Assassination," first published in *Cultural Sociology* in 2012, continues this discussion of the impact of political assassination while asking the additional question, Why does a nation remember one victim and not another? The 1978 murder of two public officials in San Francisco's City Hall—the sitting mayor George Moscone and city supervisor Harvey Milk—provides another occasion to study the impact of a shocking incident on both collective identity and collective memory. At the time of their murder, Moscone was the better known of the two victims, but it was Milk's death that has had the most lasting impact and is the most powerfully remembered. I suggest that the role played by the gay rights movement and the power of popular culture representations are the underlying reasons for this.

"Social Theory and Trauma," published in *Acta Sociologica* in 2013, uses the example of prominent intellectuals and scholars (i.e., Max Horkheimer, Theodor Adorno, Sigmund Freud and Zygmunt Baumann) to explore the differences between personal, collective, and cultural trauma. At the same time, I make the claim that these three types of trauma can intertwine and influence one another. Being European Jews confronted with the anti-Semitism of Nazi Germany and the horrors of the Second World War greatly impacted the scholarly work of all four. I use the theory of cultural trauma to illustrate this.

I have already described the next article, "The Worst was the Silence: The Unfinished Drama of the Katyn Massacre," written with Dominik Bartmanski and published in *Narrating Trauma* in 2013. This is followed by "Cultural Trauma, Collective Memory and the Vietnam War," written with Todd Madigan and Magnus Ring and first published in the *Croatian Political Science Review* in 2017. This article is related to a larger book project analyzing the memory of what Americans call the Vietnam War (hereafter referred to as "the War in Vietnam") from the perspective of its three main protagonists. Using the theory of cultural trauma as its framework, this is a study in trauma and collective memory, its impact, and the social processes through which such memory is constructed and maintained. The same framework permits us to address the same sort of comparative question asked in my earlier studies of political assassination, but with a new twist: Which of these three perspectives *on the same event* constitutes cultural trauma?

The final essay collected here also concerns the War in Vietnam, or at least one of its most infamous moments: the My Lai Massacre. The focus here is not on collective memory as much as it is on collective guilt. "Perpetrator Trauma and Collective Guilt" (2018) uses cultural trauma theory to analyze the My Lai Massacre and address the question: Under what conditions can one speak of collective responsibility when soldiers murder defenseless civilians? This well-known event for which an American junior officer was convicted of murder was the only successful prosecution of a war crime during the War in Vietnam. Legal proceedings, whether military (as in the My Lai case) or civilian, most often bring charges against individuals, something that has much to do with the stringencies involved in legal proof. However, there is also the tendency to manage and control the potential damage done to an institution should collective responsibility be sought and established. What responsibility for the actions of this junior officer and those under his command did those higher up the military chain have in the murder of more than five hundred unarmed noncombatants? What about those who designed the policies that put that junior officer in what was described as an “atrocity situation?” The wider reaches of collective responsibility for the actions of those who “kill in your name” constitute the focus of this article. The idea of perpetrator trauma, introduced into discussions of cultural trauma by Giesen in our original 2004 conceptualization is here elaborated once again. Following discussions surrounding the affect of combat, I define perpetrator trauma as moral injury, as something that can be experienced individually as well as collectively. And with this, the progression of cultural trauma has come full circle.

Notes

1. Eventually I would describe the nature of this “social fabric” as the taken-for-granted aspect of a collective identity.
2. Here I conceive of cultural trauma as a public discourse where the foundations of a collective identity are exposed to reformulation.
3. The plant was located near the border between the Ukraine and Belarus.

References

Alexander, Jeffrey. 2004a. Toward a Theory of Cultural Trauma. In *Cultural Trauma and Collective Identity*, ed. Jeffrey Alexander, Ronald Eyerman, Bernhard Giesen, Neil Smelser, and Piotr Sztompka. Berkeley: University of California Press.

Alexander, Jeffrey. 2004b. On the Social Construction of Moral Universals. In *Cultural Trauma and Collective Identity*, ed. Jeffrey Alexander, Ronald Eyerman, Bernhard Giesen, Neil Smelser, and Piotr Sztompka. Berkeley: University of California Press.

Alexander, Jeffrey, and Elizabeth Breese. 2013. Introduction: On Social Suffering and Its Cultural Construction. In *Narrating Trauma on the Impact of Collective Suffering*, ed. Eyerman, Ronald, Jeffrey Alexander, and Elizabeth Breese. Boulder: Paradigm Publishers.

Alexander, Jeffrey, Ronald Eyerman, Bernhard Giesen, Neil Smelser, and Piotr Sztompka (eds.). 2004. *Cultural Trauma and Collective Identity*. Berkeley: University of California Press.

Bartmanski, Dominik, and Ronald Eyerman. 2013. The Worst Was the Silence: The Unfinished Drama of the Katyn Massacre. In *Narrating Trauma on the Impact of Collective Suffering*, ed. Ronald Eyerman, Jeffrey Alexander, and Elizabeth Breese. Boulder: Paradigm Publishers.

Caruth, Cathy. 1996. *Unclaimed Experience*. Baltimore, MD: Johns Hopkins University Press.

Debs, Mira. 2012. The Suffering of Symbols: Giotto Frescoes and the Cultural Trauma of Objects. *Cultural Sociology* 7 (4): 479–494.

Debs, Mira. 2013. Using Cultural Trauma: Gandhi's Assassination, Partition and Secular Nationalism in Post-independence India. *Nations and Nationalism* 19 (4): 635–653.

Degloma, Thomas. 2009. Expanding Trauma Through Space and Time. *Social Psychology Quarterly* 72 (2): 105–122.

Erikson, Kai. 1994. *A New Species of Trouble*. New York: W.W. Norton.

Eyerman, Ronald. 2004. Cultural Trauma: Slavery and the Formation of African American Identity. In *Cultural Trauma and Collective Identity*, eds. Alexander, Jeffrey, Ronald Eyerman, Bernhard Giesen, Neil Smelser, and Piotr Sztompka. Berkeley: University of California Press.

Eyerman, Ronald. 2008. *The Assassination of Theo van Gogh: From Social Drama to Cultural Trauma*. Durham: Duke University Press.

Eyerman, Ronald. 2011. *The Cultural Sociology of Political Assassination*. New York: Palgrave Macmillan.

Eyerman, Ronald. 2012. Cultural Trauma: Emotion and Narration. In *The Oxford Handbook of Cultural Sociology*, ed. Jeffrey Alexander, Ronald Jacobs, and Philip Smith. New York: Oxford University Press.

Eyerman, Ronald. 2015. *Is This America?* Austin: University of Texas Press.

Eyerman, Ronald, Jeffrey Alexander, and Elizabeth Breese (eds.). 2013. *Narrating Trauma on the Impact of Collective Suffering*. Boulder: Paradigm Publishers.

Gao, Rui. 2015. The Paradoxes of Solidarity: Cultural Trauma and Collective Identity in Mao's China. *Society: Chinese Journal of Sociology* 35 (3): 108–134.

Giesen, Bernhard. 2004. The Trauma of the Perpetrators: The Holocaust as the Traumatic Reference of German National Identity. In *Cultural Trauma and Collective Identity*, ed. Jeffrey Alexander, Ronald Eyerman, Bernhard Giesen, Neil Smelser, and Piotr Sztompka. Berkeley: University of California Press.

Gill, Sandra. 2017. *Whites Recall the Civil Rights Movement in Birmingham*. New York: Palgrave Macmillan.

Hashimoto, Akiko. 2015. *The Long Defeat: Cultural Trauma, Memory, and Identity in Japan*. Oxford: Oxford University Press.

Neal, Arthur G. 1998. *National Trauma and Collective Memory: Major Events in the American Century*. Armonk, NY: M.E. Sharpe.

Onwuachi-Willig, Angela. 2016. The Trauma of the Routine: Lessons on Cultural Trauma from the Emmett Till Verdict. *Sociological Theory* 34 (4): 335–357.

Schmidt, Inge. 2013. Perpetual Trauma and Its Organizations: Mothers Against Drunk Driving and Drunk Driving Revisited. *Memory Studies* 7 (2): 239–253.

Sciortino, Giuseppe. 2018. Cultural Traumas. In *Routledge Handbook of Cultural Sociology*, 2nd ed., ed. John Hall, Laura Grindstaff, and Ming-Cheng Lo. London: Routledge.

Smelser, Neil. 2004a. Psychological Trauma and Cultural Trauma. In *Cultural Trauma and Collective Identity*, ed. Jeffrey Alexander, Ronald Eyerman, Bernhard Giesen, Neil Smelser, and Piotr Sztompka. Berkeley: University of California Press.

Smelser, Neil. 2004b. September 11, 2001 as Cultural Trauma. In *Cultural Trauma and Collective Identity*, ed. Jeffrey Alexander, Ronald Eyerman, Bernhard Giesen, Neil Smelser, and Piotr Sztompka. Berkeley: University of California Press.

Sztompka, Piotr. 2004. Trauma of Social Change. In *Cultural Trauma and Collective Identity*, ed. Jeffrey Alexander, Ronald Eyerman, Bernhard Giesen, Neil Smelser, and Piotr Sztompka. Berkeley: University of California Press.

Turkmen-Dervisoglu, Gulay. 2013. Coming to Terms with a Difficult Past: The Trauma of the Assassination of Hrant Dink and Its Repercussions on Turkish National Identity. *Nations and Nationalism* 19 (4): 674–692.

Turner, Victor W. 1980. Social Dramas and Stories About Them. *Critical Inquiry* 7 (1): 141–168.

Woods, Eric, and Mira Debs. 2013. Towards a Cultural Sociology of Nations and Nationalism. *Nations and Nationalism* 19 (4): 607–614.

Zhukova, Ekatherina. 2016a. From Ontological Security to Cultural Trauma: The Case of Chernobyl in Belarus and Ukraine. *Acta Sociologica* 59 (4): 332–346.

Zhukova, Ekatherina. 2016b. Trauma Management: Chernobyl in Belarus and Ukraine. *British Journal of Sociology* 67 (2): 195–215.

CHAPTER 2

The Past in the Present: Culture and the Transmission of Memory

Introduction: On History and Memory

In this chapter I expand on ideas presented in my book *Cultural Trauma: Slavery and the Formation of African American Identity* (2001) where I offer a detailed historical account of the role played by the representation of slavery in the formation of African American identity. The themes of that book took form while I was working with a group of sociologists at the Center for Advanced Study in the Behavioral Sciences (CASBS) at Stanford University over the 2000–2001 academic year. CASBS gathers scholars of different disciplines from around the world and is structured around a collective lunch where one is encouraged to sit with different people each day. This particular day I joined an Israeli social psychologist and an American historian deep in conversation about genocide, which was the academic specialty of the historian. The social psychologist was talking about his youthful experience as an inmate in a concentration camp in Poland during the Second World War and of his encounters with an infamous member of the Jewish camp police working for the Germans. He gave a vivid account of an incident he witnessed of the evilness of this particular person. After quietly listening, the historian politely pointed out that what he was describing could not have happened, as that guard, who was a well-known figure, was not at that camp at that particular time, which could be demonstrated by surviving documents. This shook the social psychologist, but he was sure about his memory and said he could call upon others he knew from the camp

R. Eyerman, *Memory, Trauma, and Identity*, Cultural Sociology,
https://doi.org/10.1007/978-3-030-13507-2_2

who could confirm his story. Still, perhaps because he was a scientist, he appeared willing to consider the claim. Later, the historian told me that in his research on genocide he was often confronted by the difference between narrated memory and documented history.

History began as narrative and as a formative element of collective memory and identity. I'm thinking here about the history of the Trojan War as told not only by Herodotus, but also by Homer. As Hayden White puts it,

> traditional historiography has featured predominantly the belief that history itself consists of a congeries of lived stories, individual and collective, and that the principal task of historians is to uncover these stories and to retell them in a narrative, the truth of which would reside in the correspondence of the story told to the story lived by real people in the past. (1978: ix–x)

However, as history became a discipline and a profession, its linkage with collective memory became more reflective and problematic, limited by the norms of science and the rules of evidence. Still, the narrative form and the poetic intention remains present, even with the focus on documented factuality.[1] White offers an eloquent discussion of the relation between history and memory in which he attempts to resolve the tension by placing both in temporal and socio-political context, that is, in history (1987: 58 ff.).

Sociologists do not often think about memory and not often enough about history (for the exceptions, see Misztal 2003). I want to break a little with that tradition by discussing the centrality of the past and of collective memory in identity formation. My example is drawn from my research into the making of African American identity as framed within the theory of cultural trauma. While rooted in this particular example, my presentation is structured around a more general model, centered on the concepts cultural trauma, collective memory, and narrative.[2]

Cultural Trauma

A comprehensive elaboration of the notion of cultural trauma as a theoretical frame for understanding the development of collective identity can be found in Alexander et al. (2004). I offer only a brief summary here as it relates to my own problems. Like memory, the notion of trauma, or deeply felt emotional response to some occurrence, has both individual and collective connotations. Alexander speaks of a cultural trauma as occurring

> when members of a collective feel they have been subjected to a horrendous event that leaves indelible marks upon their group consciousness, marking their memories for ever, and changing their future identity in fundamental and irrevocable ways. (Alexander 2004: 1)

Most often trauma is conceptualized on the individual level through psychological and psychoanalytical frameworks (for exceptions, see Antze and Lambek [1996] and Bal et al. [1999]). The group of us who worked together at CAS sought a more cultural notion of trauma, a theory that could help account for the emergence of new collective identities in times of social crisis. As opposed to physical trauma, which entails a bodily wound, or psychological trauma, which involves a psychic wound and the experience of great emotional anguish by an individual, cultural trauma refers to a dramatic loss of identity and meaning, a tear in the social fabric, affecting a group of people who have achieved some degree of cohesion. In this sense, the trauma need not necessarily be felt by everyone in a group or have been directly experienced by any or all. While it may be necessary to establish some event or occurrence as the significant "cause," its traumatic meaning must be established and broadly accepted by the group, a process that requires time, as well as mediation and representation. A cultural trauma must be understood, explained, and made coherent through public reflection and discourse. In modem societies, mass-mediated representations play a decisive role. Alexander calls this process a "meaning struggle" and a "trauma process" (Alexander et al. 2004), and when developing this theory we sometimes called it a "trauma drama" when, with the help of mass mediation, the collective experience of massive disruption and social crisis becomes a crisis of meaning and identity. Let me offer the more formal definition of cultural trauma provided by Neil Smelser:

> A memory accepted and publicly given credence by a relevant membership group and evoking an event or situation which is (a) laden with negative affect, (b) represented as indelible, and (c) regarded as threatening a society's [or group's] existence or violating one or more of its fundamental cultural presuppositions. (Smelser 2004: 44)

The point here is that collective identity formation, which is intimately linked with collective memory, may be grounded in loss and crisis, as well as in triumph. In fact, one way of dealing with loss is by attempting to turn tragedy into triumph, something that is one of the common themes or processes in our collaborative studies of cultural trauma (Alexander et al. 2004). This process of cultural trauma formation may take time, especially if the group in question is in a marginal or subordinate position, as is the case with American blacks.

Collective Memory/Collective Identity

As already mentioned, sociologists seldom speak about memory, except perhaps disparagingly as nostalgia. Modernity is characterized by the "tradition of the new," by an orientation toward the future, rather than the past. Central to modernity and to one classical sociological narrative is not only the idea of progress, but also that of freeing both the individual and society from the shackles of the past. As Marx put it with respect to the events of 1848, the burden of the past weighs heavily on the present. Memory is usually left to psychologists and biologists and, more recently, to the newly developed cognitive science. But memory in the form of history and tradition is central to what we mean by society and to all social interaction, which is exactly the point Marx wished to make. Memory provides individuals and collectives with a cognitive map, a map that helps orient them with regard to who they are, why they are here, and where they are going. Memory, in other words, is central to individual and collective identity.

Memory is usually conceived as individually based, as residing inside the heads of individuals. Theories of identity formation and socialization tend to conceptualize memory as part of the development of self and personality. Notions of collective identity that build on this model (e.g., the collective behavior school) theorize a "loss of self," and thus a loss of the constraints of memory (as super ego or ingrained habit) in accounting for collective behavior and the formation of new collective identities. The barrier to memory once crossed, the new collective identity is thought to emerge *sui generis*. A similar notion can be found in the classical Marxian idea concerning the emergence of class consciousness.

The Durkheimian tradition in social thought, on the other hand, has seen collective memory as central to the reproduction of society. This variant of functionalism focuses on collective events, rituals, and ceremonies in maintaining social solidarity. One can thus speak about "how societies remember," as Paul Connerton (1989) does. Within this tradition, collective memory is defined as *the recollections of a shared past that are passed on through ongoing processes of commemoration*. These commemorative processes often take the form of officially sanctioned rituals that recall a group to itself by highlighting a common heritage and a shared past.[3] Such processes are as much physical and emotional as they are cognitive in that the past is both embodied and recalled through such cultural practices. Here individual memory is conceived as derivative of collective memory. It is the collective memory that orients a group, providing the temporal and cognitive map mentioned above. Collective memory unifies the group through time and over space by providing a narrative frame, a collective story, which locates the individual and his and her biography within it, and which, because it can be represented as narrative and as text, attains mobility. The narrative can travel, as individuals travel, and it can be embodied, written down, painted, represented, communicated, and received in distant places by isolated individuals who can thereby be united culturally, if not physically, with the collective.

This process links collective memory to the formation of collective identity and brings it close to myth and to ideology. In her discussion of the role of photography in the representation of pain, Susan Sontag writes:

> Strictly speaking, there is no such thing as *collective* memory—part of the same family of spurious notions as collective guilt. But there is collective instruction. All memory is individual, irreproducible—it dies with each person. What is called collective memory is not a remembering but a stipulating: that *this* is important, and this is the story about how it happened, with the pictures that lock the story in our minds. Ideologies create substantiating archives of images, representative images, which encapsulate common ideas of significance and trigger predictable thoughts, feelings.[4] (2003: 85–86)

This explanation renders the lines between the discipline of history and collective memory sharp and distinct.

The Present as an Unfolding of the Past

From this perspective, the past is a collectively shaped, if not collectively experienced, temporal reference point that is formative of a collective and serves to orient those individuals within it. The past becomes present through symbolic interactions, through narrative and discourse, with memory itself being a product of both, "called upon to legitimate identity, to construct and reconstruct it" (Antze and Lambek 1996). While the past may be embodied in material objects, in the way a town or city is structured, or in the arrangements in a museum that are laid out to recall aspects of the past in a particular way, what the past means is always recounted, understood, interpreted, and transmitted through language and through dialogue. These dialogues are framed as stories, narratives that structure their telling and influence their reception.[5] All nations and groups have founding myths, stories that tell who "we" are through recounting where "we" came from. Such narratives form master frames and are passed down through traditions, including rituals and ceremonies, the public performances that reconnect a group and confirm its membership. Within this process "we" are remembered and "they" are excluded.

These founding narratives can be compared to discourse in Foucault's sense, especially as developed in *The Archaeology of Knowledge* (1972).[6] Where Foucault's discourses, at least as developed in this work, impose order from above and outside through disciplinary knowledge, narratives are less institutionalized, more open and malleable. Discourses offer what Stuart Hall and others in the Birmingham School call the "preferred readings" of texts in that they structure the possibility of telling and impose interpretation, producing the very objects to which they refer. In this way, discourse is said to link established power and ideology, to unify and legitimate, a diverse set of practices, thereby "establishing" a "system of relations" (Dreyfus and Rabinow 1982: 65). Even in literary fields and popular culture, discourses can be silently at work in terms of selectivity, sorting out those authors and texts that express the ideologies and values of the dominant culture. And it is precisely these authors and texts that are most likely to get published and to be read and discussed.

Both narrative and discourse have in common that they are framing structures which include and exclude, voice and silence, conditioning what can be seen and said and by whom. As opposed to Foucauldian discourse, however, collective narratives leave more room for individual agency even as they provide the framework through which individual stories gain wider meaning. While discourses are exercises in power and empower those rightly positioned, narratives can provide means for a "counter-story" for a minority or an oppressed group, in which some of the central concepts of a dominating discourse can be appropriated and given new meaning. An example is the concept of "race," which was appropriated and revalued by American blacks in their struggle to redefine their standing in society. Even here, however, those more powerful "representatives" of a marginalized group can exert a discursive influence in seeking to define how their groups should be represented.

In many instances founding narratives involve a dramatic, traumatic, occurrence from which the collective is said to emerge. In this, such narratives might be compared to myths, but they lack the all-embracing and ontological scope with which myth is usually associated. This "primal scene" is usually given positive connotation, but it can also be negative.[7] In all cases, however, it is powerful in the sense of being emotionally compelling. Founding narratives are about creating, constituting, a collective subject as much as they are about creating an "imagined" community. This process is usually studied at the level of nation states and nation-building, but I have applied it in the study of social movements and, most recently, in the study of an ethnic minority, black Americans. For the latter, a generational perspective complementing the concepts of cultural trauma, collective memory and narrative was helpful.[8]

Cycle of Generational Memory

Cultural trauma calls attention to the negotiated recollection of events and to the role of representation. There is power involved here as well, including that of political elites and mass media. This power is exercised in myriad ways, one of the most salient being through selecting what will be represented and what will not, which affects what will be remembered, as well as what will be forgotten. In the case of extremely powerful occurrences, like civil wars, there may be additional factors at work. Interpreting events may take time and a certain amount of emotional distance. Where there are winners and losers, the losers may never get their side told, or they may have to wait, sometimes even for generations.

In their study of Spanish representations of the Spanish Civil War, Igartua and Paez (1997: 83–84) list four factors in the generational cycle of memory: (1) the existence of the necessary psychological distance that remembering a collective or individual traumatic event requires; (2) the necessary accumulation of social resources in order to undergo the commemoration activities; (3) the progressive aging and the selective remembering/forgetting of those involved; and (4) the effects of this aging process on sociopolitical repression. These factors will be useful to keep in mind in what follows.

African American Collective Memory

The memory of slavery is a cultural marker, a primal scene, and a site of memory in the formation of African American identity. Succeeding generations of African American intellectuals have formed their own sense of identity and mission as they have reflected upon and reinterpreted its meaning. In the process, they articulated and reconstituted the collective narrative. The American Civil War ended in 1865 with the victory of the Union Army and the promise of emancipation as proclaimed by President Abraham Lincoln in his famous address of 1863. This ultimately resulted not only in the formal freeing of all slaves, but also in the occupation of the defeated South and institution of its Reconstruction. A central plank in this rebuilding process was creating the conditions of full citizenship for black Americans, including education for the young and active political participation for adults. The future, not the past, was the focus. The first generation of black intellectuals took form in the 1890s after what is broadly seen as the failure of Reconstruction and the reestablishment of formal segregation in the South through Jim Crow practices, as well as continued informal segregation in the rest of the nation. The meaning of the past and the memory of slavery were back on the agenda as reconciliation between North and South produced a new notion of "white-ness" in the backlash against Reconstruction. In the dominant narrative, the Civil War was reframed as a civilizing war and slavery as benevolent for blacks.

Although the black intellectuals who articulated this failure and attempted to counter this process could themselves be considered the fruit of Reconstruction and its educational policies, the crushing of raised expectations set in motion the process of cultural trauma, which involved reevaluating the past in a search for new foundations. Those who thought they would be fully fledged Americans were then forced to consider themselves as a marginalized group; in the process, and among several alternatives, the notion of "*African* American" emerged.

Two aspects of identity formation can be noted here: the creation of a collective subject and the shift of collective identity from the local community to the national and international level. Central actors in this process included Booker T. Washington, the former slave and founder of the Tuskegee Institute specializing in applied education and advocating the idea of self-help. His chief rival for the position of leading African American intellectual was the Northern-born, Harvard-educated sociologist W. E. B. Du Bois, partisan of the idea of the "talented tenth," an avant-garde made up of the highly educated that would lead black Americans along the path from the margins to the center.

Both Washington and Du Bois saw cultural politics as the chief means of gaining acceptance in American society, especially since traditional politics was essentially closed to black Americans. Du Bois propagated the idea that one could be both African and American, loyal to the nation, but not to its racist culture. Washington favored self-help and relatively autonomous, economically independent black communities. Common to both was the notion that slavery produced a unique opportunity for black Americans, providing a culture and personality and a distinctive racial mission. Slavery was, in their view, a stepping-stone to racial progress. This central idea laid the foundations for a "progressive" narrative that would be formative for the second generation of black American intellectuals.

In addition to these intellectuals, popular culture also played a formative role in the creation of the collective consciousness of this generation. The narratives of former slaves constituted the first form of black American literary expression to gain popular appeal, first as part of the anti-slavery Abolitionist movement, then as more commercialized adventure stories. Black-faced minstrel shows were extremely popular at this time, but entertainment producers also began using black performers by the end of the century. The first black novelists and poets also emerged, giving voice to a new perspective on American society, even though they were constrained by the literary genres and tastes of the dominant culture. Most important of all, perhaps, was the emergence of a distinctive folk music, the blues. This music provided a form through which black subjectivity could be publicly expressed. The blues was the singular form that could express both the collective in the individual and the individual in the collective, the "I" as well as the "We." Lines such as, "I woke up this morning, there was sorrow on my mind" are classic in the blues, as is the unspoken understanding that the "sorrow" is a collective, as well as individual, experience. Even unreconstructed intellectuals like Du Bois could locate themselves in this music, though many of the talented tenth found it too closely connected to a past they wanted to transcend, if not entirely forget. Such forms of expression transmitted the memory of slavery across generations, as it did across the expanse of the U.S. as it followed the paths of newly freed black labor.

The conditions and events that were formative for the second generation of black intellectuals after the Civil War include the participation of black Americans in the First World War and the demographic shifts that followed in its wake. Millions of blacks left rural areas and agricultural labor to find work in the urban centers of both the North and South. This Great Migration and the often-violent reactions it caused (the race riots of 1919 are a notorious example), fundamentally changed representations of black experience, where the meaning of slavery and the reinterpretation of the African past were central. These changes were also conditioned by the development of mass media beyond the printed word. The black press, which had emerged during slavery and exploded since emancipation, afforded an important collective voice that was now supplemented by radio, film, and the recording industry, forces that helped define the 1920s as the Jazz Age and the urban black as a "New Negro." The white American public became curious about the new centers of black life in cities such as New York, Chicago, St. Louis, and Kansas City. "Slumming" in white-only nightclubs located in black neighborhoods like Harlem became a defining factor in this "discovery" and commercial exploitation of black musical forms, like blues, jazz, and their accompanying dances. With these artistic innovations, it appeared that blacks had "proved" themselves worthy, at least at the level of popular culture. However, before this all collapsed in the economic depression of the 1930s, two narrative frames solidified in the discourse on the black experience since slavery: the *progressive* and the *redemptive*.

These can be illustrated through two exemplary quotations:

> Someone is always at my elbow reminding me that I am a granddaughter of slaves. It fails to register depression with me. Slavery is sixty years past. The operation was successful and the patient is doing well, thank you. The terrible struggle that made an American out of a potential slave said "On the line!" The Reconstruction said "Get set," and the generation before me said, "Go!" I am off to a flying start and I must not halt in the stretch to look behind and weep. Slavery is the price I paid for civilization, and the

> choice was not with me. It is a bully adventure and worth all that I paid through my ancestors for it. (Hurston 1928; see Watson 1995)

> We are the descendants of men and women who suffered in this country for two hundred and fifty years under the barbarous, the brutal institution known as slavery. You who have not lost trace of your history will recall the fact that over three hundred years ago your fore-bearers were taken from the great continent of Africa and brought here for the purpose of using them as slaves.... They suffered, they bled, they died. But ... they had a hope that one day their posterity would be free, and we are assembled here tonight as the children of their hope.... Each of you has a duty which is incumbent upon you. A duty that you must perform.... No grander gift can I bear to the sacred memory of the generation past than a free and redeemed Africa. (Garvey 1994 [1922]; see Van Deburg 1997)

The first quotation is by Zora Neale Hurston, a central figure in the Harlem Renaissance and the New Negro movement. Hurston was raised in an all-black town in Florida before moving to New York where she studied anthropology at Columbia University with Franz Boas and Melville Herskovits. Hurston is now well known as an ethnographer and collector of folklore. In this citation, she articulates the central notions of what I call the progressive narrative, which takes slavery as a starting point for progressive development and eventual inclusion in modern society. The second is from Marcus Garvey, founding leader of the largest popular movement in black American history. An admirer of Booker T. Washington, Garvey was born in Jamaica and made his way to New York by way of England and the Tuskegee Institute, where he arrived only weeks before Washington's death. His Back to Africa movement sought to restore pride and glory to blacks through redemption in the home country. These became the guiding ideas for all succeeding black nationalist movements.

Formative for the third generation of black American intellectuals was the Second World War and the second wave in the Great Migration, as well as the postwar prosperity that ushered in a youth-oriented consumer society and accompanying mass culture. The progressive narrative provided the framework through which the civil rights movement emerged. Begun in the mid-1950s after the landmark decision by the Supreme Court that confirmed the right of blacks to equal educational opportunities, and spurred on by black youths from segregated institutions of higher learning, the civil rights movement was largely Southern-based and religiously framed. It found its exemplary leader in Martin Luther King, Jr., a Baptist minister who gave voice to key aspects of the narrative: ever-greater inclusion in American society's dominant institutions through good works. King was able to dramatize everyday activity through linking it to religious themes long present in the black church. His speech flowed from a long history of subtle resistance transcribed into religious metaphor, both spoken and sung. Extremely powerful in the South, and also when televised to a wider audience, this type of cultural politics and political performance faltered as the movement moved northward into the much tougher conditions of the North's urban ghettos. A modernized, urban-based Black nationalism, spurred on by a new vision of Africa and its anti-colonialist movements, as well as by a reinvigorated Nation of Islam exemplified in the figure of Malcolm X, combined to revitalize the redemptive narrative.

These two representations of the black American collective, those framed through the progressive and redemptive narratives, competed for support among American blacks, a meaning struggle in which the mass media played a significant role. And the role of the mass media was made even more significant as it served to provide interpretations of black American narratives to the dominant white society. The newly developed medium of television played a major role in this case. It is not by chance that Martin Luther King, Jr. and Malcolm X became the exemplary figures they did, for both performed as well on camera as they did before a live audience. In the trajectory of the civil rights movement, one can trace a convergence of the two narrative frames, and in the aftermath, their reconciliation and institutionalization in Black Studies programs at colleges and universities across the U.S.

Conclusion

My aim in this chapter has been to outline a theory of cultural trauma with reference to the meaning and place of slavery in the formation of African American identity. My focus on representation is not meant to downplay or underestimate the real suffering or costs this involved. I have linked collective identity formation with collective memory, seeing memory as a signifying practice and a cornerstone of group identity. The notion of an "African American" emerged as part of the efforts of a generation of black intellectuals to come to grips with their collective rejection by American society after being promised full integration following the end of the Civil War. Slavery, not so much as personal experience, but as a form of collective memory, was a focal point in this process. At the same time, the dominant white society was occupied with reinterpreting the war that had torn the nation in two, and in the process slavery was consigned to the margins, along with the former slaves, themselves. This marginalization was seen as necessary for the reconciliation of a nation that had been torn asunder. For black Americans, this reconciliation meant a crisis of identity and identification. Who were these people, who were neither white nor fully accepted Americans? It was here that the notion of an *African* American was put forward, along with the idea of a *New* Negro a little later. Succeeding generations of American blacks have collectively formed themselves and renegotiated their relationship to the dominant society with slavery as an ever-present backdrop. This process occurred within the traditional arena of politics through organizations like the National Association for the Advancement of Colored People (NAACP) and established political parties, as well as through social movements and other extra-institutional means. It also occurred in the cultural arena, through struggles for representation and recognition. In all these arenas the past was always present.

The issue of the historical veracity, or fit, between the narratives and real experience remains to be explored. This in fact is part of the point of the opening anecdote concerning the often-problematic relation between history and memory. That inherited frameworks of meaning or interpretation don't "fit" a new situation is something commonly discussed in the sociological study of science in relation to crises in theory and explanation, or in the study of ideologies and their fit or reception with respect to particular social groups or classes (Eyerman 1981). Some of these issues are relevant here. The awaking of the civil rights movement in the mid-1950s occurred within the framework provided by the progressive narrative. As the movement stagnated in the South and moved northward, its focus on progressive integration as much as its principled use of nonviolence, seemed to many to be wrong or impossible in the new context. Some argued that neither the tactics nor the narrative framework of the civil rights movement fit the new situation or the new groups who were to practice them. Other frameworks and tactics were called upon to challenge the place of the civil rights movement's progressive narrative as the dominant mode of understanding. This created another form of crisis, an internal struggle to—in Erving Goffman's phrase—"define the situation" (1999) and deal with it accordingly. This, however, does not mean that the progressive narrative should be considered false or mistaken, as in the case of our social psychologist whose memory could be shown to be in error through the calling upon historical documents. Frameworks of meaning and interpretation cannot easily be falsified and rejected in this manner. They are more like the metatheoretical presuppositions that make generalization and trans-situational understanding possible. In this sense, and in the current example, such frameworks, like Kantian categories, make thinking the collective possible. There is, however, a level of pragmatism here in the sense that both narrative frames imply forms of practice, both in the long and short term. The progressive narrative implies a long-term strategy of social integration in that it aims at overcoming social marginalization. The redemptive narrative, on the other hand—especially as articulated by the young Malcolm X in his polemics against the impossible dream of integration—also has an implicit temporal dimension: How long must one wait to see who is right? One of the most famous phrases used by Martin Luther King, Jr. in his sermons was, "How long?" While for him this was a rallying cry to protest within the progressive narrative, at least at first, for Malcolm X the answer was already implicit in the question: "No longer!"

At another level of meaning, the concept of narrative can be applied directly in reference to experience.[9] In discussing the purpose and significance of the Truth and Reconciliation Commission hearings in South Africa, the writer Njabulo Ndebele (1998) is hopeful that "the narratives of memory" that are brought forth will help establish a more truthful understanding of the history of apartheid. He writes:

> time seems to have rescued the imagination. Time has given the recall of memory the power of reflection associated with narrative … narratives of memory, in which real events are recalled, stand to guarantee us occasions for some serious moments of reflection. (1998: 20)

Here, narrative is directly connected to experience and critical reflection. It is a "guarantee" and check against established discourses of power. I would call this a moral or social narrative (Cairns and Roe 2003) in that the stories constructed here are located in reference to a particular normative perspective from within which events make sense. This way of thinking is not far from the Hegelian-Marxism as developed in the early works of Georg Lukacs and the Frankfurt School (Eyerman 1981), where some dynamic event—a trauma perhaps—broke the flow of everyday life and created the possibility for critical reflection in the wake of crisis.[10] The keyword here is "critical," for criticism depends upon having some kind of perspective or standpoint from which to judge. In this more commonsensical usage, narratives are stories, in Ndebele's case true stories, which give an account of events through structuring them within a meaningful framework. There is a truth claim implied here, as such accounts can be shown to be false or mistaken, just as in my introductory anecdote. But there is a transcendent moment implied as well, in the sense that the same facts may be interpreted differently depending upon the narrative frame. For example, the American War in Vietnam could be seen as another colonial war, as many American antiwar activists saw it, or as a war for peace and democracy, as many in the American government saw it. In either case, the same number of people died. One can imagine the same in South Africa. My usage of narrative moves between these levels, the rooted commonsensical and meta-theoretical; like the notion of paradigm as developed by Thomas Kuhn, it aims to capture both the continuity and dynamism in the frameworks of understanding that guide social practices. Such narratives are both subject to the counterclaims rooted in notions of success and failure and resistant to them.

Notes

1. There are at least two distinctions and restrictions involved here. The first is to distinguish history from poetry, as did Aristotle, and the second is to regulate what type of event could properly be included as a way of separating "fact" from "fiction."
2. Bal et al. (1999: viii) distinguish three types of memory: habitual, narrated, and traumatic. Habitual memories are those taken-for-granted rules learned in childhood that guide everyday practices; narrated memories are loaded with affect, "surrounded by an emotional aura that ... makes them memorable" (1999: viii); and traumatic memories are the "painful resurfacing of events of a traumatic nature" (1999: viii). The best summation of the theories of memory and remembering can be found in Misztal (2003).
3. Working within this tradition, yet modifying it to some extent, Barry Schwartz defines collective memory as "a representation of the past embodied in *both* historical evidence and commemorative symbolism" (2000: 9). This definition allows for the distinguishing of individual and collective memory, in that collective memory is embodied in texts

and practices that have a supra-individual character. It also allows the inclusion of documentary evidence in discussions of memory, which distinguish collective memory from myth.

4. Sontag provides an eloquent discussion of the role played by images—particularly photographic images—in stirring feelings and affecting memory. She writes: "Perhaps too much value is assigned to memory, not enough to thinking.... History gives contradictory signals about the value of remembering in the much longer span of collective history. There is simply too much injustice in the world. And too much remembering ... embitters. To make peace is to forget. To reconcile, it is necessary that memory be faulty and limited" (2003: 115). In this book, she also criticizes her own previous work *On Photography* (1977) for some of its claims regarding the effects of images on memory and emotion.
5. Wertsch (2002: 55 ff.) discusses the role of narrative in relation to individual and collective memory. For him, narratives are part of a necessary and all-pervasive "tool kit" that humans use to make sense of themselves and their history. He makes the point that while narratives are universal, they are at the same time particular, rooted in "the particular cultural, historical, and institutional settings in which we live" (2002: 57). Wertsch also makes the useful distinction between the referential and dialogic function of narratives. In the former, narratives make reference to real or fictional events; in the latter, narratives refer to other narratives. In terms of another useful distinction, Muller distinguishes between collective or national memory and mass individual memory, where "the latter refers to the recollection of events which individuals actually lived through" and the former "establishes a social framework through which nationally conscious individuals can organize their history" (2002: 3).
6. I am aware that Foucault shifted his position regarding the imposing power of discourse (see Goldstein [1994] for discussion) and of the difference between archaeological and genealogical analysis in his methodology (Dreyfus and Rabinow 1982: 104 ff.). This shift is also discussed in Misztal (2003).
7. Narratives contain endings as well as beginnings, and this framing may also affect the selection and interpretation of events included in the story line. For a thoughtful discussion of this, see Wertsch (2002: 57 ff.). He also discusses tragic and progressive narratives.
8. Muller (2002: 13) discusses the role of memory in nation-building and applies a generation approach in attempting to answer the question as to why memory has become so important in recent times. He goes so far as to speak of a paradigm shift in the humanities and in the discipline of history in particular.

9. The distinction made by Muller between national and individual memory—and their use by "individuals in political reflections and decision-making processes," (2002: 3)—is pertinent here. Relevant also is his discussion of the individualization of history in Germany in the aftermath of the Second World War.
10. On the role and meaning of "crisis," see Habermas (1975) and John Keane, for whom "crisis periods ... prompt awareness of the crucial political importance of the past for the present. As a rule, crises are times during which the living do battle for the hearts, minds and souls of the dead" (quoted in Muller 2002: 3).

References

Alexander, Jeffrey. 2004. Toward a Theory of Cultural Trauma. In *Cultural Trauma and Collective Identity*, ed. Jeffrey Alexander, Ronald Eyerman, Bernhard Giesen, Neil Smelser, and Piotr Sztompka. Berkeley: University of California Press.

Alexander, Jeffrey, Ronald Eyerman, Bernhard Giesen, Neil Smelser, and Piotr Sztompka (eds.). 2004. *Cultural Trauma and Collective Identity*. Berkeley: University of California Press.

Antze, Paul, and Michael Lambek (eds.). 1996. *Tense Past: Essays in Trauma and Memory*. London: Routledge.

Bal, Mieke, Jonathan Crewe, and Leo Spitzer (eds.). 1999. *Acts of Memory*. Hanover: University Press of New England.

Cairns, Ed, and Michael Roe. 2003. *The Role of Memory in Ethnic Conflict*. Basingstoke: Palgrave.

Connerton, Paul. 1989. *How Societies Remember*. Cambridge: Cambridge University Press.

Dreyfus, Herbert, and Paul Rabinow. 1982. *Michel Foucault: Beyond Structuralism and Hermeneutics*. Chicago: University of Chicago Press.

Eyerman, Ronald. 1981. *False Consciousness and Ideology in Marxist Theory*. Highland Hills: Humanities Press.

Eyerman, Ronald. 2001. *Cultural Trauma: Slavery and the Formation of African American Identity*. Cambridge: Cambridge University Press.

Foucault, Michel. 1972. *The Archaeology of Knowledge*. London: Tavistock.

Garvey, Marcus. 1994 [1922]. Africa Is for Africans. In *The Portable Harlem Renaissance Reader*, ed. David Lewis, 1994. New York: Penguin Books.

Goffman, Erving. 1999. *The Presentation of Self in Everyday Life*. New York: Anchor Books.

Goldstein, Jan (ed.). 1994. *Foucault and the Writing of History*. Oxford: Blackwell.

Habermas, Jurgen. 1975. *Legitimation Crisis*. Boston: Beacon Press.

Hurston, Zora. 1928. How It Feels to Be Colored Me. In *The Harlem Renaissance*, ed. Steven Watson, 1995. New York: Pantheon.

Igartua, Juanjo, and Dario Paez. 1997. Art and Remembering Collective Events: The Case of the Spanish Civil War. In *Collective Memory of Political Events: Social Psychological Perspectives*, ed. James W. Pennebaker, Dario Paez, and Bernard Rim. Mahwah, NJ: Lawrence Erlbaum Associates.

Misztal, Barbara A. 2003. *Theories of Social Remembering*. Maidenhead: Open University Press.

Muller, Jan-Werner (ed.). 2002. *Memory and Power in Post-War Europe*. Cambridge: Cambridge University Press.

Ndebele, Njabulo. 1998. Memory, Metaphor, and the Triumph of Narrative. In *Negotiating the Past: The Making of Memory in South Africa*, ed. Sarah Nuttall and Carli Coetzee. Cape Town: Oxford University Press.

Schwartz, Barry. 2000. *Abraham Lincoln and the Forge of National Memory*. Chicago: University of Chicago Press.

Smelser, Neil. 2004. Psychological Trauma and Cultural Trauma. In *Cultural Trauma and Collective Identity*, ed. Jeffrey Alexander, Ronald Eyerman, Bernhard Giesen, Neil Smelser, and Piotr Sztompka. Berkeley: University of California Press.

Sontag, Susan. 1977. *On Photography*. New York: Farrar, Strauss, and Giroux.

Sontag, Susan. 2003. *Representing the Pain of Others*. New York: Farrar, Strauss, and Giroux.

Van Deburg, William (ed.). 1997. *Modern Black Nationalism*. New York: New York University Press.

Watson, Steven. 1995. *The Harlem Renaissance*. New York: Pantheon Press.

Wertsch, James. 2002. *Voices of Collective Remembering*. Cambridge: Cambridge University Press.

White, Hayden. 1978. *Tropics of Discourse*. Baltimore: Johns Hopkins University Press.

White, Hayden. 1987. *The Content of the Form*. Baltimore: Johns Hopkins University Press.

CHAPTER 3

Intellectuals and Cultural Trauma

Introduction

This chapter begins with a discussion of the role of intellectuals in the process of cultural trauma and concludes with a more general discussion of the possibility of the intellectual in contemporary society. In order to do that, I will first have to say how I conceive of these two concepts and the relation between them. The intellectual can be analytically distinguished from the intelligentsia and those who perform intellectual labor (Eyerman 1994). As is well known, the term "intellectual" came into common usage with the Dreyfus affair in France (1894–1906), during which the novelist Emile Zola wrote a politically charged open letter in a popular periodical. In the public controversy that followed this crossing of the boundary between culture and politics, Zola was accused of being a *mere intellectual*, a publicity-seeking dilettante, a popularizer who degraded cultural values in seeking a wider audience. One can see continuity in today's debate about the public intellectual, where academics are accused of crossing some imagined line between scholarship and popular writing, a point I will return to in the concluding section. In response, the term "intellectual" became a *nom de guerre* and a role to be played for those who wished to do public battle with the establishment, regardless of whether they were cultural or political figures. The idea of the intelligentsia is historically older, having roots in sections of the Russian and Polish elite in the mid-nineteenth century that identified itself with European modernity and defined itself in opposition to both

R. Eyerman, *Memory, Trauma, and Identity*, Cultural Sociology,
https://doi.org/10.1007/978-3-030-13507-2_3

the established powers and those "mere intellectuals" (Gerstein 1974). The intelligentsia achieved even greater social cohesion in taking on the missionary task of bringing enlightenment to what it considered the darker regions of Eastern Europe and Central Asia. It is a concept perhaps most useful in contexts where there exists a great disparity between the literate and the illiterate, the educated and uneducated. Conceived of as an academic (as opposed to political) category, the idea that the working population could be divided between intellectual labor (by those who produce knowledge and work with their heads) and manual labor (by those who produce goods and work with their hands) emerged in both political and academic discourse as an attempt to operationalize the concept of the intellectual. Those seeking to identify a material and objective basis for empirical investigation have projected the idea of intellectual-labor-as-the-defining-characteristic-of-the-intellectual backwards in time by (e.g., it has served as a means of distinguishing various strata of the middle class). The intellect is here treated as a source of income and status and intelligence as a personal attribute, a form of rent-bearing property (i.e., human capital). From this perspective, one may speak of intellectual types, as well as distinguishing intellectual from manual labor (Baert and Shipman 2011).

Common to these three variations is the attempt to define the intellectual in terms of a distinct social category or field and to make some judgment about function and behavior. In the 1920s, Julien Benda railed against the "treason of the intellectuals," as in his eyes this social group was not fulfilling its proper role as social reformers and critics. Antonio Gramsci distinguished "organic" and "traditional" intellectuals on the basis of their role in social change as much as on their allotted class position. Similarly, though more academically, Karl Mannheim dissected the historical position of the intelligentsia and the intellectuals as "free-floating" in the class structure. Decades later, Alvin Gouldner (1979) spoke of the intellectuals as a new class, to which Georgy Konrad and Ivan Szelenyi (1979) added the phrase "on the road to class power." John Goldthorpe (1982) proposed an opposing view, one that positioned intellectuals as a "service class" with conservative rather than radical political orientations.

In this chapter, I conceive of the intellectual as embracing the performance of a social role, one that involves the articulation of ideas communicated to a broad audience through a range of media and forums with the aim of influencing public opinion. In this understanding, artists, journalists, playwrights, and novelists, as well as factory workers writing for a union magazine can be intellectuals, while college professors and other intellectual laborers are not intellectuals in the normal course of their day. To paraphrase Gramsci's famous dictum, from the viewpoint of human potential everyone is an intellectual; who actually performs the role and becomes one is determined by social conditions. I will return to these social conditions in the concluding paragraphs.

How the intellectual-as-social-role is understood is contingent upon cultural traditions, often within a national frame. The French appear to have a fairly clear idea of what an intellectual is; as one Swedish pundit put it: "I don't know what an intellectual is, but I know the French have them." While it might be clear to the French why Jean-Paul Sartre is an intellectual, it is less clear what being an intellectual might mean in the American context. During the debate surrounding the war in Vietnam, an American vice president spoke disparagingly of "quasi-intellectuals" who opposed his government's policies, sentiments Great Britain's Margaret Thatcher would later echo against those who criticized her economic views. This is to apply the term intellectual in a slightly different way than in the original context of the Dreyfus affair, and some of the recent discussion of "public intellectuals" follows this line of thinking. Calling someone a "quasi-intellectual" at least gives some positive status to "real" intellectuals, while seeking to deny those seen as pretenders to that title (Mrs. Thatcher was to claim there were no "real" intellectuals in the UK).

Rather than taking a normative position or offering a generic definition, I define the intellectual in terms of a social role, that of articulating ideas, including problems and their solutions, in public discourses. Thus, the intellectual is neither a fixed social stratum nor a special attribute of gifted individuals; it is an emergent role constructed and performed by actors out of cultural traditions in historical contexts. This implies at least two ways of speaking about and studying the intellectual. The first is to look at the way in which various social actors take on the task of articulating ideas in public discourses. The second is to study how particular persons aspire to and perform as an intellectual, a role whose meaning they inherit as part of a tradition yet must reinvest in new and changing historical contexts. In this chapter, I will focus primarily on the first, but I will also make some reference to the second, especially in the conclusion. From this perspective, articulating ideas in a restricted public arena in a proscribed role, such as that of an elected political representative presenting an ideological argument in parliament, is not an intellectual role; however, the same person presenting the same argument in an open public debate, such as in a newspaper op-ed article, intentionally takes on the role of the intellectual. This gives the concept of the intellectual more fluidity, especially in social terms, and allows one to avoid both deterministic structuralism and a focus on unique individuals.

Cultural Trauma

By cultural trauma I mean a discursive response to a tear in the social fabric, a period when the foundations of an established collective identity are shaken by a traumatic occurrence and are in need of re-narration and repair (Alexander et al. 2004; Eyerman et al. 2011). Cultural traumas can be distinguished from the more commonly understood notions of trauma, which refers to either a physical or psychological wound. In this traditional use of the term, trauma is related to a personal experience that shocks the system, be it the mind or body. Such experience can be individual or collective, but being "traumatized" is usually restricted to the experience of individuals. Cultural traumas, on the other hand, are made, not born (Smelser 2004). While a shocking incident, like an assassination, may be necessary, the accompanying horror, anger, and grief must be narrated and represented in compelling ways. In this sense, cultural trauma can be understood as a meaning struggle, where individual and collective actors attempt to define a situation by imposing a particular interpretation on it. Intellectuals play a central role in this discursive process; they are important actors in articulating what happened, who was responsible, who the victims were, and what is to be done (Alexander 2004). Intellectuals help interpret the meaning of an occurrence, turning it into an *event*, something not only meaningful, but also significant. In illustrating this point I will draw upon recent research on political assassination. In my *The Cultural Sociology of Political Assassination* (Eyerman 2011), I compare the assassinations of Martin Luther King, Jr. and Robert Kennedy in the U.S., Olof Palme and Anna Lindh in Sweden, and Pim Fortuyn and Theo van Gogh in the Netherlands. The question I address is: In which of these cases did political assassination, a traumatic occurrence, lead to or exacerbate cultural trauma? In this chapter, I will use some specific examples from that book to elaborate on the role of the intellectual.

Making an *Event*

It might be thought that a political assassination is a significant event simply by having occurred. Yet, what constitutes an assassination, even a murder for that matter, is something that must be discursively established, and not only in a legal sense. Articulation, reconstruction, and representation are crucial to this process, and in the contemporary media-saturated society, journalists and other professionals play a central role. It is worth noting that journalists and journalism were of crucial importance in the classical understanding of the intellectual. Lenin's famous "What is to be done?" concludes with a call to start a journal, and much of Gandhi's early influence came through a journal he wrote for, though it would be stretching it to call Lenin and Gandhi professional journalists. In this connection, one can problematize the relation between routine professional activity and the role of the intellectual by asking what a journalist does in the performance of his or her job. Professional journalists perform an intellectual function when they narrate an occurrence (e.g., the murder of a public figure) and help turn this occurrence into a significant event (e.g., a political assassination). It is not so much that such occurrences are "media events" (Dayan and Katz 1992) (e.g., events made historic through television and other mass media), but rather that occurrences become understandable and then significant only through scripted narration and coded representation. In contemporary society, it is the mass media that provide these first accounts of an occurrence and make them available to a broad audience. Yet journalists are not intellectuals merely by dint of their occupation. In order to fulfill this function, journalists must shift from their typical role to something slightly different, such as when they themselves pose as "experts" in situations outside their normal work activity (e.g., when they write op-ed articles, blogs, or appear on mass-mediated panel discussions). Bloggers and blogging sites may well be considered a new forum of the media intellectual, influencing public opinion through private networks, a point I will return to.

Even as it is reconstructed through mass media, an occurrence like an assassination is not a significant event until it is accepted as such by an audience. I define political assassination as the killing of a representative figure that engages a community. This feeling of commonality and identification with the victim may well be emergent and constitutive, realized through the act of murder and the collective emotion it evokes. Here again mass media play a central role. To create such engagement, there must be some fit, some common understanding between the narration provided by journalists and their readers or viewers. The story, in other words, must be understood and resonate with those to whom it is addressed. The accounts provided through mass media thus must be constructed in such a way that they are meaningful and emotionally compelling for a particular audience. This audience, however, may be multilayered and complex, opening the possibility of different interpretations, but the frames used and the themes drawn upon are usually well-known prescriptions.

This adds another culturally specific element to the role of the intellectual. If the intellectual is understood as someone who articulates ideas and gives form to feelings, then the representative forms through which this occurs must be understandable to those at which they are aimed. In their role as intellectuals, journalists draw from a generally available yet often culturally specific reservoir of frameworks and story lines in providing their account of an occurrence. Let me give some examples to concretize what I mean. When Swedish Foreign Minister Anna Lindh was stabbed in a shopping mall in central Stockholm in September 2003, media accounts made immediate reference to the murder of Prime Minister Olof Palme, which had occurred seventeen years prior. Other references included the attack on New York's World Trade Center, now universally known as *9/11*, as Lindh died on September 11 from wounds sustained in the attack on the previous day. The fact that she had been a protégé of Palme, had spoken at his funeral, and was the mother of young children and the wife of another prominent Swedish politician were also themes which framed the narration of her murder. Her youth and promise, as well as her family ties were highlighted, leading one editorial commentator to state, "This feels worse than the Palme murder … Lindh was young and cheerful. She had most of her life in front of her" (*Kvallsposten*, September 12, 2003). There are several deep-seated cultural references here, including some that refer to Swedish history and others with a more universal grounding, like the reference to motherhood, youth, and promise. Lindh's murder was shocking and its narration compelling in part because it drew upon such themes. Narrative frames like these enhanced the significance of this murder of a political representative beyond the national community, helping turn it into a global event. Those narrating this incident, transforming it into something meaningful beyond the mere reportage of fact, performed an intellectual role, the role of mediating and translating an occurrence into an event of significance that went well beyond mere local interest.

Another group that sometimes takes on an intellectual role through its discursive construction of a significant event are those experts—academic, legal, and otherwise—who appear in the media to offer their opinions and interpretations of an occurrence. These representative figures are called upon to explain and enlighten a broad audience, and in the process they articulate various viewpoints in filling out the story as it is being constructed. And through this role, they can contribute to the process of cultural trauma formation. In all the cases of political assassination I studied, national and international political leaders, academics, and legal practitioners and scholars appeared in the mass media to express their views on the meaning of these occurrences. For that short moment, they were intellectuals. The same can be said of those personal acquaintances and friends of the victims, many of whom were well placed in the media and other culture industries, who wrote books and articles and appeared in the visual media to present their views about the victims and the meaning of their deaths. In the normal course of affairs, they were professionals of one sort or another—filmmakers, novelists, journalists, and so on—but when they appeared in the mass media or published their books and articles, they took on the role of the intellectual. To this can be added those with a professional rather than personal interest in shaping interpretation, such as the authors of biographies of the victims and accounts of the incident, as well as visual artists who in some form represent the occurrence. In the normal course of the day, all these individuals might be authors and artists, but in contributing to the public interpretation of an incident like the death of a representative figure, they took on the role of the intellectual.

There is a clear relational tension between the role of the expert, the professional, and the intellectual. Professions are connected to earning a living, to intellectual labor, and material interest, even as they imply a moral code of behavior that is meant to both temper and legitimate the pursuit of material gain. Like intellectuals, professionals define themselves as independent of outside influence, but unlike intellectuals they do so in order to speak in the interest of a client. Performing the role of expert or intellectual is somewhat autonomous of monetary and material concerns and may or may not imply a moral code of conduct. The constitutive field between the poles of the intellectual, the expert, and the professional can be understood as rooted in the tension between performing intellectual activity as either a form of communicative action or a form of intellectual labor (Arendt 1953; Habermas 1989). The former is part of the role and self-perception of the intellectual, the latter that of the professional. As the American writer and editor Irving Howe once expressed it in a debate concerning his role as an intellectual and his job as a college professor: "The problem [is] not how intellectuals earn their living, a social necessity, but whether they devote at least part of their skills to the political and cultural emancipation of humanity" (as paraphrased in Wald 1987: 324). How one understands emancipation is of course itself a matter of controversy.

From Event to Cultural Trauma

If professionals and experts become intellectuals when they contribute to public discourse about the meaning of an incident, intellectuals and the performance of the intellectual role are also important carriers and facilitators in the process of cultural trauma. In the conceptualization I have offered here, cultural traumas are public discourses in which the foundations of a collective identity are brought up for reflection, as happens, for example, in the wake of triggering incidents like political assassinations. As I have just suggested, such incidents must be narrated and framed as significant and understood as such by a collectivity. Intellectuals and professionals are central to this process, where phrases like "national trauma," "crisis," and "tragedy" are readily applied in mediated representations. In all the assassinations I studied, newspaper headlines were filled with such phrases; on editorial pages historians, social scientists, and other "experts" drew parallels with other already acknowledged significant occurrences, and medical professionals gave advice about possible long-term effects on the public's mental and physical health. After the murder of Anna Lindh, for example, the Swedish media presented expert and professional advice on how parents should talk to their children about the incident. However, it should be noted that not all political assassinations lead to cultural traumas. In these cases—as in any other such event—professionals taking on an intellectual role are significant actors in determining the result. The crisis caused by a political assassination can be managed in such a way as to prevent a spiraling into cultural trauma. Journalists can narrate the incident in a way to promote healing, rather than fanning the flames of discontent. National unity can be highlighted in what is potentially a fragmenting and polarizing situation (Pantti 2005; Panitti and Wieten 2005). Political authorities and legal professionals can perform their authoritative role in a more or less successful way, quelling and calming emotions or arousing and mobilizing them. In so doing they take on the role of the intellectual as they attempt to influence a wide range of audiences.

In the six cases of assassination I explore in *The Cultural Sociology of Political Assassination*, only in Sweden did a cultural trauma not emerge. I identify several factors that help explain this: the timing of the occurrence, the political context, how authority was performed, the type and quality of mass media representations, the presence of powerful carrier groups, and their performances. For a discussion of the role of the intellectual, the performance of authority, the style of mass media representations, and the presence and performances of carrier groups are most interesting. The performance of authority concerns more professionals than intellectuals, though there is some overlap. Important professionals in managing this sort of crisis and the process of cultural trauma itself are political authorities, such as elected officials and leaders of political parties, lawyers and judges, police officials, religious and other community leaders, as well as journalists and newscasters. In many cases, media accounts helped create a sense of national unity in a tense situation through presenting displays of collective mourning, with photos, videos, and interviews of grieving citizens, spontaneous memorials, and the like. Some accounts, however, fan the flames of anger and appear to encourage partisan reaction, or at least fear and mistrust. This was especially the case in the U.S. and the Netherlands, where collective violence was also a prominent reaction to the murders of Fortuyn, van Gogh, and Martin Luther King, Jr. Elected officials, religious leaders, and other symbolic figures, such as presidents, prime ministers, and members of the royal family (in Sweden and the Netherlands) were important actors in representing the nation and calling for calm and unity. Media images were filled with pictures and texts from these representative authorities. At the same time, there were representative figures who sought to use these assassinations for their own political gains, such as the followers of Pim Fortuyn in the Netherlands who sought to build not only on the wide public sympathy in the immediate aftermath of his death, but also by those who claimed to pick up his mantle and carry on in in the aftermath of his death. What's more, there were those, like Amsterdam mayor Job Cohen, who would later run for the prime minister post on the basis of his role in calming emotions and fears in the aftermath of the van Gogh assassination and those like Geert Wilders who opposed him by claiming the legacy of Fortuyn for himself.

The form and content of mass-mediated representation are additional significant factors in the development of a crisis into a cultural trauma. Here the articulating and representational role of the intellectual is crucial. How the murder of a political figure was framed, written about and visually represented was a significant factor in how these incidents were interpreted and reacted to. The headline of a popular Dutch newspaper after the death of Theo van Gogh read "Butchered" in bold letters (*De Telegraaf*, November 3, 2004). This exclamation was placed above the dramatic photograph of the victim's body lying in the open street with the knife and note through his chest, with an inserted black frame containing the headline "Exactly 911 days later," a reference to the time between van Gogh's and Fortuyn's murder and the attack on New York's World Trade Center, now a universal symbol of terrorism. To the left of this was a photographic portrait of van Gogh and the words "Horror and anger follow the murder of van Gogh." This "horror and anger" was intensified by reportage of the arrested perpetrator, identified as a Muslim fundamentalist and terror suspect. Conspiracy reigned, though it was never legally established. Many "experts" were then called upon, reporting through various media forums from newspaper interviews to television interviews and panel debates, to explain the meaning of this incident. While this was presented in the form of rational debate, the cumulative effect of the focus on the victim as a Dutchman and the perpetrator as a Muslim terrorist was to polarize into for and against, an easy choice for most of the audience (Eyerman 2008). All those participating were performing an intellectual role. The reference to 9/11 was different in this representation than in the Swedish one previously mentioned in the assassination of Anna Lindh. In Lindh's case the link made to the attacks on New York's World Trade Center was made through the date, as Lindh died on September 11, 2003, with the most likely intention of drawing a similarity to the grief felt by the nation for the victims. In the Dutch case, attention was drawn to the ideological motivations of the perpetrator, his immigrant background, and to an implied threat of terrorist attack. The Swedish and Dutch cases reveal two very different associations aimed at stimulating very different emotional reactions in their respective audiences.

The presence, placement, and relative strength and commitment of carrier groups are very important factors in determining whether a traumatic incident will develop into a cultural trauma. Included here would be the presence of already formed or potentially emergent collective actors, such as social movements, advocacy, and other pressure groups. Carrier groups attempt to influence the representation and thus the meaning of an incident like a political assassination, and in so doing they take on the role of the intellectual. Such agents, individual or collective, are active after the fact and are thus also concerned with how an incident and the victim will be remembered. Such carrier groups play an intellectual role and are often composed of those whom many would consider intellectuals. After the murder of Theo van Gogh, a group of his friends and colleagues organized themselves as "The Friends of van Gogh" with the aim of influencing the representation and public memory of his death. This group was composed of individuals with already-established and well-positioned roles in spheres of cultural production, such as scriptwriters, authors, and journalists. They wrote articles and books, gave interviews, and helped see to it that a memorial was erected in an Amsterdam park near the site of the murder. In their eyes, van Gogh was a martyr to free speech, and this is the message etched onto the aforementioned memorial. Van Gogh himself made a feature film on the murder of his friend Pim Fortuyn, and it is one of those historical ironies that he was murdered on his way to the studio where he was working on this film. In addition to filmmakers like van Gogh, those who attempted to influence the reception and memory of the death of Fortuyn include the political party that he founded and the popular movement that emerged around his persona. That party produced leaders and representative figures that acted as intellectuals in their attempts to represent and carry forward what they say Fortuyn's heritage was. They acted as interpreters and translators of that heritage, and, as communicators to a new public; they performed the role of the intellectual.

The accounts of journalists, photographers, artists, and authors serve not only to propel the meaning struggle which ensues after a traumatic incident like a political assassination, but also function to preserve the memory of the person and keep the circumstances alive in the public mind. At the same time, they do this from a particular point of view. They are part of the meaning struggle, offering a partisan as well as a moral framework within which to interpret this incident as an event.

As such, they can be considered part of the emotional acting out and working through, which are essential aspects of the cultural trauma process. As Felman and Donnelley (2002: 4) point out, trials can have much the same function, where the courtroom becomes a "theater of justice" and a social space for the reenactment of trauma. The trial and sentencing of alleged perpetrators in political assassinations are significant events in themselves, but they are also significant for the restoration of order and legitimacy. Even though it was clearly established that Sirhan Sirhan had murdered Robert Kennedy—and both the prosecution and defense attorneys were ready to plea bargain in order to avoid a long and costly trial—the presiding judge denied their appeal. A public trial was necessary, he stated, because the public needed it, especially since they had been denied a trial after the murder of John F. Kennedy, the former president and Robert's older brother. A public trial, even with the outcome a foregone conclusion, is a cathartic event where collective emotions can be vented. At the same time, the trial of a political assassination is also a display of civilization—of civic virtue—a vital aspect of what Jeffrey Alexander (2006) calls the civil sphere. In performing public displays of civility through their professional roles, lawyers, judges, and others perform an *intellectual* role in the processes of civic repair, though one would be hard pressed to call them *intellectuals*. Those journalists narrating these actions, framing them into a story, are closer to being intellectuals, as are the legal experts who add expert and insider commentary to these accounts in the mass media.

The Shifting Role and Possibility of the Intellectual

I have highlighted the role of the intellectual in articulating meaning and the making of events in relation to the theory of cultural trauma. Let me conclude with a more general discussion of the changing role and place of the intellectual in contemporary society. The connection between these two—intellectuals and cultural trauma and the role of the intellectual today—lies in the widespread belief that being an intellectual is no longer possible. In other words, there is a consensus that the social and cultural conditions that in the past made the intellectual possible have been irrevocably shattered, giving rise to a great sense of loss. All current discussions of the "public intellectual" are couched within this feeling of great transformation, and though this does not qualify as a cultural trauma, it does imply a meaning struggle around related issues, identifying who or what is responsible, who are the perpetrators, and who are the victims.

In a classic text on the subject of the intellectual, Regis Debray (1981) divided a genealogical account of the French intellectual into various ages of what was essentially a struggle for recognition for a distinct mode and type of being in the world. The three ages Debray identifies are rooted in the means for producing this recognition: the university, the publishing world, and the media. This periodization is more graphically captured in the English title of his book *Teachers, Writers, Celebrities.* The role of the mass media in shaping the very possibility of the intellectual is thus clearly acknowledged, though with an added sense of degradation: what was once a distinguished quest for recognition through displays of intellectual brilliance has now been reduced to sound bites and fleeting fame. The idea of the decline, disappearance, and crisis of the intellectual is by now a cliché′. However, I believe there is an important point being made here: significant changes in the context in which the role of the intellectual is made possible have greatly affected, if not entirely undermined, the traditional meaning of the term. This is the case, Debray suggests, even in France, where that meaning appears to be most clear and stable. This idea underlies some of the criticisms raised against the notion of a public intellectual, where the latter is understood as an established scholar, professional, or expert using his or her reputation in one field to make interventions in another field in full public view. Thus, Posner (2001) provides a long list of so-called public (not to say *quasi-public*), intellectuals who, in his eyes, have strayed from their professional expertise and embarrassed themselves by their public statements in other areas of knowledge than their own. The new context I would identify is the breaking down of the hegemony over the means of intellectual production and recognition by new forms of mass communication, which are much more decentralized and personalized. This leads to a central question: What is the role of the in the age of digitalized media?

The new digital age has clearly impacted the role of the intellectual; becoming an "intellectual" celebrity or a celebrity intellectual is today not limited to an occasional appearance as a talking head on a popular television discussion program as it was when Debray wrote his book. Of course, it is not only the appeal of celebrity status offered by such mediated appearances that worries Debray; it is also that the new mass media shifts the basis of power from the producers to the distributors of intellectual material. We have a new situation today, I believe, where cable television, local radio, and the internet have shifted this power back in the direction of the producer. The articulating role of the intellectual is now more readily available, as anyone with internet access can start a blog, as well as read and comment on those of others. There is a hierarchy here, of course, and also some obvious celebrities, but the hegemony of centralized distribution as channeled through the state or large commercial corporations has been greatly undermined since the 1970s when Debray was writing. These means of communication have produced their own celebrities, many of whom are far from the traditional type of intellectual. Local radio and cable television in the U.S. has produced argumentative celebrity figures like Glen Beck and Bill O'Reilly, two conservative media intellectuals with a mass following. While O'Reilly currently limits himself to televised social and political commentary, writing crime novels, best-selling books, and speaking tours, Beck is one of the leading representatives of what many consider a new social movement, the Tea Party, which is currently[1] a powerful force in American politics. Without formal academic credentials, Beck is known for his lengthy rambling speeches on American social and political history, speeches that are then recorded and distributed in both print and video. He is the owner of a media production company and thus can produce and distribute his own goods, this in addition to his widely popular syndicated radio and television shows and the online university that bears his name. While political opponents deride Beck as someone who "says what people who aren't thinking are thinking" (Jon Stewart, another very popular media intellectual), his followers say otherwise. As one put it, "He is doing the research. He is teaching us" (both quoted in *The New York Times Magazine*, October 3, 2010, pp. 37–39). The attempt to put into words—and into an ideological framework—what others are merely feeling is central to the role of the intellectual as classically understood. What has changed is not only the rhetorical devices used in this articulation, but also the way it is composed, packaged, and distributed. The messages put forward are often composed by production teams and delivered with the aid of the internet, as well as through the commercially sponsored networks. Those who can now perform the classical role of the intellectual need not have any of the credentials that appeared necessary to their forbearers. Today's media intellectuals (Jacobs and Townsley 2004) need not be men or women of letters, credentialed academics, or professionals posing as experts. They can be those like Beck, gifted monologists with access to new as well as traditional mass media who can capture the emotions of an audience. Perhaps this is just another example of what Richard Hofstadter (1962) called the "anti-intellectualism in American life," another form of American anti-establishment populism. There are certainly distinctly American aspects to figures like Beck and O'Reilly, for the scripted rhetoric and the images they draw upon reflect aspects of American life and culture (Norton 2018). Beck and O'Reilly, each in their own way, reflect a particular masculinity that might also have distinctive cultural roots: the teary-eyed emotionalism of Beck and the gruff, straight-talking, steely eyed mannerism of O'Reilly appear to speak to particular desires and images of their American audience. The French, with their own set of markers of masculinity and unique cultural desires, would presumably do it differently. However, in the Netherlands, the assassinated Theo van Gogh played a role that was not so dissimilar to that of Beck and O'Reilly. Gruff, unshaven, overweight, with a cigarette always close at hand, van Gogh made films and wrote newspaper columns that were later turned into books, all of which were meant to provoke. He was an artist playing an intellectual role in a tense political environment, and when he pushed the boundaries he was continually testing, it got him killed.

Being an intellectual in the contemporary setting is certainly not only the province of men, though the examples I have chosen might seem to suggest that. The question of whether or not it is possible for a woman to be an intellectual is one often raised, most recently by Evans (2009). The new media and means of communication offer more possibilities for women and minorities to play the role of the intellectual. Blogging, both in its individual and more formal, collectivized forms, is much more open than the insider networks, usually male-dominated and white, which defined earlier eras of intellectual performance in Western societies. Among the new media intellectuals in the U.S., one can find prominent women, from Ann Coulter on the right to Rachel Maddow and Arianna Huffington on the left. One side in a recent divisive debate concerning a proposed mosque in New York City was led by a single mother of four, through a website and a blog funded through advertisements.

Though one can raise questions about the quality of the intellectual content in these new media, as well as in the mass media generally, I believe there is something fundamental at play here. A real change in the material basis of the means of intellectual production has occurred that has permanently altered the performance of the role of the intellectual. To be sure, a more traditional idea of the intellectual is still around, even in the U.S., as is evidenced by the ongoing usage of the term and most particularly the debate regarding the public intellectual. Something has changed, however, as access to the means of intellectual recognition and opinion making has opened more widely. Is this a question of decline, as many books on intellectuals have suggested? It clearly is if one takes a normative position and understands intellectuals as "those with superior gifts to wield the power of the written word" (Diggens 2003: 91). From this perspective those persons and personalities just mentioned would most surely qualify as quasi-intellectuals and not the real thing. If, however, one takes a more neutral stance and understands the intellectual as a role aspired to and taken on, the answer is not as easy. Clearly these media intellectuals articulate sets of ideas and communicate them to a broad audience through a range of media and forums with the aim of influencing public opinion, and thereby satisfy the definition of the intellectual role I offered at the beginning of this chapter. By those criteria they are intellectuals, though a distinction can be made between "playing at" and "being"; while both imply an understanding of what an intellectual is, *being* an intellectual further involves a conscious effort of *becoming*. That is, to be an intellectual one must aspire to the role in a meaningful way. Calling oneself an artist, for example, implies awareness that this denomination involves expectations of quality and ability; it is not open to merely anyone. Even in the digital age of open access, traditional notions of the intellectual exist, and while they do not limit access to aspirants to the articulating role of the intellectual, qualitative judgment is still possible. Thus one can speak as I do of "media intellectuals," qualifying the ascription and distinguishing the role from aspiration and acknowledgment.

Another aspect of this change worth considering relates to the question of audience. If the role of the intellectual is entwined with the intention of influencing public opinion through learned ideas, one needs to ask not only about the quality of those ideas and their representation, but also about the composition of "the public" being addressed. Who constitutes "the public" in the digital age? Who is the audience of a blog? What is the assumed relation between sender and receiver? What is the assumed response or outcome? One traditional understanding of the intellectual is that of articulating, and thus simultaneously shaping, what others are feeling. In order for this to occur, there is not only a presumed end in view, but also some common ground on which to build, a foundation involving reciprocal expectations. The intellectual, in other words, addresses a known audience, either as an "organic" member of a particular group or class, or, in a more "free-floating" capacity, speaking to a known audience from what is presumed to be a more neutral position. Who is the audience for today's media intellectuals and what is their relation to that audience? What is the position from which they speak? How do we identify the public in the digital age and how is public opinion shaped? The audience for today's media intellectual is more uncertain than it was for intellectuals in Debray's other ages. Though blogging may be a form of interactive mediated conversation, there is a level of anonymity on both sides of the communication process—that of both the sender and the receiver—that was not present in earlier mediated interactions. This entails less personal responsibility and accountability for what is said. It also potentially creates a very different relationship between the parties, one where rumor and innuendo may dominate, where the force of personality, repetition, and orchestration can more easily replace the force of the better argument. One of the most prevalent techniques of presentation of the media intellectuals mentioned is bombast, the shouting down and intimidating of the listener. In this sense, much of our contemporary talk radio and "opinionated" television is as much entertainment as anything else, where "brand is everything" (a television executive, quoted in Sherman 2010: 30).

While the personality of the speaker and being entertaining were never totally excluded from the traditional role of the intellectual, it was never the main point. The form of presentation was thought to be appropriate to the topic and to the presumed intelligence of the intended audience. The position from which the media intellectual speaks is thus different from that of the traditional intellectual. In the latter, the intellectual spoke from a moral, political, or intellectual high ground, which, it was claimed, permitted him or her to see more clearly. There is of course a form of elitism implied here, but this was often tempered by the form of presentation, by the desire to communicate and convince without offending and alienating. Of course, media intellectuals vary in their positioning vis-à-vis their audience: not all blogging is ungrounded and not all opinions are presented through bombast. The possibility of a reasoned reply is made more difficult, however, in a situation where the senders are few and the receivers are potentially in the millions. Arguments can be presented in a forceful, emotional way without the chance of reply and the likelihood of a "culture of critical discourse" (which Alvin Gouldner saw as formative of intellectuals—both as individuals and as a community), is minimal. It was this community reared in a culture of critical discourse that functioned as a form of quality control. It was this that helped make the intellectual, as a form of being in the world, a role worth aspiring to.

Being an intellectual is also a matter of being recognized as such. Media intellectuals put heavy emphasis on "media" and less on "intellectuals." In fact, in the tradition of American anti-intellectualism, media intellectuals like Beck and O'Reilly view intellectuals with disdain, labeling them with pejorative terms, like "pinheads" (the title of a best-selling book by O'Reilly). While aspiring intellectuals like C. Wright Mills moved to New York City in the 1940s to be at the center of intellectual life, a world of small literary magazines and radical politics, Beck and O'Reilly moved to New York to be at the center of media production, the world of radio and television. For those whose medium is the internet, there is no center to move to: they can work from home in any locality. While media intellectuals may perform a similar role as the more traditional intellectual, the quality of that performance leaves much to be desired.

Note

1. In 2011, the time of the original publication of this piece.

References

Alexander, Jeffrey. 2004. Toward a Theory of Cultural Trauma. In *Cultural Trauma and Collective Identity*, ed. Jeffrey Alexander, Ronald Eyerman, Bernhard Giesen, Neil Smelser, and Piotr Sztompka. Berkeley: University of California Press.

Alexander, Jeffrey. 2006. *The Civil Sphere*. Oxford: Oxford University Press.

Alexander, Jeffrey, Ronald Eyerman, Bernhard Giesen, Neil Smelser, and Piotr Sztompka (eds.). 2004. *Cultural Trauma and Collective Identity*. Berkeley: University of California Press.

Arendt, Hannah. 1953. *The Human Condition*. New York: Doubleday.

Baert, Patrick, and Alan Shipman. 2011. Transforming the Intellectual. In *The Politics of Knowledge*, ed. Fernando Rubio Dominguez and Patrick Baert. London: Routledge.

Dayan, Daniel, and Elihu Katz. 1992. *Media Events*. Cambridge, MA: Harvard University Press.

Debray, Regis. 1981. *Teachers, Writers, Celebrities*. London: New Left Books.
Diggens, John Patrick. 2003. The Changing Role of the Public Intellectual in American History. In *The Public Intellectuali*, ed. Richard M. Zinman, Jerry Weinberger, and Arthur M. Melzer. Lanham, MD: Rowman & Littlefield.
Evans, Mary. 2009. Can Women Be Intellectuals? In *Intellectuals and Their Publics*, ed. Christian Fleck, Andreas Hess, and E. Stina Lyon. New York: Routledge.
Eyerman, Ronald. 1994. *Between Culture and Politics: Intellectuals in Modern Society*. Cambridge: Polity Press.
Eyerman, Ronald. 2008. *The Assassination of Theo van Gogh: From Social Drama to Cultural Trauma*. Durham, NC: Duke University Press.
Eyerman, Ronald. 2011. *The Cultural Sociology of Political Assassination* New York: Palgrave Macmillan.
Eyerman, Ronald, Jeffrey Alexander, and Elizabeth Breese (eds.). 2011. *Narrating Trauma: On the Impact of Collective Suffering*. Boulder, CO: Paradigm Publishers.
Felman, Shoshana, and Thomas E. Donnelley. 2002. *The Juridical Unconscious: Trials and Traumas in the Twentieth Century*. Cambridge, MA: Harvard University Press.
Gerstein, Linda. 1974. Ivanov-Razumnik: The Remembrance of Things Past. *Canadian-American Slavic Studies* 8 (4): 532–538.
Goldthorpe, John. 1982. On the Service Class, Its Formation and Future. In *Social Class and the Division of Labour*, ed. Anthony Giddens and Gavin Mackenzie. Cambridge: Cambridge University Press.
Gouldner, Alvin. 1979. *The Future of Intellectuals and the Rise of the New Class*. New York: Seabury.
Habermas, Jurgen. 1989. *The Structural Transformation of the Public Sphere*. Cambridge: Polity Press.
Hofstadter, Richard. 1962. *Anti-Intellectualism in American Lifei*. New York: Vintage Books.
Jacobs, Ronald, and Eleanor Townsley. 2004. Media Intellectuals and Public Sociology: The Case of Op-Eds in the *New York Times*. Paper Presented at the Annual Meeting of the American Sociological Association. Available at http://www.allacademic.com/meta/p108954_index.html.
Konrad, Gyorgy, and Ivan Szelenyi. 1979. *Intellectuals on the Road to Class Power*. London: Harvester Press.
Melzer, Arthur M., Jerry Weinberger, and M. Richard Zinman (eds.). 2003. *The Public Intellectual*. Lanham, MD: Rowman & Littlefield.
Norton, Matthew. 2018. A Structural Hermeneutics of *The O'Reilly Factor*. *Theory and Society* 40 (3): 315–346.

Pantti, Mervi. 2005. Masculine Tears, Feminine Tears, and Crocodile Tears: Mourning Olof Palme and Anna Lindh in Finnish Newspapers. *Journalism* 6 (3): 357–377.

Pantti, Mervi, and Wieten Jan. 2005. Mourning Becomes the Nation: Television Coverage of the Murder of Pim Fortuyn. *Journalism Studies* 6 (3): 301–313.

Richard, Posner A. 2001. *Public Intellectuals*. Cambridge, MA: Harvard University Press.

Sherman, G. 2010. Chasing Fox. *New York Times*, October 11.

Smelser, Neil. 2004. Psychological Trauma and Cultural Trauma. In *Cultural Trauma and Collective Identity*, ed. Jeffrey Alexander, Ronald Eyerman, Bernhard Giesen, Neil Smelser, and Piotr Sztompka. Berkeley: University of California Press.

Wald, Alan M. 1987. *The New York Intellectuals: The Rise and Decline of the Anti-Stalinist Left from the 1930s to the 1980s*. Chapel Hill: University of North Carolina Press.

CHAPTER 4

The Assassination of Harvey Milk

Introduction

In November 1978, Mayor George Moscone and City Supervisor Harvey Milk were assassinated at San Francisco City Hall. At the time of his death, Milk was one of the first openly gay men to hold political office in the U.S. His life story has since been recounted in books, plays, and films; ordained as "Saint Harvey," he has become a symbol of gay liberation and a cult-figure known the world over. Harvey Milk has recently been honored posthumously with both the Presidential Medal of Freedom and a memorial day in the country of his birth. George Moscone is largely forgotten outside of San Francisco. In this chapter, I apply and develop the theories of social drama and cultural trauma to help explain how and why these murders became a significant event. The framework of social drama (Turner 1974, 1980; McFarland 2004) allows one to isolate an incident, like an assassination, and study its various layers of meaning, while the theory of cultural trauma adds to this both a historical and emotional dimension (Eyerman 2008, 2011).

As hard as it may be to imagine today, it was not immediately obvious that Harvey Milk would be granted iconic political status, and it is one of my objectives in this chapter to elucidate how that was attained. At the time of the murder, George Moscone was the better-known figure. Not only was he the mayor of a major American city, he was also active in state and national politics, known for his liberal ideas and his skill in handling racial, ethnic, and sexual conflicts. Harvey Milk had achieved

R. Eyerman, *Memory, Trauma, and Identity*, Cultural Sociology,
https://doi.org/10.1007/978-3-030-13507-2_4

national recognition as one of the first openly gay men elected to public office. In the context of the time, this was a mixed blessing, as homosexuality was even more contentious an issue then than it is today. Even in San Francisco, a city on the verge of becoming the home of the largest concentration of gay people in the country, if not the world, sexuality and sexual politics were still very controversial subjects. In fact, part of Milk's ascent to prominence began with his very visible opposition to a campaign to remove homosexuals from teaching positions in California public schools (D'Emilio 1993). To run for public office as a gay person, even—or perhaps especially—in a district with a large number of homosexuals was seen as a courageous, dangerous, and potentially suicidal act. Indeed, Milk specifically anticipated his own death by assassination. In a message recorded before his death, Milk said:

> This is only to be played in the event of my death by assassination. I fully realize that a person who stands for what I stand for, an activist, a gay activist, becomes the target or the potential target of somebody who is insecure, terrified, afraid or very disturbed themselves. Knowing that I could be assassinated at any moment or any time, I feel it is important that people know my thoughts.... I have always considered myself part of a movement ... everything was done through the eyes of the gay movement. (musicmedia10 2008)

It is striking how significant Milk was in shaping both the narrative and the political consequences of his own death. That Milk died in a public building and that he saw himself as representing a movement helps us to understand, but does not entirely explain, why he would be remembered and honored in 2008 with the Presidential Medal of Freedom and, in 2009, commemorated by the state of California with a Memorial Day. It is here that the theories mentioned above become useful.

As will be elaborated in greater detail below, the theory of social drama allows us to view the murders of Moscone and Milk as an ordered and structured performance in which the actions of individuals are understood as meaningful both to themselves and to others in the context of a shared cultural world. It is through reconstructing these frameworks of meaning that we can make sense of what happened and why. This reconstruction can emerge from the point of view of the protagonists as well as from those looking on. Included in the latter are not only the onlookers at the scene and those immediately affected, such as family members, political constituents, legal authorities, and various others, but also the mass media. It is the mass media that create the collective representations that most will see, hear, and read.

The specific social spaces in which actions are performed are part of their meaningful nature and must also be included in any reconstruction, as certain actions only make sense in relation to their context. That the murders occurred at San Francisco City Hall was not incidental; from the perspective of Victor Turner's theory of social drama, it was a central part of its meaning. The model of social drama can be applied in mechanical fashion, passing through its various stages, from the initial breach to an eventual reconciliation and reformation of a collective identity. My approach to social drama is more contingent, where an initiating occurrence, already dramatic-in-itself, opens a liminal space in which interpretations compete and where several outcomes are possible. There are three levels in this analysis: that of social interaction, where a performative approach is applied (Alexander et al. 2006); a discursive analysis of the way these actions were reconstructed in mass media; and finally an analysis of long-term impact through the theory of cultural trauma (Alexander et al. 2004; Eyerman 2001, 2008, 2011).

By focusing on the wider contexts and the discursive processes within which collective foundations or "root paradigms" are articulated, the theory of cultural trauma adds a historical dimension to the analysis (Eyerman 2008; Wagner-Pacifici 1986). From this wider perspective, the wounds and scars of previous crises can be called upon to explain the emotional power and impact of the current drama, in what can be thought of as a cumulative effect mediated through collective memory. The systems of collective representation that are called into play in the analysis of a social drama are—from the point of view of a cultural trauma—laden with emotionally charged memory. They are much more than words on a page or acts upon a stage: they are representations of past actions and experiences that are freighted with emotion. And this affective dimension can be cumulative, making responses to current events much more powerful. With its focus on the dramaturgical and the discursive, as well as its underlying concern with repair and reconciliation, the model of social drama lacks an emotional as well as historical component, something that cultural trauma provides.

Cultural trauma theory also calls attention to collective memory and its construction as part of the meaning struggle that is at its core. This meaning struggle involves not only how current occurrences will be understood, but also how they will be remembered. The theory helps us identify those carrier groups that are important agents in this process. It will be important not merely to identify these carrier groups, but also to reconstruct what they actually do. Armstrong and Crage list three primary activities of those they call "symbolic entrepreneurs" (2006: 736): (1) constructing interpretations of events as important and identifying what about the event is salient; (2) disseminating this particular viewpoint over time and space; and (3) locating these interpretation within "well-developed commemorative repertoires" to which they have access. From within the theory of cultural trauma, I will map this process in order to explain why it is that Harvey Milk, rather than George Moscone, became the most idealized and commemorated figure to emerge out of the murders at San Francisco City Hall.

That Fateful Monday

In the late morning of November 27, 1978, the recently resigned city supervisor Dan White walked into San Francisco City Hall and killed Mayor George Moscone and Supervisor Harvey Milk. A former police officer, White used his old service revolver to murder his colleagues. Leaving the building, he drove to a nearby diner in a car borrowed from an aide on his way out. Soon after this, White surrendered to old police colleagues, and one of his best friends took his testimony and recorded his confession. Moments earlier, in the same police station, detectives had cheered as a radio bulletin announced the news of the murders, so hated were the two city officials (Weiss 1984).

Though some might have cheered, these cold-blooded killings shocked the city and the nation at large. That public officials could be gunned down in their offices during working hours was devastating, especially in a city still recovering from other tragic news. Eight days prior, the mass suicide at Jonestown, Guyana, in which more than 900 people died, had been initiated by a well-known city resident and former public official: Jim Jones, pastor of San Francisco's People's Temple. The news of Jonestown filled the headlines of the city's two leading newspapers for the entire week. On November 18, California Assemblyman Leo Ryan, himself a former mayor of San Francisco, had been murdered by members of the People's Temple. There were rumors that hit squads from the Jones congregation were in the city targeting other public officials, with Mayor Moscone said to be a prime target.[1]

In order to enter City Hall with a concealed weapon and a pocket full of shells and avoid the metal detector at the front entrance, Dan White climbed through a basement window. Dressed in his best three-piece suit, the well-known White moved easily through the building. He came unannounced, yet was somehow expected at the mayor's office. A few days earlier, in a fit of anger and disappointment, White had resigned his post; he had since changed his mind and Moscone agreed to consider reinstating him. But now there were rumors that Moscone would appoint someone else, and White wanted to confront the mayor about this. Indeed, Moscone had called a press conference for that afternoon to announce the new supervisor, and it was not Dan White. Although Moscone and Milk had conspired about the new appointee, Milk was also being misled as to just who the person might be. White was furious over this deception. He was let into Moscone's office, where he was told of the decision. Moscone then suggested they move to a more comfortable back office to have a drink, presumably to soothe the disappointment. After sitting for a moment in these intimate quarters, White rose to his feet and shot Moscone at close range, the first shots knocking his victim to the floor. In all, White used four of the five bullets in his revolver. He then walked down the hallway to where his own office and that of Harvey Milk were located. White invited Milk into the hall and from there they moved into White's old office. "What the hell are you doing to me?" White yelled. "Why do you want to hurt my name, my family? You cheated me" (Weiss 1984: 253). He then drew the newly reloaded revolver and shot Milk five times, in much the same manner as Moscone, with a final shot to the head to make sure.

Though a jury would later find otherwise, the style of these murders was that of an execution. When later asked why he did not just punch Moscone and Milk in the nose instead of shooting them, White replied that would have been unfair, since he was so much larger than either of them. This may sound ridiculous, but it is more understandable given a culturally bound sense of fairness relating to size and physical strength. Killing someone with a gun, especially for someone with the proper training, might seem more just, since it was less dependent on physical prowess. If this was about honor, then a revolver was the appropriate weapon for an ex-policeman, just as city hall in broad daylight was the appropriate setting. Fists or even a knife would have made these killings more personal and less professional and, while they were personal, the killings were carried out in a manner befitting a trained and disciplined professional.

The Players

Dan White was 32 years old when he shot Moscone and Milk. The son of a firefighter, he was raised in a Catholic household consisting of nine children in a working-class district on the southeastern outskirts of San Francisco called Visitacion Valley. While some things from the time of his childhood had changed by the mid-1970s, many things remained the same. Weiss describes the neighborhood this way: "[I]n 1977 you would … still have to search diligently to find a registered Republican, a college graduate or somebody who earned more than $20,000 a year" (1984: 39). After a troubled youth, White was a star athlete in high school and served seven years (1965–1972) as an enlisted man in the U.S. Army, including a tour of duty as a paratrooper in Vietnam. When he returned to San Francisco, White joined the police force but resigned following conflicts with other officers, whom he found too brutal and cynical about their work. In what was the final straw, he accused a fellow officer of mistreating a black prisoner. White then followed in his father's footsteps and became a firefighter. In 1977, White won the election for city supervisor in the newly created District 8, which incorporated his old neighborhood with those surrounding it. He campaigned as a conservative Democrat in a time of growing concern with urban violence and demographic shifts. Many of his constituents were worried about such changes and White promised to restore their neighborhoods. Just before the election, White's image was featured in the local media when he rescued a woman from a burning building. He was deemed a hero just as his father had been. With this unexpected publicity, White won the election handily. One frustrating year later, after failing to live up to his campaign promises and much bickering with his fellow supervisors, he suddenly resigned his position.

Unlike White, Harvey Milk was not a local hero. Milk first moved to San Francisco from New York in 1969, two years after the "Summer of Love." He returned to stay in 1972. Born in 1930 to a Jewish household in Woodmere, a Long Island suburb of New York City, Milk was 48 years old when he was killed. Like White, Milk was also a high school athlete and saw military service during wartime. Milk was a naval officer during the Korean War after graduating from college. Where White was self-enclosed and inward looking, Milk was gregarious and outgoing. After military service, Milk returned to Long Island and taught high school mathematics. In the early 1960s, he worked on Wall Street and was highly successful in the financial world. A conservative Republican, he worked on Barry Goldwater's campaign during the latter's unsuccessful presidential bid in 1964. At that time Milk was living an openly gay lifestyle. By 1969, Milk had left Wall Street and, together with a friend, a theater stage manager, moved to San Francisco with the touring company of the Broadway musical *Hair*. From a Goldwater conservative Milk had transformed himself into a counterculture hippie. A 1972 *New York Times* article covering developments in the theater described Milk as a "sad eyed man—another aging hippie with long hair, wearing faded jeans and pretty beads" (Gruen 1972: 14). Making the move to San Francisco permanent, Milk opened a camera store on Castro Street, the heart of a vibrant and expanding gay community. At the time of the Watergate hearings, angered by the local bureaucracy and the direction of national politics, Milk decided to run for elected office. He ran as a liberal Democrat and as openly gay. On his third try, Milk was elected to represent the Castro district as city supervisor.[2] By this time he had cut his hair and retrieved some of his earlier political beliefs. No longer a hippie, he was now a small business owner with a social conscience and an interest in the civil rights of minorities. From this position, Milk could more easily represent a large swath of his district, especially the largest segment of his constituency: young, well educated, gay men.

Like White, Moscone was a local hero. Born in San Francisco in 1929 in an Italian-American household, Moscone attended Catholic schools and was a star high school athlete. He had just celebrated his 49th birthday when he was killed. A lawyer by training, Moscone entered politics in 1960 when he ran for the California State Assembly as a Democrat. He lost that election but garnered a seat on the San Francisco Board of Supervisors in 1963. In 1966 he was elected to the California Senate, representing a San Francisco district. Reelected in 1970, he also served as Senate Majority Leader. He was a liberal Democrat in the Kennedy mold, known for his legislation supporting minority rights, including those of homosexuals. Moscone became mayor of San Francisco in 1975, when he defeated both the conservative candidate John Barbagelata and Diane Feinstein, a more centrist Democrat who would succeed him after his death. Moscone won by the very small margin of 3000 votes and would acknowledge the significance of the gay vote in his victory (D'Emilio 1993: 72). In recognition, the newly elected mayor appointed Harvey Milk "to an important City Hall post as a member of the Board of Permit Appeals" (Castells 1983: 144). Moscone was also helped in winning the election by members of the People's Temple who distributed leaflets around the city for Moscone and other liberal candidates. Jim Jones would be rewarded for these efforts with an appointment as Chairman of the San Francisco Housing Commission. Later reports suggested voter fraud in connection with the People's Temple (Binder 1978: 12). Jones also supported the election of Milk. Moscone made some other controversial appointments as mayor, including that of a liberal police chief, something that made him very unpopular with rank-and-file officers. Members of the police force were also angry with the mayor for his support of minorities, including gays and lesbians, both on the force and in the city generally. Moscone and Milk saw themselves and each other as part of a liberal coalition against big business and the tourist industry; included in the latter was Feinstein, as well as White, whom they saw as her protégé. In spite of this, both tolerated White at first, thinking that some common ground could be forged, especially concerning the protection of local neighborhoods. However, the longer the political term wore on, the more problematic these relationships became. No one really knew where White stood; perhaps he did not even know himself.

The Trial

The issue of why Dan White killed George Moscone and Harvey Milk was central to the trial held in San Francisco's Hall of Justice in the spring of 1979. Since White had turned himself in and confessed to the murders directly after the fact, there was no question of his guilt. The issue was not *if* White murdered the two public officials but *why*. The prosecution and the defense argued over White's life—whether or not he would die in the gas chamber—not over whether he had killed the two men. The issue of whether this was assassination and not merely murder was never articulated, perhaps because of a tacit agreement not to bring the sensitive issue of local politics into the courtroom (Weiss 1984). For the prosecution, the matter was settled—the facts added up to murder in the first degree and warranted the death penalty. White had clearly intended to kill, and he came to city hall fully armed and prepared to do so. He had knowingly avoided the metal detector, appeared calm and determined, and reloaded his weapon in between the killings; all this pointed to premeditated murder.

For the prosecution, White's motivation was revenge; he wanted to punish those who had taken away his political position. The defense argued otherwise: White was an upstanding citizen and a "good person" who had not intended to commit murder but had been driven over the edge of sanity by financial pressure and family responsibility. White was portrayed as an honest man who was unable to carry out his masculine duty while trapped within the pressure cooker of local politics. This viewpoint had already been articulated in a headline in the *San Francisco Examiner* (November 28, 1978: 1) the day after the murder: "Dan White: 'casualty of pressure.'" Such "pressure" could make anyone "snap." Carrying a weapon in a hostile and threatening atmosphere, as San Francisco was portrayed at the time, was described as normal, and when questioned about this, former board president and current mayor Diane Feinstein admitted to having done so on occasion. Feinstein also testified that White was not the type of man to shoot people. White's mental state at the time of the murder was thus important, and several psychiatrists were called to testify that White was driven to murder by factors outside his control. The most controversial was the so-called Twinkies Defense, named after a popular sugary cake, where it was claimed that a high intake of junk food could result in diminished mental capacity. This was the same "diminished capacity" defense strategy employed by the attorneys for Sirhan Sirhan ten years earlier, though there was no mention of junk food on that occasion. When White's recorded confession was played in court, his sobbing claims of being under tremendous pressure from work and family responsibility moved many to tears, including members of the jury. The effect, unanticipated by the prosecution but planned by the defense, was to turn sympathy from the actual victims to White himself. The perpetrator was now victim, driven by uncontrollable emotion to commit murder. From this perspective, George Moscone was not killed because he was mayor of San Francisco. Likewise, Harvey Milk was killed neither because he was city supervisor nor because he was an openly gay politician. By the same reasoning, Dan White did not commit murder as a politician, but as an individual who snapped under pressure and acted in a despondent state.

The jury found Dan White guilty of voluntary manslaughter, and the judge sentenced him to seven years and eight months in prison. In prison, in one of those ironies of history, Dan White and Sirhan Sirhan, the killer of Robert Kennedy, would become jogging partners and good friends (Weiss 1984: 422). White was released from prison in 1984 and returned to San Francisco soon after. When the announcement was made of his release on parole, two hundred police officers in riot gear stood outside San Francisco City Hall "just in case" (Gorney, *Washington Post*, January 3, 1984). In October 1985 White committed suicide in the garage of his house while listening to a tape playing the Irish folk tune, "The Town I Loved So Well."[3]

Reactions

If White's defense attorneys had been able to convince the carefully selected jury (anyone with a "pro-gay" attitude was carefully weeded out) that he had acted in a momentary fit of rage and had *not* murdered for political or cultural reasons, this was not how others viewed things. The broadly conceived San Francisco gay community reacted to the verdict very differently from the way it had reacted to both the murder and the trial. The deaths of Moscone and Milk were initially cause for a massive outpouring of sorrow and mourning. Milk's funeral brought tens of thousands of people together in a peaceful candlelight march through the Castro. The march made for an unforgettable sight as row after row of people with candles in their hands walked slowly through the darkened streets, the flickering lights stretching for miles. Five months later, when the verdict was announced, there was another massive outpouring of emotion, but this time it was anger. Police cars were burned, the windows of City Hall broken, and the building itself set on fire, resulting in what has come to be called the White Night Riots. Like the murders themselves, the highly anticipated announcement of the verdict evoked distinctive responses, as vividly described by Mike Weiss:

> Radio and television stations interrupted their regular programming beginning at 5:30 for bulletins ... On a live radio hookup, Clive Jones [an aide to Milk] said: "This means that in America it's all right to kill faggots." The police band radio also announced the verdicts and somebody began to sing: Oh Danny boy, the pipes are calling.... (1984: 405)

Though these opposite reactions reflected two separate constituencies, the meaning was essentially the same; Dan White had gotten away with murder. For the police corps and the gay community—or at least for groups within these constituencies—Dan White and Harvey Milk were representative figures and their fate reflected upon those they represented: a police officer had been exonerated and a gay man had been assassinated. Within this polarization, the figure of George Moscone began to fade into the background.

The rioters outside City Hall who were chanting, "Dan White was a cop," "Avenge Harvey Milk," and "Kill Dan White" (Weiss 1984: 408) looked past the individuals whose names they shouted, invoking social categories and identifying themselves with one and against the other. The deed described inside the courtroom as the act of one individual against another was here negated and redefined. From this vantage point, White acted as a representative of a group with a distinctive view of the world, and he murdered in their interests. This appeared to be confirmed in the reactions of at least some in the police corps and throughout the city at large. His victim, Harvey Milk, was from this point of view killed for more than narrow political reasons; he was killed because of what and who he represented, confirming what he had predicted himself.

But what exactly did Harvey Milk and Dan White represent? The 1960s and 1970s marked a major transition in San Francisco. From a city dominated by its harbor and run by a Democratic political machine, it had slowly been transformed into a tourist and convention city, with a service-oriented economy. Working-class occupations and neighborhoods began to decline, and along with Asian immigrants, more highly educated young people began moving in. Immigration and westward migration has long been part of U.S. history but, for the most part, this was a new sort of migrant, better educated, individualistic, and highly self-defining. A large subgroup among these migrants consisted of young gay men, many with middle-class backgrounds and college degrees, ready to take their place in the growing service sector. In one sense, Harvey Milk represented this group, but in another he did not. Though well educated and with a background in finance and investment, Milk came to San Francisco from New York more as part of the 1960s counterculture than the 1970s gay migration. He came to escape the corporate world, not to join it. To mark this he grew a beard and long hair and opened a second-hand camera store in what was then a neighborhood in transition. As mentioned above, after being defeated in a couple of elections, Milk modified his public persona. He campaigned for City Supervisor in a newly created district, clean-shaven and in second-hand, three-piece suits. In addition to the gay residents, he counted among his supporters the local unions, including the firefighters. He campaigned against the "downtown machine," as well as the "Uncle Toms" of the gay movement. As Frances FitzGerald eloquently put it:

> As an outsider running against liberals, he became at once a fiscal conservative and a populist: he was for 'the little people' in the neighborhoods against the downtown interests and the landlords: he was for better schools, better city services for the elderly ... but in the end his main supporters were the thousands upon thousands of young gay men settling in the Castro. (1986: 56)[4]

What Milk had in common with them was his sexual orientation, but he differed from many in his political views. For him, the gay movement was a countercultural movement and he viewed gays as a marginalized and oppressed minority who should seek coalition with other minorities. This feeling was in part generational, but it was not incidental that Harvey Milk was Jewish, for this feeling of being a minority among other minorities has as much to do with liberal Jewish sentiment as with generational politics. In contrast, many of the newly arrived gay men had another perception of themselves and seemed less interested in coalition politics.[5] On the contrary, despite the homophobia of the dominant culture, they viewed themselves in positive rather than negative terms, as discriminated against professionals and business owners whose interest in equality appeared to center largely on sexual orientation. At least at first, what fused Milk with this new generation of gays was primarily how they were viewed by others, not necessarily how they viewed themselves. He became their leader, and later their martyr and icon, because he was gay and proud of it, not because they necessarily shared a broader worldview. For this movement and for the mass media, homosexuality was Milk's defining characteristic; his name could not be mentioned without also mentioning his sexual orientation.

If Dan White viewed himself as representing a threatened, ethnic white working class, he was portrayed by the gay community as homophobic and reactionary—this despite the fact that his campaign manager had been openly gay. For them, White was a police officer and a bigot who was out not only to represent what they viewed as reactionary economic and political interests but also an equally threatened masculinity. White was identified as a "law and order" politician with a traditional view of family and gender relations. After a few attempts to work with him, this was pretty much how Milk saw him, as well. Milk also viewed

White as in coalition with big business and the tourist industry, which had no real interest in protecting working-class neighborhoods or occupations. As for what White might have represented for others, Frances FitzGerald (1986) ends her reportage on Milk and the Castro district with a possible set of motivations that led to White's murderous actions. What the prosecution could have argued, she writes, was this:

> Dan White had resigned from the Board of Supervisors for purely personal reasons.... Being politically naïve, White did not realize the political consequences of his private decision to quit the board until the real-estate men and the police came to him. What kind of pressure was put on him remains unknown, but the pressure was certainly great enough to make him put himself in the embarrassing position of asking the Mayor to give him his job back after only four days. (FitzGerald 1986: 69)

To the extent this is true, it was the dishonor of letting down his friends and supporters in the police and fire departments that led White to kill Moscone and Milk when the mayor reneged on his promise and when he heard that Milk had lobbied against him. Shame and dishonor were the motivating emotions in this account, with economic and political interests thrown in, which is to say that Dan White saw himself as an honor-bound member of an occupational group with ethnic and class ties. In an article entitled "Dan White's Last Confession" (*San Jose Mercury News*, September 18, 1998), Mike Weiss recorded White's 1985 conversation with his friend Frank Falzone, the police officer who had recorded his original confession one hour after the murders in 1978. When asked again what happened the day of the murders, White replied: "I really lost it. I was on a mission. I wanted four of them ... Carol Silver—she was the biggest snake of the bunch. And Willie Brown. He was the mastermind of the whole thing." Carol Silver was also on the Board of Supervisors and a friend and ally of Harvey Milk, and Willy Brown was a State Assemblyman, a friend and ally of George Moscone. If this is true, it raises not only the issue of White's motive, but also who the real target was.

Mediated Representation

After reporting the facts about the murders, much of the early media representations focused on the city of San Francisco, its mayor, and the sexual orientation of Harvey Milk. The front-page banner headline of the *San Francisco Chronicle* the morning after the shooting read: "City Hall Murders, Moscone, Milk Slain—Dan White is Held." All these names would be well known to readers and there was no need for further elaboration. Under a photograph of White being escorted by police authorities was a smaller headline: "Feinstein Becomes the Mayor." To the right of this was a description of the facts as then known and portrait photographs of the two victims. Inside, the *Chronicle* offered reactions from residents and the headline: "Stunned Silence in San Francisco, The Horror that Swept City Hall." Many of those interviewed worried about the city's image and that of the state of California, for the murders quickly became a major theme in national media representations. Along with the issue of public safety and the security of public officials, shock and sadness was another theme on this first day of reportage. "It's incredibly shocking … this feels something like a reprise of the Kennedy assassination" (*San Francisco Chronicle*, November 28, 1978: 2), said one of those interviewed. Many on the steps of City Hall were "too shocked to speak" to reporters.

The edition of the *San Francisco Examiner* published on the afternoon of November 28 carried the banner headline: "A City in Agony," draped in black. Underneath, in bold letters, it proclaimed: "White Charged—Faces Death." Given that most readers already knew the basic facts, its reportage primarily concerned what had happened since, the reactions of individuals, and on the broader background. The *Examiner's* first-page report on the perpetrator came under the headline "Dan White: 'casualty of pressure.'" White was crying in his jail cell, the story began, and then quoted a city supervisor: "I think everyone has a breaking point … and if indeed as it looks, there was a breaking point for Dan, I can understand it." He went on to characterize White as a "normal, devoted, young father … a casualty of pressure." If Milk were always represented as a "gay politician," White would be represented as an "ex-fireman" and a "family man," a man surrounded by his wife and son, and as this report noted, his parents and his three sisters, who visited him in jail. Writing in 1984, while awaiting White's release from prison, *Washington Post* reporter Cynthia Gorney summarized his media representation as "a local boy, local hero, policeman, fireman, Catholic schools, Catholic church, wife and child, old San Francisco" ("Waiting for Dan White," *Washington Post*, January 3, 1984: B1). Moscone was represented somewhere between the two as a "liberal mayor" and a family man, the latter being something that apparently further angered local police, since Moscone's reputation as a womanizer was something they gossiped about. Summing up the hatred between the San Francisco police and its mayor, Gorney, quoting Mike Weiss, writes:

> They hated him because he turned the city over to Them. But that was political hatred, and political hatreds don't run very deep in most cases. With George, it was the added dimension of, "He turned the city over to them, and he's not good to his wife. Everybody in the city knows he's running around." (Gorney 1984: B1)

The unstated "them" was clearly gays and the other minorities moving into the city. The newsweeklies followed Diane Feinstein's lead in linking the murders of Moscone and Milk to Jonestown, as well as to other violence in the region. A three-page report headlined "Day of the Assassin" (*Newsweek*, December 11, 1978: 26–28) immediately drew the two together in what it called the "San Francisco syndrome": "a mindless streak of violence that has afflicted the Bay Area with nearly 100 bomb blasts and more than a dozen murder victims in the past ten years" (p. 26). The report went on to describe the murders of Moscone and Milk, complete with a graphic detailing of the events in City Hall. In this reportage, most of the biographical segments focused on Moscone and White, with Milk receiving only a few lines. The prime message, however, was that of a troubled city in the midst of turmoil and soul-searching. Juxtaposed to this reportage was a long article, "Ghosts of Jonestown," which also made the link to San Francisco. The city itself, it seemed, was as much the perpetrator as Dan White. According to the *New Yorker* as reported by Frances FitzGerald (1986), it was a combination of local political intrigue and long-term structural changes affecting the city that were the root cause of White's murderous act. White was of course the perpetrator at a surface level—no one could deny that—but they suggested there were deeper underlying structural changes in motion that must be accounted for in understanding his actions. These included not only a shifting occupational structure and population but also the reorganization of political boundaries and how all this affected local politics. The City Board of Supervisors had just been restructured to accommodate newly reconfigured districts. It was this restructuring that allowed both Dan White and Harvey Milk to enter the political scene. All the central players in this drama—Dan White, George Moscone, and Harvey Milk—were representative figures acting on an unsteady, shifting stage. In such an environment, the positions of victim, perpetrator, and audience become fluid.

Memorialization

In addition to the media coverage of the murders and the trial of Dan White, there have been annual memorial celebrations in the city to commemorate the victims. At first these marches and the accompanying speeches concerned both Moscone and Milk, but as time went on it was the commemoration of Harvey Milk that gradually came to dominate. Why this occurred can be traced to two related processes. On the one side was the mobilizing potential of Milk's memory, which was greater that Moscone's, and on the other, the presence of activists, or movement entrepreneurs, who recognized and drew upon this potential. By the 25th anniversary in November 2003, the *Chronicle*'s headline (p. A1) read, "City Hall Slaying: 25 Years Later; From Milk's times to our times; It's hard to fathom gains for gay rights since the death of 'St. Harvey.'" Reportage focused entirely on Milk, or as they wrote, "Milk as myth." Harvey Milk had transcended not only George Moscone and Dan White, but also himself; he was now a movement icon and a measure, at least for this newspaper, of the movement's success.

Why was this the case? As a leader and public figure, Milk was no more powerful than George Moscone, and measured in terms of local politics, much less so. There are two factors that help us understand why Milk became such a prominent figure in the public memory, and both of them are related. The first has to do with the way he died, the victim of assassination in a public place by a man whom he had known and befriended. This tragic story included Moscone as well, but Milk was killed not only because of what he did, but also because of who he was as a person, not merely as a politician. He was both a symbolic and an organizational leader in the sense meant by Klapp (1964). Harvey Milk was an elected public official in the same way as George Moscone, but Milk's public, as well as his public persona, was easily identified and identifiable—he was a *gay* politician.

As one of the first openly gay public officials in the country, Milk was newsworthy over the long run in a way that Moscone was not. A gay man in politics, one not afraid to speak his mind and to express his sexual identity, was clearly news of extraordinary interest. From his side, Milk's public proclamations concerning his sexual orientation were both strategic and courageous. Milk's power as a political operator and his ability to influence policy was rooted in his claim to represent a large and, at least on certain issues, relatively unified constituency. He was able to use this power in helping see to it that Dan White was not reinstated, something that contributed, as we have seen, to his own death. In this sense, White murdered Milk because he was gay, a representative of a constituency from whom White was increasingly alienated.

The second factor that helps us understand the longevity of Milk's memory lays with the community—or more precisely, the marginalized social group with whom he identified and in so doing helped identify. Milk was an important figure in the attempts to mobilize a social movement around gay rights. He was important during his lifetime and then again after his death. In death, he became a martyr to the cause and an emblematic figure in the continuous process of mobilization. The annual memorial marches in his name are as much about this as about Harvey Milk—in fact the two became intertwined. As Castells puts it, "Gay culture is inseparable from gay politics" (1983: 163). Large-scale public activities are a central part of this mix of culture and politics, and there are many occasions for popular celebration beyond the memorial marches. Especially in San Francisco, the figure of Harvey Milk is omnipresent in these mobilizing events. While marginalized by the mainstream society, members and supporters of this particular group were making significant inroads into the sphere of cultural production far beyond San Francisco, something that permitted crucial access to mass media, including not only newspapers, radio, and television, but also film, theater, and the other arts. It should also be said that the deaths of Milk and Moscone had a significant effect on the local gay community. Although acting mayor Feinstein appointed a gay man, Harry Britt, to replace Milk, under pressure from other forces in local and state politics, she also initiated an anti-pornography bill that led to a crackdown on central gay institutions, such as bookstores, bars, and theaters (D'Emilio 1993: 75).[6]

In 1984 a documentary entitled *The Times of Harvey Milk* was released to national acclaim and an Academy Award. It was this film, rather than Randy Shilts' biography (1982), that set the narrative tone for how Milk would be remembered. As noted earlier, the film begins with real television footage of Diane Feinstein's announcement of the murders to a shocked public. One can hear cries of "Oh, no!" in the background. This scene is followed by a photograph of Milk as we listen to his voice in the recorded message about the possibility of being assassinated because of his gay-rights activism. The film then moves back in time to recount the rise of Harvey Milk to national prominence. It is a powerful story with a well-known sentimental theme: the rise of an ordinary man to notoriety who in the midst of his success dies tragically. It is probably no coincidence that this documentary was made during what was by that time identified as an AIDS epidemic, which was then having a devastating effect on the gay community, most notably in the Castro district of San Francisco. Just the year before, French researchers had isolated the virus that was the cause of these deaths, which had been known at least from 1981 as a "strange type of cancer." With so many dying, there was a sense of a world disappearing, and the documentary portrayed Milk as a representative figure from a happier time.

In 2008, just days before the 30th-anniversary commemoration of Milk and the release of the Hollywood version of this story, the director of the 1984 documentary, Rob Epstein, was asked if any progress in terms of gay rights had been made over the ensuing years. "In some ways, it's clear that we've made such incredible strides, and in some ways it seems like we're exactly where we were 30 years ago.... Be it teachers in 1978, or the institution of marriage in 2008, it's still up against the same fears" (Willmore 2008), he lamented.

The identification with Milk and the movement he represented seems clear in these sentiments. In response to a question about when he decided to make the film, Epstein replied:

> I had already started the project before Harvey was killed. I started to do a film about the Briggs initiative—Proposition 6 [a proposal on the California ballot to fire any teacher found to be "advocating, imposing, or promoting" homosexuality in the classroom].... That's what I was interested in, that fight, which was new then, and then it all became Harvey's story. That was all part of it, which is why I ended up doing a film that was more about the times, and showing Harvey as a man of history—that particular history—than a biopic documentary.

What began as a documentary of a political conflict ended up as a story of a man's life and times. One reason for this shift of narrative focus seems clearly to be the way Milk died. It was the drama of assassination that sparked the telling of a wider story, and it was this story—this plot structure—that has come to be definitive. The catastrophic effect of the AIDS epidemic on the gay community combined with the way the murder of one of its leaders was treated by the legal system were contextual conditions that helped transform Harvey Milk into a martyr and an icon.

In the more recent (2008) Hollywood remake of this documentary, entitled simply *Milk*, the nostalgia is even more apparent. AIDS is conspicuously absent in this story. What we have instead is a rallying cry, a sense of pride in being gay, with death as political and heroic, not biological and excruciatingly personal. No doubt, the film may have contributed to a more positive view of the gay community against another wave of conservative reaction. It also contributed, as noted above, to the Governor of California changing his mind about a Harvey Milk Memorial Day. There were other political moments: upon accepting the Academy Award for his role as Harvey Milk, the actor Sean Penn used the occasion to criticize opponents to gay marriage. Even as Hollywood epic, Harvey Milk remains a mobilizing force, one that has moved beyond the movement that made him.

Remembering and Forgetting

All this is not to say that Moscone has been entirely forgotten. An interesting controversy emerged in 1980, two years after the assassination. After the construction of the Moscone Convention Center and Exhibition Hall, a commission was awarded to sculptor Robert Arneson to create a monument to the fallen mayor to be placed in its center hall. Arneson was known for his irreverent portraits, and he produced a powerful, expressionist bust of the mayor that, when previewed by the mayor's widow, received her approval. However, what Mrs. Moscone did not see during her preview was the pedestal upon which the bust was resting; the artist had covered it up in anticipation of her visit. The 58-inch pedestal was an integral part of the work, embodying "graffiti-like scrawls and five bloody bullet holes" and the words "Bang, Bang, Bang" along with newspaper clippings about the assassination (Weiss 2000). The "Portrait of George," which measured 94 inches in height and weighed over 500 lbs., was finally rejected by Mayor Diane Feinstein as too controversial after the artist refused to remove the pedestal and redo the work. It is now owned by a private collector in Arizona, but has been shown in San Francisco's art museum.

Both Moscone and Milk have schools named after them, they are linked together on a Facebook memorial site, and there is a memorial to both in San Francisco City Hall; there is also one at Harvey Milk Plaza. San Francisco has the Moscone Convention Center and a Moscone Recreation Center. The disparity comes in the breadth of the commemoration. There are several factors that help explain this. The role of carrier groups—in this case the gay movement and the powerful position of some of its representatives and sympathizers—is of crucial importance, but there are other factors as well. Would the killing of Milk alone have lent itself to commemoration? Possibly, but in a much more restricted sense. Milk's murder could have functioned as the so-called Stonewall Riots, becoming a significant event in the formation of a group identity and formative, even foundational, to its collective memory (Armstrong and Crage 2006). But that Moscone was also murdered was very important for the intensity and the scope of the initial media coverage. The murder of two public officials became a significant event through mass-mediated coverage and construction. Had Moscone been absent, that coverage, and the ensuing broad-based reaction, would most likely have been much narrower and less intense. The fact that the mayor of San Francisco was also a victim not only conditioned public reaction in the city, but also around the nation; at the same time, it widened the range of possibilities for movement activists in their mobilization of public support for their cause. Even as Moscone's part in the drama began to fade from popular memory, his name and position could be invoked to broaden the appeal.

Not every incident is a candidate for reconstructing collective memory; some are more likely than others to have long-term impact. This is in part dependent on carrier groups, but it also has something to do with the occurrence itself, its own inherent power to evoke emotional recall. Political assassinations carry this potential, especially when they involve a cast of characters and an outcome like this one. What Marshal Sahlins (1981; see also Armstrong and Crage 2006; Sewell 1996) calls the "structure of the conjuncture" (i.e., the local conditions that help determine which events become "transformative") is important as well. While Sahlins and others focus on institutions and social structures, I would also include the symbolic structures of the occurrence itself. This means that the same type of occurrence—in our case, a political assassination—might be transformative of collective memory at one point, but not at another. Such local conditions would have to include the wave of violence and death that had recently struck San Francisco, as well as all the structural changes that were affecting the city. Emotions in the city were high, and the atmosphere was tense, and this contributed to the intensity of the public reaction to the murders. In this sense, the murders can be seen as the culmination of a series of occurrences that, when experienced as linked together through mass-mediated narrative reconstructions, added to the depth and breadth of their impact. These were then broadly disseminated. However, had only the mayor of the city been involved, the occurrence might well have remained a local one, fashioned into the memory of those present, commemorated once or twice, but soon forgotten. Because a gay activist was also killed, the reconstructed event took on greater significance. This was due to a combination of local reactions, mass media representations of the occurrence itself, and the narratives constructed by movement intellectuals who retold the story in more partisan terms and disseminated it far beyond the location where it occurred.

Local conditions are important in explaining why the murder of two local public officials is still commemorated in San Francisco, but not sufficient to explain its wider impact. There is also the capacity of the occurrence to evoke powerful emotions and the capacity to create carrier groups with will, skill, and position. Such groups are not always already there, and an occurrence may or may not be a catalyst to their formation. This formative potential, if it is present, must also be continually renewed and rejuvenated. It is here that the qualities, as well as quantities, of these carrier groups are a very important variable in explaining why some dramatic events enter the wider collective memory. One important quality is the forcefulness and the receptive power of the narrative they construct and disseminate. Carrier groups are not only bearers of a message; they must also shape and spread it in an effective way.

The meaning attributed to the death of Harvey Milk transcended local conditions because they were framed and interpreted as universal. Milk's life was narrated as the quintessential American success story, a veteran and high school teacher who overcame adversity to do good for both himself and others. This story had an appeal that transcended the merely local. This familiar narrative frame resonated with a much broader group than the gay community within which it was produced. When Governor Schwarzenegger proclaimed Harvey Milk Day a statewide day of remembrance, it was as much because of this narrative as the pressure brought to bear by interested parties. Milk had been turned not only into a symbol of a gay movement, but also of America itself, a nation where minorities could win acceptance.

"Memory may be the last weapon of the dead" (Meir Shalev quoted in Vinitzky-Seroussi 2009: 21) is a sentiment proclaimed by one of the friends of the assassinated Israeli Prime Minister Yitzhak Rabin, and to accomplish this retribution, he pointed out, the friends of the murdered individual "must fashion the sword and keep it from rusting" (Meir Shalev quoted in Vinitzky-Seroussi 2009: 21). This is close to the role of the audience in Hannah Arendt's (1953) discussion of action, where the audience is witness, judge, and recorder of the actions of individuals. Within the audience, the storyteller or recorder weaves individual actions into a coherent tale, making it available to those not present, including future generations. In and through these narratives and their ritual retelling, a group reconstitutes itself at the same time it makes its story available to others. The storyteller, a concept Arendt borrowed from her own friend Walter Benjamin, is comparable to the "friends" who forge the narrative sword, keeping alive their fallen hero by recalling for themselves and for others the words and deeds that constitute the collective memory of the community. This narrative can be forged in pictures as well as through words, and it can also be integrated into speeches in the legislative battles over commemoration. This was the case in the 1984 documentary mentioned earlier and in the struggle to get the state of California and the U.S. president officially to honor the memory of the slain Harvey Milk. Here the friends of the fallen acted as an interest group as well as a communal carrier of memory. In terms of formal political power, one would have thought that the friends of George Moscone would have more influence in seeing to it that the murdered mayor of San Francisco and former state representative would be commemorated, especially within the state of California. To a degree, this was so. But that Harvey Milk would be afforded national recognition and commemoration did not depend on political influence in the narrow sense of the term. What brought this honor on Milk was not only the way he was killed, which of course also affected the commemoration of Moscone, but also the power and influence of his friends within the social group and social movement he represented: the gay community. Randy Shilts, the writer of Milk's definitive biography, was a self-proclaimed member of the community, as were those behind the award-winning documentary and the Hollywood film. Behind them stood the gay movement, a powerful force in the identity politics in the U.S. over the last few decades. Well placed in the means of cultural production, members of this self-identified community were able to disseminate representations of Milk that helped transform him into a mythic figure—a martyr and a representative figure of a once marginalized and threatened community, a community that has now become powerful enough to effectively challenge the sexual politics and proclivities of the dominant culture. In this social drama, Moscone and White were important supporting actors, but Milk was the leading character.

From Drama to Trauma

The question of where to begin the narrative is a contested matter in the making of any significant event (Vinitzky-Seroussi 2009). In Victor Turner's (1980) view, a social drama begins with the transgression or breach of a well-established norm in a public arena and evolves toward attempts at repair and reconciliation. In the present case, the social drama begins when White, illegally carrying a concealed weapon, climbed through a window in order to avoid the metal detector at the main entrance of City Hall. From there followed the shooting of Moscone and Milk. These actions not only broke various laws for which White would be tried and convicted, but also transgressed social norms in a very public arena. Clearly, the murder of any public official constitutes a breach that must be repaired if a collective is to continue. Calling this an assassination points not only to motive, but also to the seriousness of the rupture and the depth and direction of the process necessary to repair it. From the perspective of social drama theory, the story should end with closure, a sense of moving on, and the reconfiguration of collective identity. This would come after some form of ritualized reconciliation, a period of grieving and mourning and institutionalized commemoration. In the case of Milk and Moscone's murders, after the funeral and an outpouring of public grief, the city moved on, appointing and then electing a new mayor and a suitable replacement for Harvey Milk. The wound opened up again with the trial and the hotly contested verdict. The scars had not healed and several violent confrontations occurred that some deemed a "civil war." The final culmination of this social drama, at least from the point of view of supporters of the victims, appears to have come in 2009 with the establishment of a Harvey Milk Memorial Day in California. In between, besides the death of Dan White, were a long series of commemorative events, including anniversary celebrations, the naming of schools and other public buildings, an award-winning documentary, a Presidential Medal of Freedom, a major Hollywood film and awards, a debate in the California legislature, a veto by the state's governor, and finally the passage of the commemorative legislation.

A social drama is a narrative in which the actions of various protagonists can be reconstructed as attempts to define the situation. Each protagonist has his or her ideal plot: how he or she would have the story unfold and be interpreted. One task for the analyst is to reconstruct these ideal plots as conceived by each protagonist in order to gain a fuller meaning of the event at the level of social action. We must ask, for example, what the ideal plot and ending might be from Dan White's perspective. Perhaps that the murders of Moscone and Milk would expose the collusion and corruption that he felt existed at City Hall, where political power and—from his perspective, perverse sexuality—formed an unholy alliance against solid and virtuous working-class values. White saw himself as a representative of those values, and he thought he reflected them in his actions as city supervisor and the representative of a largely working-class district. White went to City Hall that day aggrieved because he felt Moscone (who had at first promised to reinstate him), Milk, and several others had conspired to prevent his reinstatement.

As victims of White's crime, neither Moscone nor Milk entered this drama as protagonists, except perhaps in their concerted effort to keep him from returning to office. Only if we view them as individuals and as representative figures, the way White did, can we try to reconstruct their respective ideal plot in the unfolding drama. Moscone had appeared friendly to White when the latter assumed his post as city supervisor, and even when he spoke with White about the possibilities of being reinstated. This was done with all the savvy of a political operator, but Moscone also because seemed genuinely taken with White's Boy Scout seriousness and open-faced honesty, qualities so out of place in a world of backdoor wheeling and dealing. Moscone used White when he could, but their political interests were mostly at odds. He was probably sincere when he told White that he would consider reinstating him to his post a few days after he had so impulsively resigned. Yet upon further reflection, with input from Harvey Milk and others, Moscone became convinced that he should use this opportunity to appoint someone closer to his own political views. That Moscone never informed White of this change of mind—until their final, fatal conversation—only confirmed White's view that the mayor was a devious politician, another representative of that corrupt system of government. Moscone's ideal plot would most surely have been for White to accept his fate and quietly disappear from local politics. The same was probably true for Harvey Milk. The mass media played a key role in the unfolding drama. This was so in more than the usual sense of reporting and reconstructing the occurrence—their influence impinged much more directly upon the ongoing process itself. It was a telephone call from a radio reporter the night before the murder that might have helped pushed White over the edge, from frustration and depression to action. Hearing the news that Moscone was about to appoint someone else to the post, the reporter called White at his home for a reaction. After receiving the call, White was up all night pondering just that (Mann 1997; Weiss 1984).

The symbolic terms that script social drama must also be specified and analyzed. These can be approached from both the point of view of the actors and that of the mass media that reconstructed the narrative of the occurrence, turning it into a significant event for a much wider audience. Two of these symbolic terms were *family* and *community*. Dan White saw himself as not only representing a specific community, but also beholden to his family. He followed in the footsteps of a father he admired, especially when he became a firefighter and an on-the-job hero by rescuing a woman from a burning building, just as his father had. In fact, this widely reported heroism helped clinch his election (Geluardi 2008; Weiss 1984). At least in his public representation, it was in consideration of his family responsibilities that he sought to be reinstated as city supervisor, a job that involved practices he found morally despicable. Harvey Milk also viewed himself as representing a community, the San Francisco gay community, and as a representative figure with moral as well as political responsibilities. He had to appear as a good public official in part because he was so visible a representative of a marginalized social group only recently making itself felt in the public arena. He was more adept at performing the other side of politics than White. Milk was skilled in backroom negotiation, having worked in the financial world in New York. He had a different class background and a different range of social competencies from White. Like Moscone, Milk had befriended White because he was genuinely taken by White's political naivety, but he also thought he could make strategic use of him.

Other symbolic terms that informed this social drama were *civic violence* and *terrorism*. From the actors' point of view, violence was an active agent in the San Francisco of the 1970s. The homes of local politicians, including the district attorney and that of Diane Feinstein, then a city supervisor, had been bombed. Many other local politicians had received death threats, including George Moscone and Harvey Milk. This threatening atmosphere was one of the reasons given to explain why White carried a loaded pistol into City Hall the day of the murder. Others admitted to doing the same on occasion. There were rumors of terrorist groups, such as those from the Jonestown collective, plotting to kill city officials. Testifying at White's trial, Mayor Diane Feinstein recalled, "I had several threats from the New World Liberation Front terrorist organization" (Weiss 1984: 310). An October 1975 *Time Magazine* article on California's underground described the New World Liberation Front as "composed of about 25 middle class whites and possibly some black ex-convicts, the group has claimed responsibility for 23 terrorist bombings in the Bay Area and Sacramento since Sept. 3, 1974."[7] Just a week before the murder, the mass suicide at Jonestown rocked the nation and dominated the headlines for nearly a week, with each day bringing more horror and higher body counts, not dissimilar to the Vietnam War coverage a few years prior. As already noted, Jonestown had an even greater impact upon the San Francisco audience, since its leader, the notorious Jim Jones, had been a local pastor active in the Moscone campaign who had been rewarded with a position in his administration.

Interpretation through social drama provides an insight not only into motive, but also into alternative readings of the event. There were two dominant narratives to emerge out of the San Francisco murders. The one established at the trial was that of an honest man who had temporarily "snapped" in the face of great disappointment; the other told of two community leaders tragically struck down in a city known for violence. If White's actions are placed in the context of the violence of the time, it is still tragic (for both the victims and perpetrator), but also more easily understood. As a soldier in a wartime army, White had been trained to kill and, as a police officer, violence was part of his daily life. It was also part of the daily, mass-mediated American experience in the 1970s, when violence seemed to be everywhere, from the televised coverage of the Vietnam War, to the mass suicide in Guyana, to the continuously reported violence on the nation's city streets. In this context, responding to the perceived threat to family and community with violence did not appear that strange. This perspective allows us to better address the question, Who was Dan White when he engaged in the act of murder? Was he a man temporarily of "diminished capacity," whose ability to react rationally to disappointment had been radically distorted by a junk food diet, as his defense attorneys successfully argued? Or was he an individual shaped by his age and background, acting desperately to right a wrong through means that appeared appropriate to the circumstances? Was he a representative figure acting out class and gender ideals in a corrupt world he could no longer understand, much less control, as his own family and community appeared to think?

Conclusion

The assassination of Moscone and Milk was a very public occurrence. Once it happened, it could not be denied and led to a cascade of significant consequences. In addition to the law against violence against other persons, the norms of the democratic process had been breached and a vacuum created at the top of local government. The three persons involved were all well-known members of the civic community, and the violence of their interaction reverberated widely. Beyond their immediate family and friends and law enforcement authorities, the governing of the city was disrupted and, once reported, the mass media turned the eyes of the nation and the world toward the city. One of the victims was a prominent member of a vibrant community-in-formation, a man whose death caused a tear in a fragile social fabric, leaving an indelible mark and spurring a cultural trauma.

From the point of view of social drama, the story could have concluded after the funeral and mourning. All that remained was a denouement consisting of a few annual commemorative events, some streets and public buildings named for the victims, and perhaps a monument or two constructed in the city. However, several circumstances intervened to shift the narrative. The initial response of city residents to the murders was an outpouring of grief and a peaceful march in honor of the fallen victims. The gay community turned out in the thousands to mourn the loss of both Moscone and Milk, though the emphasis was clearly on the latter. Had the trial been the more or less ritual act of justice and reconciliation that one could have expected, things might have ended there. But the sense of outrage that the verdict evoked was impetus to a new wave of protest and a new narrative structure. The murders became seen more clearly as assassinations, the killing not only of two political leaders, but also of a sense of justice. Through this verdict, many members of the public, especially those within the gay community, felt that the core, anti-gay values of American society were revealed; homosexuals were not real members of society, for they could apparently be legally assassinated. This feeling ignited a cultural trauma in a collective that was gaining a new sense of self. The gay community in San Francisco, already a strong political force, was through these occurrences further consolidated. Just as he was in life, the figure of the slain Harvey Milk became a catalyst to mobilization and collective identity. With heightened awareness of its own vulnerability, the gay community mourned the loss of one of its representative figures as it was forced to re-narrate its relations to the wider society. In that ongoing process, the assassination of Harvey Milk became an iconic event that has now, with the aid of mass-mediated representations, inspired actors and activists around the globe.

Notes

1. One of the conspiracy theories circulating after the murders alleged that it was Jones's representatives who had ordered the murder of Moscone and Milk.
2. Regarding those previous electoral attempts, Castells writes: "In his first election race, in 1973, Harvey Milk attracted 17,000 votes and came eleventh in a field of 33 candidates. Although it was an excellent showing, it was, at the same time, a sign that he also had to address a broader liberal constituency. In his second electoral attempt, in 1975, while he was still a gay candidate, he also dealt with the more general issues, particularly emphasizing the need to control real estate speculation. He assumed a 'straight image,' and his support jumped to 53,000 votes, but he still lost" (1983: 143).
3. White had a romantic attachment to Ireland and identified himself as Irish-American. On the day he killed Moscone and Milk, he carried a book cover in his breast pocket from a book about Ireland. Commenting on this, one blogger wrote: "'The Town I Loved So Well' says a lot to me about Dan White. White was a boy in San Francisco in the Fifties and Sixties. SF in those days was half the size it is now; a small comfortable livable city … The Sunset District epitomizes White … in the Forties and Fifties [this district was] working class Irish or Italian … Until the 1970s, the Sunset was Dan White's "The Town I Loved So Well" … a big Asian influx started in the late Seventies, and the Sunset District is now 75% Asian, mostly Chinese. White was alive when the other Irish neighborhood, the Castro, became the gay ghetto. The Castro was a pretty rundown area in the early Seventies. First hippies moved in. Then gays began to buy up rundown houses and gentrify the neighborhood. Most of the Irish left and the hippies moved to the Haight" (Patrick Joubert Conlon, March 29, 2009, www.bornagainredneck.blogspot.com. Accessed February 11, 2010).

4. John D'Emilio has another perspective on Milk's political views and his relation to George Moscone: "[D]uring 1978 [Milk] helped push Moscone away from mainstream liberalism and toward a populist-style coalition politics. By the time of the November election, Milk had become one of the most popular politicians in San Francisco and had achieved wide voter recognition throughout the state" (1993: 73–74).
5. FitzGerald (1986) points out that it was largely gay men who were moving into San Francisco in the 1970s and who formed the bulk of Milk's constituency. She points out that gay men and lesbian women often had different political and cultural priorities. Milk surprised many when he chose a lesbian to serve as his chief aide.
6. According to one account, Milk "clearly designated the names of four persons who could replace him as supervisor" (Castells 1983: 164). Among them was Harry Britt.
7. Accessed at http://www.time.com.

References

Alexander, Jeffrey, Bernhard Giesen, and Jason L. Mast (eds.). 2006. *Social Performance: Symbolic Action, Cultural Pragmatics, and Ritual*. Cambridge: Cambridge University Press.

Alexander, Jeffrey, Ronald Eyerman, Bernhard Giesen, Neil Smelser, and Piotr Sztompka (eds.). 2004. *Cultural Trauma and Collective Identity*. Berkeley: University of California Press.

Arendt, Hannah. 1953. *The Human Condition*. New York: Doubleday.

Armstrong, Elizabeth A., and Suzanna M. Crage. 2006. Movements and Memory: The Making of the Stonewall Myth. *American Sociological Review* 71 (October): 734–751.

Binder, D. 1978. Reports Conflict on Status of Jones Cult's Finances. *The New York Times*, December 16, p. 12.

Castells, Manuel. 1983. *The City and the Grassroots*. Berkeley: University of California Press.

D'Emilio, John. 1993. Gay Politics and Community in San Francisco. In *Psychological Perspectives on Lesbian and Gay Male Experiences*, ed. Linda Garnets and Douglas Kimmel. New York: Columbia University Press.

Eyerman, Ronald. 2001. *Cultural Trauma: Slavery and the Formation of African American Identity*. Cambridge: Cambridge University Press.

Eyerman, Ronald. 2008. *The Assassination of Theo van Gogh: From Social Drama to Cultural Trauma*. Durham, NC: Duke University Press.

Eyerman, Ronald. 2011. *The Cultural Sociology of Political Assassination*. New York: Palgrave Macmillan.

FitzGerald, Frances. 1986. A Reporter at Large: The Castro-1. *The New Yorker*, July 21, pp. 34–70.
Geluardi, John. 2008. Dan White's Motive More About Betrayal Than Homophobia. *San Francisco Weekly*, January 30.
Gruen, John. 1972. 'Do You Mind Critics Calling You Cheap, Decadent, Sensationalistic, Gimmicky, Vulgar, Overinflated, Megalomaniacal?' 'I Don't Read Reviews Very Much,' Answers Tom O'Horgan. *The New York Times Sunday Magazine*, January 2, p. 14.
Klapp, Orrin E. 1964. *Symbolic Leaders*. Chicago: Aldine.
Mann, Emily. 1997. *Testimonies: Four Plays by Emily Mann*. New York: Theater Communications Group.
McFarland, Daniel A. 2004. Resistance as a Social Drama: A Study of Change-Oriented Encounters. *American Journal of Sociology* 109 (6): 1249–1318.
musicmedia10. 2008. November 18, 1977 Harvey Milk Speaks, Audio Tape He Recorded. YouTube Video. Available at http://www.youtube.com/watch?v=Y-9dGPVVUQ. Posted November 17, 2008. Accessed February 11, 2010.
Sahlins, Marshall D. 1981. *Historical Metaphors and Mythical Realities: Structure in the Early History of the Sandwich Islands Kingdom*. Ann Arbor: University of Michigan Press.
Sewell, William H., Jr. 1996. Historical Events as Transformations of Structure: Inventing Revolution at the Bastille. *Theory and Society* 25: 841–881.
Shilts, Randy. 1982. *The Mayor of Castro Street: The Life and Times of Harvey Milk*. New York: St. Martin's Press.
Turner, Victor W. 1974. *Dramas, Fields, and Metaphors: Symbolic Action in Human Society*. Ithaca, NY: Cornell University Press.
Turner, Victor W. 1980. Social Dramas and Stories About Them. *Critical Inquiry* 7 (1): 141–168.
Vinitzky-Seroussi, Vered. 2009. *Yitzhak Rabin's Assassination and the Dilemmas of Commemoration*. Albany: State University of New York Press.
Wagner-Pacifici, Robin E. 1986. *The Moro Morality Play: Terrorism as Social Drama*. Chicago: University of Chicago Press.
Weiss, Mike. 1984. *Double Play: The Hidden Passions Behind the Double Assassination of George Moscone and Harvey Milk*. Reading, MA: Addison-Wesley.
Weiss, Mike. 2000. Art That Captured a City's Pain: It's Been a Long, Strange Trip for Bust of Slain Mayor. *San Francisco Chronicle*, November 26, p. A1.
Willmore, A. 2008. Interview: Rob Epstein on 'The Times of Harvey Milk'. Available at http://www.ifc.com.

CHAPTER 5

Social Theory and Cultural Trauma

Introduction

In this chapter I use three classic works of social theory to discuss how the personal trauma of their authors' has influenced their writings. The books are Sigmund Freud's *Moses and Monotheism*, Zygmunt Bauman's *Modernity and the Holocaust*, and *The Dialectic of the Enlightenment* by Max Horkheimer and Theodor Adorno. I use "trauma" here in its common meaning as the impact of shocking occurrences that profoundly affect an individual's life. Such "inner catastrophes" leave wounds and memory scars that cannot easily be erased and that influence later behavior in unexpected and unpredictable ways. While all of these authors were directly affected by the "outer" catastrophe that struck European Jews during the Second World War, none had direct experience of what came to be called the Holocaust. The trauma they experienced was not that of a camp survivor, and these texts cannot be called testimonial (Zolkos 2010). Yet they do bear witness to that catastrophe in the indirect sense of those who could well have been victims but who managed to escape, leaving a feeling of consternation that finds expression in their work.

In what follows I describe the origins of the concept of "trauma" and give a brief outline of how personal and collective trauma affected the books by Freud and Bauman. This is followed by a longer account of Horkheimer and Adorno, where I include an article by the latter, "What does it mean to work through the past?" written in 1959 after the pair

R. Eyerman, *Memory, Trauma, and Identity*, Cultural Sociology,
https://doi.org/10.1007/978-3-030-13507-2_5

had returned to Germany. Here the aim is to illustrate the concept of cultural trauma, a concept that incorporates both individual and collective trauma within it. These works were selected in other words to illustrate distinctive notions of trauma: individual, collective, and cultural.

Trauma: Individual and Collective

The word *trauma* stems from the ancient Greek term for "wound" (see Leys (2000) for a full genealogy). In contemporary medical and psychiatric literature, "[t]he term *trauma* is understood as a wound inflicted not upon the body but upon the mind" (Caruth 1996: 3 ff.), a wound inflicted by an emotional shock so powerful that it breaches "the mind's experience of time, self and the world" (Caruth 1996: 4) and eventually manifests itself in dreams and flashbacks. In this conception, an occurrence is traumatic not simply because it is forceful, but because it is *unthinkable* in that it "resists simple comprehension" (Caruth 1996: 6) and cannot easily be assimilated into already established frameworks of understanding. The actual trauma itself, however, is not the only aspect that is harmful to the victim; it is the repression of its memory that brings forth the symptoms. Freud first associated trauma with hysteria in women before later adapting this term in an attempt to explain the long-term, recurring effects of industrial and transportation accidents in the late nineteenth century. This notion was further modified and elaborated in connection with his treatment of victims of trench warfare during the First World War. In all these cases, trauma makes reference to a real occurrence, a physical or emotional blow that overwhelms the senses and against which the mind and body must defend itself. In addition to physical numbness, a condition where the capacity to feel pain is temporarily suspended, amnesia and repression are defenses of the mind against such an intrusion. The victim simply forgets or denies that anything has occurred. In developing a dynamic model of trauma, Freud called this forgetting a period of latency, a time during which the trauma victim can appear quite normal in carrying out everyday routines. There is no exact time frame for the latency period—it could last for days or even years—but the effects of the original experience will at some point emerge and manifest themselves, either in nightmares or some otherwise inexplicable abnormal behavior. Freud's notion of trauma thus builds around the direct experience of an actual occurrence and clearly identifiable individual victims. For later theorists in this tradition, Auschwitz and Hiroshima fully disclosed the catastrophic potential of modernity, and trauma and modernity were intimately linked in a much more general and abstract way (Fassin and Rechtman 2009; Kaplan 2005). From this perspective, one of the manifestations of a catastrophic age is taken to be the insufficiency of word and narrative to capture the affect of traumatic experience, making reading and writing about trauma a problematic exercise (LaCapra 2001).

Contemporary revisions of the classical notion of trauma focus on two aspects: first, the traumatic effects on the victim, the recurrent unwanted intrusion of memory and its affect on behavior; second, on the possibility—or the "impossibility" (Caruth 1996)—of memory. In such conceptualizations, reading and writing about trauma opens up to literature a specific kind of experience, one that becomes available not merely to the therapist but also to the theorist. Studies of trauma reveal a previously uncharted world to the observer and thus in a tragic way create an opportunity to see what would otherwise remain deeply hidden. In this sense, trauma at the individual level resembles crisis at the societal level. A crisis, such as a severe economic depression, is a shocking occurrence that can cause a breakdown in daily routines and at the same time expose the largely taken for granted values that guide them; crises in this sense reveal to a collective the grounds of its collective identity (Habermas 1975). Like individual trauma, a societal crisis is both a shock to established routines and taken-for-granted identities and an opportunity, because to the trained eye it reveals what otherwise remains deeply hidden. While at the individual level trauma is inclusive, at the collective level it can be exclusive as well, a process in which old collectivities can be reaffirmed and new ones created. Kai Erikson formulates it this way: "trauma has both centripetal and centrifugal tendencies. It draws one away from the center of group space while at the same time drawing one back" (1994: 232).

Individual and collective traumas both issue from shock, and in each instance the wounds that incur are collective and social as much as they are individual. Individual and collective trauma may also be thought of as reinforcing one another, compounding the shock and sense of loss experienced. In economic crisis—as in war—one's personal loss is intimately tied to that suffered by others. The cumulative impact intensifies the trauma, where a sense of belonging, a shared collective identity, is shattered along with one's individual identity.

Cultural Trauma

With reference to individual and collective trauma as described above, cultural trauma is a dimension apart as it refers to more abstract and mediated notions of collective identity, including religious and national identity. Cultural trauma is usually connected with a traumatic incident and thus with individual and collective trauma, but its occurrence is contingent on a number of factors that might or might not be present (Eyerman 2011). In an insightful discussion of the difference between psychological and cultural trauma, Neil Smelser finds one essential difference in the fact that cultural traumas are made, not born. He goes on to define a cultural trauma as "an invasive and overwhelming event that is believed to undermine or overwhelm one or several essential ingredients of a culture or the culture as a whole" (Smelser 2004: 38). Though acknowledging the discursive aspect of cultural trauma, Smelser grounds the process in an actual event. I think, however, that the key phrase here is "*believed* to undermine," a notion that undercuts any idea that an event could be traumatic in itself. This invites two vital questions: (1) Can *any* occurrence or event whatsoever be made traumatic? In other words, Can *everything* potentially be "believed to undermine" an established collective identity? And if not, (2) What is it that permits some occurrences to become traumatic in this sense and not other seemingly equally powerful or shocking occurrences? (This is precisely the issue raised in the opening paragraph of this chapter.)

The first question raises the issue of the power to create belief. A radical social constructivist might argue that, given the ultimate power to persuade, one could turn any occurrence into a "trauma."[1] This would be to push the idea that "traumas are made not born" to its limits. At the other extreme, a strong naturalist or lay trauma account would make the claim that certain events are traumatic in themselves, i.e. are the direct cause of traumatic affect (Alexander 2004a). In previous works (Eyerman 2001, 2008) I have tried to make the case for a middle position, arguing that certain occurrences—political assassinations, for example—might create conditions conducive to setting in motion a process of cultural trauma, understood as a public discourse in which the foundations of collective identity are opened for reflection and debate (Eyerman 2011). This will not happen without the aid of meaning making forces, including the mass media and certain carrier groups like intellectuals, who influence the formation and direction of a process of cultural trauma.[2] However, not just any interpretative frame will "fit" or make sense in a particular case; there must be some relation, real or perceived, between the interpretive frame and the actual experience. Cultural traumas are not things, but processes of meaning making and attribution, a contentious contest in which various individuals and groups struggle to define a situation and to manage and control it. I would add that these forces are unlikely to create a trauma out of nothing; there is likely to be some powerful, shocking occurrence that creates the possibility and provides the opportunity to mobilize opinions and emotions. There are thus two sides to a cultural trauma: an emotional experience and an interpretative reaction. Shocks arouse emotion by breaking everyday routines (behaviors as well as cognitive frameworks) and as such demand interpretation. This demand for interpretation in turn opens a discursive field where well-placed individuals can play a determinate role. In modem societies, access to mass media is significant in this process. The polarity and disparity between perpetrator and victim are what distinguishes cultural trauma as discourse. In this sense, cultural trauma is a contentious discursive process framed by a dichotomy between perpetrator and victim that is spurred by a powerful, unforgettable occurrence. Cultural trauma is also characterized as discourse in that through the process of trauma creation, an established collective identity is shaken and its foundations called into question. It is a discursive process in which the emotions that are triggered by a traumatic occurrence are worked through and an attempt is made to heal the collective wound.

Freud and Bauman

Moses and Monotheism, Freud's final book, was written in three parts in two locations. Its opening chapters were composed in Vienna in the mid-l930s, while the final sections were written in London after Freud and his family had left Austria in the wake of the German invasion in March 1938. The author dutifully explains all of this to the reader:

> In truth [this book] has been written twice over. The first time was a few years ago in Vienna, where I did not believe in the possibility of publishing it. I decided to put it away, but it haunted me like an unlaid ghost and I compromised by publishing two parts of the book independently.... The rest, which might give offence and was dangerous—namely, the application of my theory to the genesis of monotheism and my interpretation of

> religion—I kept back, as I thought, forever. Then in March 1938 came the unexpected German invasion. It forced me to leave my home, but it also freed me of the fear lest my publishing the book might cause psychoanalysis to be forbidden in a country where it was still allowed. No sooner had I arrived in England than I found the temptation of making my withheld knowledge accessible to the world irresistible, and so I started to rewrite the third part of my essay. (Freud 1967: 132)

The irony is manifest: the "freedom" to publish this work was gained only through forced exodus and exile, a path similar to the one Freud traces in his history of the Jews. Habermas's insight—that the "myth of origin involves the *double meaning* of "springing from": a shudder at being uprooted and a sigh of relief at escaping" (1987: 107)—is apt: "springing from" can mean both a shudder and a sigh of relief. *Moses and Monotheism* concerns myths of origin and is the only work of Freud's where Judaism is the central focus. I suggest that this is explained by the conditions under which it was written, the rise of fascism and the new wave of anti-Semitism devouring Europe at the time of the book's writing, from the cumulative shock of collective identification and personal displacement. This might seem obvious, but what is not so obvious is how the topic of this work might have been influenced by the personal trauma affecting Freud and his family. Freud's central claim is that Moses was not a Jew, but an Egyptian who was later murdered by the Jewish people he helped create.[3] In Freud's account, the formation of the Jewish people is rooted in a wounding occurrence, a primal scene, which must be repressed and denied. Thus the history of the Jews is rooted in a trauma that only becomes available for the author and the reader through Freud's own trauma. The disruption of his own life creates the conditions, the "freedom" for understanding. Equally significant for our purposes are Freud's ruminations over the historical roots of the violent hatred being inflicted upon Jews: "Whence comes this resistance of the Jew and how his character is connected with his fate are things one would like to understand better" (Freud 1967: 134). "Resistance" here means the stubborn resilience through which Jews "defied misfortune and ill-treatment, developed special character traits, and, incidentally, earned the hearty dislike of all other peoples" (Freud 1967: 134). The solace-giving belief that they were God's chosen people became an anchor in the Jewish religion and, according to Freud, created a distance and even an arrogance that he then offers as one of the explanations of this hatred. The victim in other words bears at least some responsibility for the crime being perpetrated. Not only Freud himself, but also his family—Freud's daughter Anna was interrogated by the Gestapo just before they left the country—are now threatened because of a religious identification they had never fully embraced. This ascribed and imposed identification was now responsible for a forced exodus and self-reflective theoretical speculation. In the process, personal and collective trauma became intimately entwined in life and in the form and content of *Moses and Monotheism*.

Zygmunt Bauman's *Modernity and the Holocaust* (1989) can be read in a similar way. Like Freud, Bauman is clear about his book's genesis.[4]

> Having written down her personal story of her life in the ghetto and in hiding, Janina thanked me, her husband, for putting up with her protracted absence during the two years of writing, when she dwelled again in that world "that was not his." Indeed, I escaped that world of horror and inhumanity when it reached out to the most remote comers of Europe. And like so many of my contemporaries I never tried to explore it after it vanished from earth, leaving it to linger in the haunted memory and never-healing scars of those whom it bereaved or wounded. (Bauman 1989: vii)

Through his wife's memoirs of the Warsaw ghetto Bauman confronted his own past, though he frames this confrontation through a polemical dialogue with the discipline of sociology. Reading this profound work through the lens of trauma provides insight into its forcefulness and power. Bauman was forced out of Poland in 1968 when a wave of anti-Semitism swept the country, and while he, like Freud, never fully identified himself with the Jewish faith, others made that identification for him. And again, like Freud, he too ended up in England. It was not this forced exile, however, that spurred him to write about this event that would become so closely identified with Jews and Jewish history. Instead, it was the 1986 publication of his wife's memoirs of ghetto life—written more than forty years after the fact—that spurred Bauman to reflect on the meaning of the Holocaust for his own life and work. This period of latency, spanning the time between the initial shock of the occurrence (the experience of war and the discovery of the extent of its horror) and the interpretive reaction (the writing of *Modernity and the Holocaust*), was ended by a cumulative series of shocks, including forced exile and forced confrontation with the past.

Although the central thesis of *Modernity and the Holocaust* is that the Holocaust, by now universalized as absolute evil (Alexander 2004b), should not be viewed merely as part of Jewish history, but more broadly as a consequence of modernity, the book can also be seen as an outpouring of traumatic recollection, one that led him down the path previously traveled by Horkheimer and Adorno and Freud. As in the case of Freud's *Moses and Monotheism*, one finds in this book the author's need to understand and explain what has been denied or repressed, a memory best forgotten, but which somehow cannot be erased. And like *Moses and Monotheism*, *Modernity and the Holocaust* is fragmentary and disjointed (although this may be more the result of institutional causes than personal trauma). However, beyond the form of the text, one can uncover trauma in the content itself. Unlike many of his previous works (the exceptions being *Legislators and Interpreters* and *Freedom*), *Modernity and the Holocaust* is essayistic and highly polemical in tone. It is argumentative and accusatory, containing a powerful mixture of empirical claims and moral philosophy. This is quite different from Bauman's earlier writing, especially in his Marxist period. There is more than a stylistic break apparent though, because after this work Bauman came to identify himself as a "postmodernist" or at least as a sociologist of postmodernity, marking a fundamental shift in perspective. Similar to Lyotard (1984), Bauman proclaims (often implicitly) the end of grand historical narratives, for both himself and society at large. Upon reflection, the Holocaust marks the end of an epoch, after which things are never the same.

In his introduction to *The Longest Shadow* (1996), where he reflects on "writing trauma," Geoffrey Hartman notes: "There is always a decision for or against silence" (1996: 3). He implies that anyone who has experienced trauma has to decide both whether or not to speak and when something might be better left unsaid since, "to integrate the Holocaust into our image of human nature is to despair of humanity, as well as of language" (1996: 4). From this perspective, it might be that Bauman chose to remain silent about the Holocaust earlier in his life precisely because to speak about it would have deeply challenged his belief in humanity, a foundational belief of Marxist thought. By his own account, however, such a decision was never consciously made. The Holocaust was "an experience that was not experienced, yet had an exceptional presence," to paraphrase Hartman. I will return to this discussion of silence later with reference to Adorno and Horkheimer.

Dialectic of Enlightenment

Like Freud and Bauman, Horkheimer and Adorno are also explicit about the genesis of their collaborative work *Dialectic of Enlightenment*. In the preface written for the 1969 edition, they explain that the book was written in America but published in Amsterdam. The work was written in when the end of the Nazi terror was within sight; nevertheless, in not a few places the reality of our times is formulated in a way no longer appropriate to contemporary experience. And yet even at that time, our assessment of the transition to the world of the administered life was not too simplistic (1972: ix).

Neither a monograph nor a collection of essays, *Dialectic of Enlightenment* "comprises an essay of something over fifty pages, two excursuses, and three appendixes," as Habermas (1987: 107) put it.[5] This disjointedness has led many in search of the main lines of argumentation, as well as an explanation of the book's long-standing appeal. If a central intellectual claim can be uncovered, it is that of an alliance between reason and domination. The European Enlightenment, the philosophical impulse that was to provide the conditions for human liberation through the construction of a social order based on human reason, has shown itself to lead to the opposite. Worse, this was not merely a question of German exceptionalism, but of modernity as such. These broad claims are contained in the famous opening sentence: "In the most general sense of progressive thought, the Enlightenment has always aimed at liberating men from fear and establishing their sovereignty. Yet the fully enlightened earth radiates disaster triumphant" (Horkheimer and Adorno 1972: 3).[6]

While the actual conditions of writing were comfortable, even idyllic, there is both a sense of urgency and despair that comes through the prose. Horkheimer and Adorno, along with the latter's wife and parents, were once again united and living comfortably in the U.S. Freed from institutional obligations, they approached their task with apparent enthusiasm (Muller-Doohm 2005a). Yet the despair and fragmentation that would mark the text was something deeply felt. In writing about modem music a few years before starting *Dialectic of Enlightenment*, Adorno wrote that authentic modern music "has its happiness in the perception of misfortune" and, since it is fragmentary, "no one ... wishes to become involved with it ... it is the surviving message of despair from the shipwrecked" (quoted in Muller-Doohm 2005a: 277). *Dialectic of*

Enlightenment may have been written in idyllic conditions, but this was happiness grown out of misfortune, containing the same sort of "message of despair from the shipwrecked." Like a message in a bottle cast into the sea, *Dialectic of Enlightenment* had no clear addressee. It was meant for no one and for everyone, a cry in the wilderness from those who might on the surface appear to be free-floating intellectuals, but who beneath that sunburned veneer were castaways adrift in a meaningless void.

The effects of exile and the culture shock experienced in an indifferent America during the years of writing (1939–1944) can be pointed to in order to explain the often exaggerated prose and fragmentary nature of *Dialectic of Enlightenment.* The actual manuscript existed in at least two different forms when they first appeared in a mimeographed copy in New York in 1944. How much this version differed from the one published in Amsterdam three years later has been analyzed by several scholars, including Ziege (2009) and van Reijen and Bransen (2002). These authors and others have pointed out the significant changes made in those intervening years (something entirely denied by Horkheimer and Adorno in their introduction to the 1947 edition), most pointedly those related to the removal of Marxist concepts. The explanation offered for such changes is usually framed in terms of internal theoretical debates, or of not wanting to offend their American hosts. This may well be correct, but I would also suggest their own experience, their trauma, as a primary cause of this fundamental shift.[7] Adorno would later write,

> After the Second World War, everything, including a resurrected culture, has been destroyed without realizing it; humankind continues to vegetate, creeping along after events that even the survivors cannot really survive, on a rubbish heap that has made even reflection on one's damaged state useless. (Adorno 1991: 244)

The capitulation of the working classes in Germany and Italy, and their accommodation in France, helped create a sense of loss and disbelief for those who believed in a Marxist theory of history. It is true that earlier studies, such as that carried out by Erich Fromm in Weimar in the late 1920s, already hinted at "working class authoritarianism" and a potential accommodation to both authoritarian dictatorship and the "command economy," such as that installed by the Nazis; however, the seeming total collapse of working-class solidarity was unexpected. The idea of class struggle as a source of redemption was lost to Horkheimer and Adorno forever, and this idea had formed the basis of their analysis of contemporary society much more than any economistic notion of class. The loss of this historical agent, combined with their personal experience of being outcasts, fostered a sense of hopelessness and disillusionment. To this one can add both the traumatic memory of the suicide of Adomo's close confidant and mentor Walter Benjamin (Benjamin killed himself in the midst of a failed attempt to flee the Nazis) and the knowledge that two colleagues, Karl Wittfogel and Paul Massing, had been imprisoned in concentration camps. Benjamin's death is claimed by one historian (Wiggerhaus 1995) to be the "guiding star" that unified this fragmentary work. A final blow came with the revelations about the fate of the Jews near the war's end. It was this disclosure that prompted the inclusion of the chapter on anti-Semitism in the final version of the book (Rabinbach 1997).[8]

Habermas (1987) described *Dialectic of Enlightenment* as a distinct break with Horkheimer and Adorno' s previous reflections on the aims of critical theory. Heins makes the stronger claim that critical theory itself emerges from trauma. He writes: "I … depict Critical Theory as a trauma narrative in which a particular group of people affected informs the public about the nature of a great injury" (Heins 2011). For Heins the desire to publish, to objectify—and in this sense make permanent—was a form of witnessing, an attempt to preserve from extinction a form of thought against the changing tides of history.

As with Freud and the writing of *Moses and Monotheism,* I suggest that one could call the cumulative effect of such experience *traumatic* in the classical sense outlined above. That forced mobility affected the form of the book is clear. It is also important to consider that the book is a collaborative effort (something very new for Adorno) by two individuals known for their independence of thought. The strong personalities of the authors, however, does not by itself account for the passion expressed on the pages of *Dialectic of Enlightenment.* Rather, it is their emotional state that is most significant, their sense of despair that the attuned ear hears and recognizes as the sound of intellectuals cut adrift from their moorings. Reading this text "as trauma" reveals a shattered sense of identity and meaning, individually felt but with a collective referent. Despite this, however, one also finds a biting rhetorical style (most probably Adomo's) that one can say is appropriate to their message, at least if the text is read as literature, as well as social theory. The future may look dim for those who truly believed in critical Marxist theory, but this has not dampened the ability to witness its collapse with caustic irony. The authors of *Dialectic of Enlightenment* may be grieving, but they disguise it with their rhetorical style. The text is full of shifts and twists of language, especially when they are speaking about mass culture and the emergent power of the "culture industry," a concept coined in this work that helps explain its continuing relevance.

Few who read *Dialectic of Enlightenment* today would view it as documentation of traumatic experience, though they might wonder about the forcefulness of the writing style and its powerful sense of urgency. Sympathetic readers are more likely to find the analysis insightful and as alive and compelling as if were only just written. This is in part due to the insights offered into the nature and structure of modem society, that is, the knowledge gained in reading the text as social theory. The authors were correct when they retrospectively wrote, "our assessment of the transition of the world of the administered life was not too simplistic" ("Preface to the New Edition," 1969). Indeed, their analysis of the role of mass culture and the culture industry seems even fresher today than when originally written. Now at least there is an audience. Horkheimer and Adorno may have written with the intention of bearing witness to the death of a Marxist-inspired critical theory, but they also witnessed the birth of mass consumer society. Their trauma provided the grounds for that insight, making it available to later generations of readers.

From Trauma to Cultural Trauma

One of Adomo's most quoted reflections is the pronouncement that writing poetry after Auschwitz would be barbaric (1967: 34).[9] Poetry here may stand for all literature and, perhaps, aesthetic representation generally. Heins (2011) suggests that Auschwitz came to symbolize modernity as such in Adorno's mind, and he used the term as shorthand to communicate its dark side to a new generation of Germans who had experienced neither the Second World War nor the Holocaust first hand. Taken in the narrower sense to mean literary expression and representation, much has been said about what this pronouncement might mean (see Rothberg [1997] for a perceptive analysis). Should one remain silent in the manner of Bauman or speak in the manner of Primo Levi, Nelly Sachs, or Paul Celan? Did this prohibition include only art and literature, or also social theory, such as the works of Hannah Arendt? Was silence the only alternative to public recognition of the Holocaust? What, after all, does silence mean?[10]

In a speech to German schoolteachers in 1959, Adorno addressed this issue in terms of public education. This speech was later published as "What does it mean to work through the past?" Its German title, "*Was bedeutet: Aufarbeitung der Vergangenheit*?" is a play on the title of Immanuel Kant's famous essay, "What is Enlightenment?" (Olick 2003). Adorno's title also makes clear reference to the psychoanalytic project of working through a neurosis or trauma through honest and fearless confrontation. Adorno and his Frankfurt colleagues had recently (1950–1951) completed a large-scale empirical study of German "non-public opinion," where findings indicated the continuing presence of authoritarian tendencies among the German populace (Adorno 2010).[11] Adorno gave the talk twice, once before and then again just after a new wave of anti-Semitism swept through the German Federal Republic. According to Anson Rabinbach (1997), this new publically expressed anti-Semitism "demonstrated the failures of postwar denazification" (Olick 2003: 550). In his talks, Adorno traced this failure to the lack of any real attempt to confront—and thereby work through—the past. As he commented in his opening remarks before the second presentation (made at the invitation of what was to become the leading German radical student organization, the German Socialist Student Association [SDS] on May 22, 1962):

> please understand my reflections [on the possible reemergence of fascism in Germany] as a contribution to the attempt to deal with the threat not through fruitless indignation and cosmetic measures, but rather by comprehending it in its deeper dimensions. Some suggestions for praxis nonetheless may follow, even if one does not imagine the path from insight to action to be as short as so many well-meaning people today seem to believe it to be. (Adorno 2010: 308)

As an important public figure, as well as a respected academic, Adorno was to be a significant force in the German debates about the Nazi era and its meaning for the nation that would emerge through the new generation and the social movements of the 1960s. His postwar books and articles were printed in the thousands, and between 1950 and 1969 Adorno participated in more than 160 radio programs (Pickford in Adorno 2010: viii). Adorno was a representative symbol, a German Jew returning from forced exile, as well as a leading figure of one of the most influential intellectual traditions of prewar Germany. He and Horkheimer had returned to help reinstate and rebuild the nation's higher education system, as well as its intellectual standing in the world. A fundamental premise of this project, as of the ongoing American occupation, was the elimination of all traces of the Nazi past and the creation of a democratic society with a robust public sphere where this past could be honestly acknowledged and discussed. That this had not occurred in more than what he considered a cosmetic way was Adorno's central point; rather, the past had merely been repressed. However, in the coming years a new generation would form itself in part by confronting its elders about their role during the Nazi era (Giesen 2004). In this confrontation, Adorno would be viewed as both an intellectual hero and, at one and the same time, a figure of ridicule. His "old-fashioned bourgeois" manners, including his attitudes toward women, were mocked by student radicals at the same time as they honored him as a living memento of prewar critical theory. Through his person, a new generation of students worked through the German past. As Giesen reveals this was but one small part of a wider national and generational confrontation that I call a *cultural trauma*, an emotionally charged meaning struggle over the foundations of collective identity in which perpetrators and victims are named and the past as collective memory is re-narrated as it is worked through. Along with other forums and forms of public expression, literature and the arts would play a central role in this meaning struggle over the foundations of collective identity. Social theorists in the role of public intellectuals, like Adorno and Habermas, if not social theory itself, would also play an important part along with the student activists they taught and confronted (Muller-Doohm 2005b).

Personal and Cultural Trauma

Personal trauma is difficult to narrate while it is being lived through. It is formidable, not to say impossible, to grasp the meaning of shocking occurrences as they are experienced. It is typically only after the fact that interpretation and real understanding become possible. Freud saw the process of trauma, from occurrence to understanding, as one in which forgetting was an essential element. For Holocaust survivors such as Primo Levi, who were at first totally baffled by the obscene reality they faced, narration was nearly impossible. It took years to find a form proper to what was experienced. Finding an audience willing to listen was also not an easy matter. The first accounts written by Holocaust survivors and others appeared almost directly at the war's end but found little interest from either publishers or readers.[12] Whether or not one calls this temporal dimension "latency" or "necessary distance" is a matter of the framework of interpretation one applies. However, whichever term one might choose, time and distance, as well as a form proper to representation, appear necessary when dealing with experiences that so powerfully shock one's accustomed being in the world. When this shattering of the taken-for-granted occurs at a collective level, we may speak of the beginnings of cultural trauma. Cultural traumas begin with disruptions to the established foundations of collective identity, something that can entirely destroy a collective, or at the very least demand a re-narration of the myths and beliefs that ground that collective.

Literature and the arts have proven to be of central importance in the process of re-narration, something I discussed in a previous work on slavery and the formation of African American identity (Eyerman 2001). In that case, works of fiction and the visual arts were especially important in articulating and communicating a form of experience that had been made invisible, namely, that of black Americans. This too was the case in Germany with regard to the Nazi past, and most especially with regard to those the Nazis victimized. In 1969, when an art student named Anslem Kiefer performed an illegal Hitler salute in a bathtub, it was cause for outrage, especially when this was done outdoors in the public squares of European cities (Anderson 2008: 129). A few years earlier, the film director and author Alexander Kluge produced a series of "biographies" of perpetrators and victims of the war. After Gunter Grass's path-breaking *Tin Drum* (2009 [1959]) and a few other novels and plays, such as those by Rolf Hochhuth (*The Deputy*, 1964 [1963]), Peter Weiss (*The Investigation*, 2010 [1965]) and Heinar Kipphardt (*In the Matter of J. Robert Oppenheimer*, 1997 [1964])—all influenced by the Eichmann trial in 1961 and the Auschwitz trials in 1963–1965—German literature did not really engage with the Holocaust, anti-Semitism, and the darker sides of the Nazi past. This would have to wait until after the 1968 student uprisings. And it was in this context that *Dialectic of Enlightenment* was rereleased. More than a document from a traumatic past, it became an intervention in the ongoing German cultural trauma, as well as a call to arms for student activists around the globe. Who in 1944 would ever have imagined?

Conclusion

One can read a text in many ways. Texts in social theory are not usually judged aesthetically or evaluated for any deeper meaning beyond their explicit arguments (exceptions to this include Marxist and feminist ideology critiques that seek to expose underlying bias). By aesthetic reading I mean paying attention to the *mode of presentation*, peering beyond logical argumentation and the careful use of factual information and reference. That which is generally assumed to be important in reading social theory is not the mode of presentation, but what one "acquires" from a text. Social theory texts are meant to provide information and knowledge, and in rare cases a new way of viewing the world. While this latter may share certain aspects with literature, the difference is that literary texts are *meant* to be read aesthetically. Here the act and experience of reading itself is central, and "the reader's primary concern is with what happens *during* the act of reading" (Rosenblatt 1978: 25). Though form is paramount, literary texts, of course, can also perform a therapeutic function for their writers as well as their readers. Writing and reading about grief and other strong emotions, either through fiction or memoir, can offer temporary relief to the author while at the same time being met with empathetic understanding from the reader. Literature can also be a means of communicating an unacknowledged or unimagined experience, such as Toni Morrison's novels about the American slave experience (Eyerman 2001). Bearing witness to catastrophe can be done in a literary mode, as fact or fiction (Zolkos 2010). Like social theory, the literary form offers the writer distance from emotion while at the same time exercising its ability to draw in the reader in unexpected ways.

In this chapter, I have read social theory texts in the aesthetic mode. Like appreciating abstract art, reading social theory in this manner requires a certain disposition and willingness on the part of the reader. Reading social theory as an expression of trauma means looking through the text for an underlying rupture—what Hartman called the "original inner catastrophe"—that disrupts the flow of argumentation and helps account for any sudden breaks, lapses, and absences. Reading social theory in light of trauma theory is to find meaning in what might otherwise look like exaggeration, fragmentation, or obvious inconsistency. The three texts discussed above show elements of all of these, something uncommon in works of social theory, where the norms guiding the logic of presentation are stringent. Freud's *Moses and Monotheism* is a highly unusual book for an author with realist pretensions. The argument moves forward in starts and stops, changes course, and then starts over again. I believe such ruptures are directly connected to the trauma Freud was both personally experiencing and trying to understand at one and the same time. *Modernity and the Holocaust* expresses personal trauma of another sort. Like *Dialectic of Enlightenment,* Bauman's reflections are those of the consternated survivor. In his writing as in his life, Bauman is more activist than victim, and he engages his subject with more distance than Horkheimer and Adorno, being more than forty years removed from his topic. Bauman speaks in the name of morality and responsibility to an audience of academics who in his mind have not taken proper heed of the Holocaust. In *Dialectic of Enlightenment,* there is no clear addressee, for in the mind of its authors there is no one who cares to listen. This too is part of the trauma reflected in the text. Especially during the 1960s, after the Eichmann and Auschwitz trials, the book suddenly finds its audience; the opening in the public discourse affords Adorno an opportunity to expand his public voice. In this new context, personal trauma and cultural trauma coalesce. While social theory is not poetry, one might still raise the question, Is writing social theory after Auschwitz barbarism? Adorno remained ambivalent about the possibility of a critical social theory in postwar Germany and approached his topic with uneasiness. Bauman reveals neither ambivalence nor uneasiness. Critical social theory is not only possible; it is necessary, even if the audience might be a restricted one. However, he agrees with Adorno that social theory should offer no solace. And while it might not change the world, it could at least reflect on its condition. A voice in the wilderness is better than no voice at all, and personal trauma helped him find that voice.

Notes

1. This is a different way of speaking about "radical constructivism" than LaCapra (2001: 8), who uses the term in the context of the line between history writing and fiction. In his sense, those like Hayden White (1990), who argue that on the formal level there is no fundamental difference between writing history and writing fiction (because both necessarily make use of narration) are radical constructivists. For White the form itself imposes an interpretation.
2. A parallel might well be the Marxian idea of class-consciousness and the distinction between class-in-itself and class-for-itself.

3. Edward Said (2004) thought *Moses and Monotheism* a major work by a major European. In *Freud and the Non-European*, reprinted from a lecture Said held at London's Freud museum, he found in Freud's book grounds for criticizing Israeli policy vis-à-vis Palestinians. In his view, the argument that Moses was an Egyptian revealed the non-Jewish precedents to Jewish identity.
4. I am aware of the ongoing discussion about the relation between Bauman's biography and his published works. My position in the case of *Modernity and Holocaust* is that biography and history played an extremely important role in the book's emergence, though not in the usual sense of that relation. Here the connection was filtered through denial and trauma.
5. Habermas, who had firsthand knowledge of both authors, also writes

   Dialectic of Enlightenment is an odd book. A substantial part of it is composed of notes taken by Gretel Adorno during discussions between Horkheimer and Adorno in Santa Monica, California. ... The impact of this book—through which Horkheimer and Adorno exercised a special influence upon the intellectual development of the Federal Republic of Germany, especially in its first two decades—stands in curious relation to the number of its purchasers. (Habermas 1987: 106 ff.)

6. In a recent English translation, this is rendered as:

   Enlightenment, understood in the widest sense as the advance of thought, has always aimed at liberating human beings from fear and installing them as masters. Yet the wholly enlightened earth is radiant with triumphant calamity. Enlightenment's program was the disenchantment of the world. (2002: I)

7. Heins makes a similar claim when he writes

   Ziege regards these changes as no more than tactical adaptations to the emerging culture of the Cold War, whereas my suspicion is that with their sharply dichotomizing discourse Horkheimer and Adorno were on their way to declaring that modem society as a whole is a traumatizing evil. (2011: 37)

   To the extent that this is true, the claims made by Bauman in 1986 mirror this view. Yet there is a difference between them. One of Bauman's claims is sociological and historical: it was modem technology, including the railroad and bureaucratic administration (and the workaday attitudes created by the latter) that made the mass killing of Jews possible. This claim can be assessed through empirical argument (however, it should be noted that this sort of assessment would be more difficult in judging the moral claims of the book). On the other hand, Horkheimer and Adorno make the more abstract, philosophical claim that Auschwitz emerges out of the mythical origins of the modem "enlightened" world-view. Historical and empirical argument purporting to show that modem technology did not play much of a role in the Holocaust would not, for example, pose the same challenge to their argument as it would to Bauman's. Their argument is so rooted in their own traumatic experience that it is difficult to think of how one could counter it, though Habermas (1987: 106 ff.) does make an attempt.

8. Their understanding of the grounds of anti-Semitism has some similarity with that traced by Freud in *Moses and Monotheism*. Anti-Semitism has religious roots, they claim, and Jews can bear some responsibility for the hatred against them. But the fate of Jews at the hands of the Nazis was more a matter of chance and opportunity where the "rage is vented on those who are both conspicuous and unprotected … the victims are interchangeable: vagrants, Jews, Protestants, Catholics, so each of them can replace the murderer" (Horkheimer and Adorno 2002: 140).
9. These words appear in the article "Cultural Criticism and Society" reprinted in *Prisms*, but written in 1949 and first published in 1951 (Schlant 1999: 246). Schlant also points out that Adorno was later to change his position, at least with reference to Holocaust poetry. In 1966 Adorno wrote: "The enduring suffering has as much right to expression as the tortured man to scream; therefore it may have been wrong that after Auschwitz poetry could no longer be written" (quoted in Schlant 1999: 9). Rothberg (1997) offers a slightly different analysis, suggesting not that Adorno changed his position, but that the social conditions in Germany had changed and that Adorno was adjusting his message to fit.
10. Schlant (1999: 7–15) offers a perceptive discussion of the possible meanings of "silence" with reference to the Holocaust and Adomo's proclamation. Rothberg (1997) gives a broader interpretation of the alternatives for making art through a close reading of Adorno's later work, especially his literary criticism, where Beckett's plays are seen as exemplars of how one could write after Auschwitz.
11. This study has recently been translated and published in English in two books, *Group Experiment* (Adorno 2010) and *Guilt and Defense* (Adorno 2010), both edited, translated, and introduced by Jeffrey Olick and Andrew Perrin. *Group Experiment* followed on the heels of Adorno's participation in the American based *Authoritarian Personality* (Adorno et al. 1950) and reproduced in a modified form some of the methodology from that study.
12. This should perhaps be clarified a little. It appears that publishers were more willing to publish firsthand factual accounts of war experience,

including testimonials from survivors, than readers were willing to buy and read. Such accounts fit with the "need to know" and also with the desire to prosecute and blame.

References

Adorno, Theodor. 1981 [1967]. *Prisms*. Cambridge, MA: MIT Press.

Adorno, Theodor. 1991. *Notes to Literature*. New York: Columbia University Press.

Adorno, Theodor. 2010. *Guilt and Defense*. Cambridge, MA: Harvard University Press.

Adorno, Theodor, Else Frenkel-Brunswick, Daniel J. Levinson, and Nevitt Sanfo. 1950. *The Authoritarian Personality*. New York: Harper & Row.

Alexander, Jeffrey. 2004a. Toward a Theory of Cultural Trauma. In *Cultural Trauma and Collective Identity*, ed. Jeffrey Alexander, Ronald Eyerman, Bernhard Giesen, Neil Smelser, and Piotr Sztompka. Berkeley: University of California Press.

Alexander, Jeffrey. 2004b. On the Construction of Moral Universals: The 'Holocaust' from War Crime to Trauma Drama. In *Cultural Trauma and Collective Identity*, ed. Jeffrey Alexander, Ronald Eyerman, Bernhard Giesen, Neil Smelser, and Piotr Sztompka. Berkeley: University of California Press.

Anderson, Mark M. 2008. Documents, Photography, Postmemory: Alexander Kluge, W. G. Sebald, and the German Family. *Poetics Today* 29 (1): 129–153.

Bauman, Zygmunt. 1989. *Modernity and the Holocaust*. Ithaca, NY: Cornell University Press.

Caruth, Cathy. 1996. *Unclaimed Experience*. Baltimore, MD: Johns Hopkins University Press.

Erikson, Kai. 1994. *A New Species of Trouble*. New York: Norton.

Eyerman, Ronald. 2001. *Cultural Trauma: Slavery and the Formation of African American Identity*. Cambridge: Cambridge University Press.

Eyerman, Ronald. 2008. *The Assassination of Theo van Gogh: From Social Drama to Cultural Trauma*. Durham, NC: Duke University Press.

Eyerman, Ronald. 2011. *The Cultural Sociology of Political Assassination*. New York: Palgrave Macmillan.

Fassin, Didier, and Richard Rechtman. 2009. *The Empire of Trauma*. Princeton, NJ: Princeton University Press.

Freud, Sigmund. 1967 [1939]. *Moses and Monotheism*. New York: Vintage.

Giesen, Bernhard. 2004. The Trauma of the Perpetrators: The Holocaust as the Traumatic Reference of German National Identity. In *Cultural Trauma and Collective Identity*, ed. Jeffrey Alexander, Ronald Eyerman, Bernhard Giesen, Neil Smelser, and Piotr Sztompka. Berkeley: University of California Press.

Grass, Gunter. 2009 [1959]. *The Tin Drum*. New York: Harcourt.

Habermas, Jurgen. 1975. *Legitimation Crisis.* Boston, MA: Beacon Press.
Habermas, Jurgen. 1987. *The Philosophical Discourse of Modernity.* Cambridge, MA: MIT Press.
Hartman, Geoffrey H. 1996. *The Longest Shadow.* New York: Palgrave Macmillan.
Heins, Volker. 2011. *Beyond Friend and Foe.* Leiden: Brill.
Hochhuth, Rolf. 1964. *The Deputy.* Baltimore, MD: Johns Hopkins University Press.
Horkheimer, Max, and Theodor Adorno. 1972. *Dialectic of Enlightenment.* New York: Herder and Herder.
Horkheimer, Max, and Theodor Adorno. 2002. *Dialectic of Enlightenment.* Stanford, CA: Stanford University Press.
Kaplan, E. Ann. 2005. *Trauma Culture: The Politics of Terror and Loss in Media and Literature.* New Brunswick: Rutgers University Press.
Kipphardt, Heinar. 1997 [1964]. *In the Matter of J. Robert Oppenheimer.* New York: Hill and Wang.
LaCapra, Dominick. 2001. *Writing History Writing Trauma.* Baltimore, MD: Johns Hopkins University Press.
Leys, Reys. 2000. *Trauma: A Genealogy.* Chicago, IL: University of Chicago Press.
Lyotard, Jean-Francois. 1984. *The Postmodern Condition.* Minneapolis, MN: University of Minnesota Press.
Muller-Doohm, Stefan. 2005a. *Adorno: A Biography.* Cambridge: Polity Press.
Muller-Doohm, Stefan. 2005b. Theodor W. Adorno and Jurgen Habermas—Two Ways of Being a Public Intellectual. *European Journal of Social Theory* 8 (3): 269–280.
Olick, Jeffrey K. 2003. What Does It Mean to Normalize the Past? Official Memory in German Politics Since 1989. In *States of Memory*, ed. Jeffrey K. Olick. Durham, NC: Duke University Press.
Rabinbach, Anson. 1997. *In the Shadow of Catastrophe.* Berkeley, CA: University of California Press.
Rosenblatt, Louise M. 1978. *The Reader, the Text, the Poem.* Carbondale, IL: Southern Illinois University Press.
Rothberg, Michael. 1997. After Adorno: Culture in the Wake of Catastrophe. *New German Critique* 72: 45–81.
Said, Edward. 2004. *Freud and the Non-European.* London: Verso.
Schlant, Ernestine. 1999. *The Longest Silence.* New York: Routledge.
Smelser, Neil. 2004. Psychological Trauma and Cultural Trauma. In *Cultural Trauma and Collective Identity*, ed. Jeffrey Alexander, Ronald Eyerman, Bernhard Giesen, Neil Smelser, and Piotr Sztompka. Berkeley: University of California Press.
Van Reijen, Willam, and Jan Bransen. 2002. The Disappearance of Class History in 'Dialectic of Enlightenment'. In *Dialectic of Enlightenment*, ed. Max Horkheimer and Theodor Adorno. Stanford, CA: Stanford University Press.

Weiss, Peter. 2010 [1965]. *The Investigation*. London: Marion Boyars.
White, Hayden. 1990. *The Content of the Form: Narrative Discourse and Historical Representation*. Baltimore, MD: Johns Hopkins University Press.
Wiggershaus, Rolf. 1995. *The Frankfurt School: Its History, Theories and Political Significance*. Cambridge, MA: MIT Press.
Ziege, E. 2009. *Antisemitismus und Gesellschaflstheorie: Die Frankfurter Schule im amerikanischen Exil*. Frankfurt: Suhrkamp.
Zolkos, Magdalena. 2010. *Reconciling Community and Subjective Life*. New York: Continuum.

CHAPTER 6

The Worst Was the Silence: The Unfinished Drama of the Katyn Massacre

(with Dominik Bartmanski)

On April 7, 2010, Russian Prime Minister Vladimir Putin made an unprecedented symbolic gesture. He placed a wreath at a burial site near the Russian village of Katyn in a ceremony to commemorate the seventieth anniversary of the massacre of Polish military officers and elite civilians in the early stages of World War II. In his speech Putin paid tribute to "Soviet citizens, burnt in the fire of Stalinist repression of the 1930s; Polish officers shot on secret orders; soldiers of the Red Army, executed by the Nazis" (*New York Times* April 8, 2010, A16). The story of responsibility for this mass murder of Poles is one of dispute, suppression, protracted marginalization, and "the great efforts of obfuscation of Soviet propaganda" (Snyder 2002). Therefore, Putin's words came as an unexpected but promising sign of much-needed change. Three days later, on April 10, 2010, the airplane carrying Polish President Lech Kaczynski, high-ranking Polish officials, and the heads of the Polish military crashed nearby while on their way to similar ceremony. All people on the plane died in the crash. Upon hearing of these deaths, former Polish president and leader of Solidarity, Lech Walesa said, "This is the second disaster after Katyn. They [the Russians] wanted to cut off our head there, and here the flower of our nation has also perished" (Walesa 2010). Shortly afterward, Wiktor Osiatynski, a Polish professor

R. Eyerman, *Memory, Trauma, and Identity*, Cultural Sociology,
https://doi.org/10.1007/978-3-030-13507-2_6

of law, provided a general context for understanding this and many similar responses to the catastrophe when he wrote in the *New York Times*, "By the time Mr. Kaczynski took office, Katyn had gone from a secretly remembered event to a symbol of Polish heroism and independence" (Osiatynski 2010). This chapter unpacks the mechanisms and meanings of this remarkable transformation.

In what came to be called the Katyn Massacre, the precipitating occurrence was the mass murder of over 14,500 Polish military officers and over 7000 other Polish citizens rounded up by the Soviet army and executed by the NKVD. This transpired in April 1940 following the Soviet invasion of eastern Poland on September 17, 1939. When some of the corpses were first discovered in the spring of 1943, the Soviets claimed the Germans were the perpetrators. The directly affected groups were the Polish military, at that time under attack not only from the west by the German army but also from the east by the Soviets, as well as by the families and friends of those killed. However, neither the army nor the relatives of the murdered soldiers knew the precise circumstances of what happened. This was partly due to the fact that Poland and the Soviet Union were not at that time officially at war and that the relations between their armies were not clearly defined or understood. It took years to establish the historical facts and to narrate them in a coherent and meaningful way. Another reason was the concerted attempts made by the wartime governments in the U.S. and Great Britain to silence any public discussion (based on their fear of alienating their Soviet ally), as well as the systematic attempts by the latter to cover up the facts. These efforts, combined with the knowledge that the Germans had committed many other atrocities, lent credence to the Soviet claim of German responsibility for the crimes in Katyn. Any attempt on the part of Poles to raise the issue of possible Soviet guilt was treated as pro-German treason: During the war it formed a pretext for Stalin to break off diplomatic ties with the Polish government-in-exile, and after the war an anti-Soviet, counter-revolutionary caveat would be added.

As time passed, the directly affected collectivities expanded from the Polish military and relatives of the victims to include the entire Polish nation as such. Once construed as trauma, Katyn became an important symbol in the struggle for Polish independence from Soviet domination. It was this potential as anti-Soviet propaganda that in large part motivated a renewed official interest in the U.S. and Great Britain during the Cold War. For those affected family members, however, the murders always remained an issue.

Because of all this contestation, as well as the horrendous context of mass murder in which it occurred, this particular war crime could emerge as a cultural trauma capable of deeply affecting whole collectivities only insofar as the claims to truth could be firmly established and the symbolic attribution of suffering and guilt effectively enacted in the form of a story couched in generalizable moral terms. With numerous other incidents of mass killing having occurred during the war, an important question to ask is, Why was it that Katyn emerged with such symbolic force? The present project aims at answering this question by exploring the social conditions under which these claims were made, as well as the cultural trajectory of the trauma narrative that followed the incident. We will investigate how the war crime of Katyn entered Polish collective identity, when and how it unfolded, and the results of the transformation of that crime into a major cultural crisis that to this day overshadows Polish–Russian political relations.

While looking at the historical facts concerning the Katyn Massacre, there are several important social processes to consider. From the very beginning the construction of the trauma narrative of the victims was accompanied by what we call a *counter-trauma narrative.* This oppositional narrative was propounded by the perpetrators who sought to set forth a false attribution of responsibility for the war crime and to actively conceal its circumstances. We recognize that the unequal distribution of political and military power during the Second World War—not only between Poles, Germans, and Soviets, but also between Poles and their Western allies—played an important role in conditioning the context of the whole story. In fact, we claim that a distinctive characteristic of traumatic narratives is an asymmetrical relationship between perpetrator and victim, and that this in part is what gives rise to cultural trauma. Another complicating factor is the Soviet Union's false attribution of German guilt, for during and immediately after the war this carried a high degree of plausibility not only for those inside Poland but also for those abroad, as well. Finally, after the war's end, there existed groups within Soviet-occupied Poland (ethnic Poles among them), who resisted the generalizing efforts on the part of the victims, considering such efforts a symptom of reactionary nationalism.[1] In fact, the Katyn Massacre can be described as the emergence of a dialectic between a trauma narrative of relatively weak victims based on strong premises, on one hand, and the counter-trauma discourse of relatively strong suspects based on weak premises, on the other. While this power distribution matters, it is also necessary to consider the cultural and social conditions under which the correct attribution of responsibility for the massacre was prevented, the controversy sustained, and an eventual resolution made possible. We recognize that it was not only the sheer power of political and military control but also the intellectual attachments and emotional dispositions of various social groups on all sides that played a significant role in framing and handling the issue. These attachments, a set of time- and place-specific cultural codes and attitudes, shaped the ways in which the incident was approached both during the war and after. These embedded cultural codes initially obscured and suppressed the tragedy of Katyn. From the perspective of cultural sociological theory, the suppression of this painful memory—not just the murders themselves—contributed to the emergence of collective anxiety and enabled victims to construct yet another dimension of their collective injury. As a family member of one of those murdered in Katyn put it,

> The worst was the silence, the prohibition against speaking openly of their death, of a dignified, burial, for half a century. It was forbidden even to visit the places of execution. My younger sister, Zosia, always envied those friends of hers whose parents had died in Auschwitz. They at least could go to the gravesites, and didn't have to hide the truth.... (Stanislawa Dec quoted in Kaczorowska 2006: 150)

The memory carried by the families of the victims was suppressed through the political control the Soviet Union effectively exerted in Poland between 1945 and 1989. As a result, discussion could not be introduced into the domestic public sphere, the locus of crucial engagement with the incident. However, public discussion was possible, at least to a certain extent, throughout the Polish diaspora, especially in France, Great Britain, and the U.S. The publicized trauma narrative of Polish emigrants and exiles was fueled by their own private memories and the pain of the relatives of those killed who remained in Poland. However, as long as the Cold War status quo buttressed the political and cultural structures that suppressed the discourse of Katyn, there could be no collectively felt trauma, since public discourse was impossible. The potential symbolic power associated with private suffering can only be fully actualized in the broad public sphere. Cultural trauma became possible only when the directly affected individuals and communities were able to express themselves verbally and visually in a sustained way and project their personal tragedies onto the larger moral screen of the nation.

In this sense, the story of Katyn as cultural trauma is different from others discussed in this volume. It is a story of the power of both political authorities to suppress and carrier groups to resist—and ultimately it is the story of a wound that would not heal.

In analyzing the cultural trauma process of the Katyn Massacre, we distinguish three crucial expatriate carrier groups: survivors, relatives, and the intellectuals and politicians who were vital to the process of creating and sustaining the trauma narrative. While these groups maintained their own organizations, they also attempted to make use of the public institutions of their host countries. Some of them delivered extraordinary testimony replete with thick descriptions that almost single handedly established Katyn as a collective tragedy. These vivid accounts endowed the incident with great moral significance and historical authenticity for a public that stretched far beyond the carrier groups themselves (e.g., Józef Czapski's *Inhuman Land* published in England in 1951). However, it was in the context of the changing political and cultural conditions following the rise to power of Mikhail Gorbachev in the Soviet Union and the 1989 Autumn of Nations that this traumatic memory could truly become a powerful public phenomenon, a grand trauma drama. For the first time in the postwar period, it became possible for public representations to widely surface in Poland and an international discourse to emerge. In short, the incident at Katyn underwent a metamorphosis from a military and political conflict and tragedy known by few to a case of class- and ethnic cleansing discussed by many. In the process the Katyn Massacre became completely transformed from a war crime to a cultural crisis in which the foundations of collective identity were brought into play, what we call a cultural trauma.

The most recent visualization of Katyn by the well-known film director Andrzej Wajda (2007)—as well as the whole gamut (and lack) of response to his film—have created a cultural story whose complexity reflects that of the actual trauma construction. As we will discuss below, there are at once compelling personal, national, international, moral, and intellectual aspects to this film and its reception that help illuminate the cultural trauma process. Since this response was brought to public light by a single event of artistic intervention, an analysis can contribute to the understanding of the wider process of trauma construction by adding a performative aspect to the more traditional historical presentation of the story. Such extraordinary individuals as Czapski and Wajda, both at once visual artists and intellectuals, were very much aware that even tragic events require powerful representation if collective memory is to be firmly entrenched. This is the case not only for those who directly identify with the murdered individuals and their families because of national and civic ties but also for those who empathize with the victims because of more general moral ties. Wajda (2008) emphasized the importance of "showing Katyn to the world" and anticipated a moral and cultural shock in response to the film. Thus we have to recognize an iconic aspect of trauma construction, as well as the more discursive aspects. In the introduction to *Inhuman Land* (in the 1984 edition), Józef Czapski mentions that his greatest reward was that so many years after the incident, people still wanted to hear his Katyn story. His mission, he thought, had thereby been completed. From the very beginning, however, Czapski was convinced there was a profound paradox involved in the unwillingness to remember such tragedy: "it would be impossible to live, impossible to smile, if one always remembered things and never erased any memories" (Czapski 2001: 96). Yet because of the official denial, such remembering was in this case paramount. The reception to the artistic representations of Czapski and Wajda, as well as their own attitudes toward them, should be culturally unpacked, for they contain a possible key to understanding what it really means to assert that social actions become cultural events through the process of symbolic construction, not simply through their own inherent force. This is one of the central insights that the Katyn case study can provide sociological theory.

A Timeline of the Occurrences

On August 23, 1939, the governments of Germany and the Soviet Union signed a nonaggression agreement, popularly known as the Molotov–Ribbentrop Pact. This agreement essentially eliminated Poland from the map, since it divided its territories between Germany and the Soviet Union. The document also contained a secret agreement that legitimated the elimination of Poland's intelligentsia, presumably because such eradication would make the occupation of the territories that much easier and secure. In early spring of the following year, approximately 14,500 Polish citizens (the issue of whether or not they were prisoners of war is a legal issue, as no formal declaration of war against the Soviet Union was made), primarily reserve and regular military officers, but also members of the police corps, were murdered in several killing grounds on the eastern front.[2] These individuals were generally recognized as the cream of Polish society.[3] The killings were carried out with German-made revolvers by the Soviet secret police (NKVD); the victims were executed individually with a single shot to the back of the head and their bodies were buried in stacked layers in tightly packed mass graves.[4] The style of execution was well-known and associated with the Soviet secret police. The prisoners, mostly men but also at least one female officer, had been held in three separate camps and were killed within a period of a few weeks. Many prominent Polish Jews were included among the victims; about 5% of the inmates of one of the three camps (Kozelsk) were Jews according to one account, among them the chief rabbi of the Polish army (Paul 1991: 70).[5] There were also Muslims among the dead, and the monument that has been erected in the memory of the Katyn Massacre contains four different religious symbols.[6] The extent and impact of these murders only slowly emerged after the betrayal of the nonaggression pact and the German invasion of the Soviet Union in June 1941.

On April 13, 1943, in a broadcast carried by all German-controlled radio stations, including those in occupied Poland, Radio Berlin announced that, "the local population indicated a Soviet execution site at Kosogory … about 3,000 bodies … had already been uncovered in a huge pit" and that these were the bodies of "thousands of officers of the former Polish army, interned in the U.S.S.R. in 1939 and bestially murdered by the Bolsheviks" (Paul 1991: 128, 210). Four days later, the Polish government in exile requested that the International Red Cross (IRC) investigated this claim. Coming as it did in the wake of the defeat at Stalingrad, the discovery of the bodies at Katyn, which the German command mistakenly thought represented all the murdered Polish officers, presented a significant opportunity in the propaganda war. "Goebbels now saw an opportunity to divide the Allies. He wrote in his diary that as soon as he heard of this statement, he secured Hitler's sanction for the German Red Cross to ask the IRC for an investigation of the Katyn graves" (Cienciala et al. 2007: 218).[7] This ensured that any investigation of the graves at Katyn would necessarily be couched within the wider political conflicts and intrigues of the war.

Following the German request for an investigation, an international commission of forensic experts was deployed to the Katyn forest to exhume the bodies. This occurred between April 28 and 30, 1943. The commission produced a 350-page report identifying the bodies and establishing both the cause and approximate time of death.

The Polish Red Cross, which at first refused to participate for fear of supporting German propaganda (and indeed the Germans thought Polish representation necessary to making their case believable), was represented at the site by a group of forensic specialists and other technicians, including some who were active in the Polish underground. However, the advancing Soviet army and the lack of further discoveries caused the Germans to suspend operations, and by June 1943, the Polish representatives returned with their information to occupied Poland.[8] Their personal testimony strongly suggested Soviet guilt, but the use of German pistols and the difficulty in establishing the exact date of the executions, along with the clear propaganda motivations of the Germans, allowed doubts to continue, at least among those predisposed toward skepticism. In addition to the periodic radio pronouncements (the names of the dead were solemnly and repeatedly announced over loud speakers in Krakow and other major occupied cities), lists of the dead were published in German-language newspapers throughout occupied Poland. But the question of who carried out the killings was publicly disputed; the Germans accused the Soviets and vice versa. Two days after the Berlin announcement (April 15, 1943), Moscow fired back with this statement: "In launching this monstrous invention the German-Fascist scoundrels did not hesitate at the most unscrupulous and base lies in their attempts to cover up crimes which, as has now become evident, were perpetrated by themselves" (Paul 1991: 211). Stalin took the cooperation between the Polish Red Cross and German authorities as a pretext to break off relations with the London-based Polish government, referring to them as "Hitler's Polish collaborators." This became one of the interpretative frames that would define any attempts by Poles to dispute the Soviet claims of German guilt (at least until the end of the war).

The long list of known German atrocities and the equivocal material evidence in the case (e.g., the inability or unwillingness to establish the exact date of execution or origin of the weapons used) contributed to the uncertainty of just who exactly the perpetrator was. Who the victims were was, of course, clear. What they represented, and to whom, was also relatively clear. For the Germans the dead represented proof of Soviet ruthlessness, something to counterbalance their own image in the eyes of the world. The discovery of the bodies also helped alleviate some of the sting of their failing military strategy, at least at the level of political propaganda. For the Soviets, the dead bodies were useful as yet another signifier of German barbarism, an aid in their own propaganda efforts to convince Poles and the rest of the world of their good intentions that they were protecting and liberating rather than occupying their country. Their attribution of German responsibility was made all the more believable by Allied propaganda and by the ruthlessness of the German forces in Eastern Europe. For the Poles, the dead represented yet another example of their victimization, part of a long history of being caught between powerful and aggressive neighbors. It also meant a blow not only to their military but also to their desire for sovereignty. There might have been some Poles who saw Katyn as a tragedy but did not share the national aspirations of many of their countrymen; in this case, they might have viewed the massacre in exclusively military terms. If this perspective did exist, one can speculate that those who adhered to it would be members of the Soviet-sponsored Polish army and the communist wing of the underground in occupied Poland. While they make no mention of Katyn, some of Wajda's earlier films explore this tension within the Polish resistance. Finally, there were also ethnic minorities within the shifting Polish borders for whom the uncovered graves might have meant something else altogether.

Katyn and the cry for vengeance became a strong motivating agent in both forces of the Polish military fighting in the war. The Soviets would name a tank the "Avenger" with this in mind. It was also a strong motivating force in the Polish resistance and in what was called the Home Army, the force behind the tragic Warsaw Uprising in 1944. The Soviets viewed the Home Army through the same lens it viewed the London government-in-exile: as Polish nationalists who were a threat to Soviet aims in the region. The Soviets did all they could to discredit and destroy both.

At the Nuremberg tribunals in 1946, the prosecution of the perpetrators of the Katyn Massacre fell under Soviet jurisdiction as it had occurred in the zone allotted to the Soviets. The indictment read, "In September 1941, 11,000 Polish officers, prisoners of war, were killed in the Katyn woods near Smolensk." While it did not name the Germans as perpetrators, it was clear from the dating of the event where the blame lay, as the region was at that point under German occupation. The case presented was based on the findings of the earlier Soviet report (Paul 1991: 335). German lawyers put up a strong defense and there was much suspicion of Soviet guilt. In the end, the Soviets formally withdrew their claims, and the case was omitted from the final verdicts announced in late September 1946.

Besides the general ambivalence among the Allies, another reason given for the withdrawal of charges was that the Nuremberg tribunal was concerned only with German war crimes. Great Britain and the U.S. were reluctant at that point to confront their Soviet allies on this matter and sought to bury the issue. The Polish government-in-exile had expected this and sought, unsuccessfully, to have the issue of Katyn excluded entirely from consideration at Nuremburg. It is now assumed that the Soviets decided not to press the issue because their case was weak and the possibility of exposure strong. One can speculate that had the Katyn Massacre been fairly and completely treated at Nuremberg, the cultural trauma tied to the event might never have developed. Presumably the killings would have been treated as one war crime among many, and the issue would have been resolved with the appropriate attribution of guilt and allocation of punishment. In this case, perhaps a memorial would have been constructed and Polish families given a site to grieve and remember their lost loved ones. However, the politics of war and peace made that impossible.

With the continued Soviet presence, any discussion of Katyn was strictly forbidden in postwar Poland. For an account of what happened, Poles were directed to the official account of the war given in the *Great Soviet Encyclopedia*. As something publicly forbidden, reference to Katyn was kept within the bounds of the private sphere, while in the underground of public memory it became a symbol of Soviet oppression. For those Poles who actively participated in and supported the Communist government, any reference to Katyn was interpreted as nationalistic propaganda and thus reactionary, regardless of who the perpetrator was deemed to be. For them, the issue was best considered another tragic event of war, a war that had in the end led to a revolutionary change in direction. However, while public discussion was forbidden in Poland, this was not the case for émigré Polish communities in the West.

During the Cold War and under pressure from Polish Americans and the Polish American Congress (PAC, founded in 1944), the American Committee for the Investigation of the Katyn Massacre (a.k.a., the Lane Committee) was established. In 1951 the U.S. House of Representatives established a select committee to investigate "the facts, evidence, and circumstances of the Katyn forest massacre" (Sanford 2005: 142). Some of the witnesses called to testify wore hoods to avoid identification, fearing for their relatives in Poland. Hearings were held throughout 1952 amidst the highly politicized atmosphere of the Cold War. In its final report published in December 1952, the committee named the Soviets a responsible agent and recommended referral to the United Nations' the International Court of Justice. It also called for the establishment of an international commission to investigate Katyn and other crimes against humanity perpetrated by the Soviet Union. The USSR was denounced for "one of the most barbarous crimes against humanity" (Sanford 2005: 144).

In 1965 a postage stamp was issued in the U.S. commemorating the victims of the Katyn Massacre. The stamp was sponsored by Edward Derwinski, an Illinois congressman from Chicago, a city with a large Polish American population at the time.[9] At about the same time, a campaign to establish a Katyn monument in Great Britain was initiated, a campaign that was strongly supported by the American-based Polonia (a Polish American association). Books also began to appear on the topic in Great Britain, and in 1971 the BBC broadcast a program that raised the issue of Soviet responsibility. In the following year, the British *Daily Telegraph* printed the headline: "Russian guilt for Katyn Reaffirmed" (Sanford 2005: 180). Finally, in 1976 a memorial monument was erected in London (although it eschewed mention of the massacre's perpetrators).

Knowledge, Remembrance, and the Meanings of the Katyn Massacre in Poland: 1943–2008

The sixty-five-year Katyn trauma drama in Poland has constituted a narrative of protracted civil struggle for historical transparency and moral repair. To state briefly the difference between the postwar situation of the Polish diaspora in Western Europe and the U.S. on one hand and the in-country citizens on the other, one could say that while the story of Katyn was an inconvenient truth in public discourse in the West, it remained a rather cumbersome official lie and a publicly suppressed issue in Eastern Europe until 1989. In fact, it continued to be politically taboo in the official discourse of Russia after 1989, as well, a circumstance that sheds additional light on the conditions of Soviet occupation in the region and its cultural legacy.

The time between the April 1943 emergence of public information regarding the existence of mass graves in the Katyn Forest and the first official celebration of the Katyn Remembrance Day on April 13, 2008 was a period during which this issue gradually became a key signifier of

Polish victimhood, especially with reference to the Soviet Union. Much of this time was consumed by civil perseverance and moral dedication to an issue that was silenced and consigned to oblivion by the highest echelons of authority. To many, the issue seemed almost lost; to others, it remained vague or virtually unknown.

For those Poles who knew the facts as established in 1943, this was a dramatic period, not only because of the emotional character of the knowledge they possessed but also due to the fact prior to before 1989, (1) this knowledge had been suppressed for decades; (2) its bearers were systematically persecuted, threatened, or socially marginalized; (3) a false account of the incident was disseminated from the outset of People's Republic of Poland; and (4) the issue was ignored altogether from the 1960s on in the official media. Beyond this, there were an even greater number of individuals for whom the drama consisted of an anguish of uncertainty intertwined with the premonition that the Katyn killings were not an isolated incident. As time elapsed, the worst-case scenario was finally confirmed. Prior to that confirmation, however, Katyn symbolized in an incrementally increasing number of circles the array of physical and psychological damage historically inflicted upon the Polish people. It signified at once the extermination of Polish prisoners of war in the Soviet Union; a long-lasting uncertainty and confusion concerning the facts; the brutally enforced silence; the gaping lack of information about those "lost in the east"; and official hypocrisy, obfuscation, and deception. The specificity of Katyn consists then not simply in the systematic nature of the atrocities committed and groups targeted but also in the fact that the mass killings were cynically appropriated and used by the Nazi and Soviet governments for their own political purposes, initially with the more than tacit support by other governments.

Knowledge of the murders was scattered, incomplete, and overshadowed by the perpetrators' counter-narrative. Since memory and recall are indispensable for the experience of trauma, and since recall does not exist without a cognitive referent, the conditions for the emergence of cultural trauma might seem unfavorable. Indeed, the Soviet political realism of the time conditioned an overwhelming corruption of reality, a paradigmatically Orwellian situation in which control of the present depended upon strict control of the past. The latter meant the destruction and falsification of any contrary evidence, the psychological and physical torture of inconvenient witnesses, and above all the blurring of key social meanings and the degrading of individual life. In this process, language itself was permeated by sayings such as the ambiguous Russian phrase, “to lie like an eyewitness” (Nim 2008: 22). All this ensured a situation of perennial fear and disorientation. However, this particular circumstance appears to have multiplied and congealed the emotional trauma felt in thousands of Polish households. Katyn began to emerge not only as a tragedy of individual grief but also a trauma narrative of scant, stolen, and persecuted collective memory. This concerned and encapsulated not only what was coded as extraordinary injury but also the necessity of dealing with silence, uncertainty, and falsehood in the course of ordinary daily life.

Actual memory of the occurrence was relatively scarce for the simple reason that only some 394 out of the thousands captured left the detention camps alive, spared by NKVD and initially grouped in a separate camp. As Józef Czapski (himself one of the survivors) noted, the prisoners had not even considered the possibility of mass extermination (2001: 71). The very few who survived and could be regarded as witnesses at first did not realize what exactly was going on in fall of 1939 and spring of 1940. For many Polish citizens, the first weeks of terror and havoc caused by the joint invasion of Poland meant a brutal confrontation with the informational chaos and political arbitrariness of an invading power. For this reason, it seems more adequate to speak here of the tedious processes of ascertaining and verifying knowledge, about channels and frameworks of communicating and disseminating it, and finally about acts of commemoration, artistic representation, and responses to them.

A key sociological issue concerns how the witness-based remembering of individuals is conveyed and translated up to the collective level and subsequently transformed into sustained social remembrance. In addressing this, we emphasize the role of discursive frames and visual representations predicated on specific cultural binaries that, in turn, are infused with emotional attachments. First of all, there is the dichotomy of truth and falsehood employed in all the narratives surrounding this case. This fundamental binary is often accompanied by other oppositions, such as innocence and guilt, decency and perfidy, and openness and secrecy. Second, in addition to the fundamental division of the public and the private, one can speak of the dichotomy of the official and the underground—the state and civil society. However, these binaries are not stable and discrete; it is important to recognize that under the Soviet regime they often overlapped.

The transmission of private narratives into public discourse was severely restricted in Poland and, in the case of Katyn, nearly impossible during the closing years of the Second World War and its immediate aftermath. It is not until the so-called political thaw of 1956 that one can notice a narrative shift from the claims of German guilt to a muffled silence on the part of the authorities. Nevertheless, public discussion continued to be seriously hampered until the political collapse of 1989. But this is not to say that the discourse was altogether absent. Private discussion and familial transmissions of memory could never be completely eradicated, and these eventually carved out a significant social niche whose meanings and cultural relevance began to be publicly felt. As we shall demonstrate below, this particular tension between state order and social order can easily be reinscribed within the mythical tragedy of Sophocles' play *Antigone*, which as Breese demonstrates with reference to Becket's *Waiting for Godot*, helped articulate the feelings held by many Poles when performed in the immediate postwar period and then reframed in Wajda's *Katyn*.

In addition to this, we also examine yet another set of binaries, namely that between what can and cannot be spoken, what can (and should) be told and discussed and what constitutes the unspeakable. On the one hand, speech and text are connected to an anthropological imperative to express oneself, to witness and testify (Suleiman 2006). As the Lithuanian author Tomas Venclova writes, "speaking and writing means overcoming and transcending" (1999: 129). Some, of course, might disagree or point to a danger inherent in such speech. This seems to be the case when Adorno made his famous remark about the impossibility of poetry after Auschwitz. Certainly speaking and writing about the forbidden truth of Katyn, whether in private or in public, was one of the few forms of overcoming and transcending the Communist regime that suppressed it. The construction of cultural trauma involves a specific distribution of the sacred and profane and an understanding of the symbolic borders of its representation and reception. According to Izabella Sariusz-Skapska, "to not cross the border between testimony and the silence of things that are ineffable is a condition of reliability of representation" (2002: 22). The "ineffable" is here understood as something that cannot be fully communicated, not only because of the limitations of the language employed by storytellers but also because of the impossibility of full entrance into the narrative on the part of recipients. Moreover, there are borders to what should be communicated, and there is a risk associated with crossing such borders; to do so can mean either the banalization of the victims' suffering or a deranged fascination with the profane and evil, a point made by Adorno in the reference above. Therefore, while researching forms of knowledge, remembrance, and post-memory, one faces a twofold problem: on one hand, the politically molded possibility to represent, and on the other, the culturally molded ability to speak out and be heard in a particular social context.

If we take into account the politically shaped possibility of public expression, we can distinguish at least three general periods within the temporal brackets we've already established in demarcating the processes of collective trauma construction. This begins with the obtaining and transmitting of knowledge of the incident. It includes the remembrance enacted and the transformation of a tragic occurrence into a significant event, intellectually and artistically represented under various social conditions in the following heuristically delimited political eras: 1943–1956, 1956–1989, and 1989–2010. With reference to the second criterion of the culturally shaped ability to communicate, a specific periodization is much harder to establish. Such a process is always affected by political conditions, but it is also responsive to various other circumstances that have their own often-nonlinear logic of temporal change. However, one can distinguish one particular circumstance that crucially affected the emergence and maintenance of cultural trauma with reference to Katyn: the lack of symbolic closure in the trauma drama. A recurrent string of metaphors that are intuitively crucial in this respect are injury, wound, and scar. A cultural trauma emerges with recognition, symbolic elaboration, and meaningful representation of social wounds that are felt to remain open. It continues to exist as a cultural process that tends, as it were, to turn wound into scar, something healed but still present as meaningful referent. Symbolic closure is vital at this point; the lack thereof keeps the wound open and fosters anxiety derived from deprivation of coherence in a narrative marked by tragic occurrence.

The specific carrier groups with firsthand knowledge of the mass killings, along with those who harbored the most emotionally charged memory of the massacre, such as the families of the murdered, were either hunted or closely watched by the authorities. Polish forensic specialists and other experts who visited Katyn in 1943 were understood by the communist regime to be one of the most significant among these carrier groups. Though the few surviving eyewitnesses either fled the country or ended up imprisoned, some did manage to pass on their knowledge to specialists and lay people, and in this way they contributed to the more general framing of the incident. But it was the personal trauma of the families, especially of the wives, mothers, and children of those killed that supplied the critical mass of highly emotionally charged tragic narratives (see, for example, those collected in Kaczorowska 2003 in Polish and 2006 in English). Their situation became particularly dramatic as any inquiries concerning the fate of "the lost in the east" and the public sharing of knowledge and opinion about Katyn began to be prohibited and persecuted. Yet thousands of women waiting in vain for their husbands, brothers, and sons formed one of the key groups that slowly but surely undermined the official discourses. The forced silence of this group during the first decade following the war compounded their sense of helplessness and initially confined their suffering to the private sphere. The dissemination of "false information about the Katyn crime" was punishable by a two-year sentence of forced labor. Acts of invigilation targeting the families took place and those caught spreading "false knowledge" could even be accused of espionage (Oseka 2007: 7). If one was identified as a child of those "lost in the east," the entrance to higher education and other institutions and occupations could be seriously hampered or made impossible (Kaczorowska 2006). Once drafted into the Polish army, the sons of those murdered could be directed to work in mines and other industrial locations controlled by Communists (Bartmanski interview).

Under such strenuous political and social conditions, the family members of the murdered officers were important carriers of remembrance, not only because of the knowledge some possessed but also—and most importantly—because of their emotional attachment to the wider case. The atmosphere of fear engendered by the strict official control of the Katyn narrative fostered general suspicion toward the government and its official propaganda. As members of elite families, many came to feel responsible for saving the traces of what was for them their true Polish heritage, the vestiges of their life-world that was now in the process of being systematically erased. That feeling was buttressed by the fact that many in this category belonged to the first generation raised and educated in the independent Poland created in 1918 after 123 years of political nonexistence (Ksiazek-Czerminska 1999: 7). For some, the imposition of a Communist regime might have appeared as a continuation of previous Russian domination under a different banner.

The disappearance of their relatives and their inexpressible fate was thus intimately linked to the Soviet occupation of Poland, and within that, the binary of truth and falsehood was mapped onto the division of state and society. Although not quite underground heroes, the relatives of the murdered formed one of the key mechanisms of transmission of remembrance into the public sphere. In the first period this transmission remained almost completely "privatized" and only occasionally found public expression in the form of distributed leaflets and individual acts of sabotaging official propaganda. As their official and personal abandonment persisted, their fate eventually became emblematic.

In short, the first period of the emergence of the trauma narrative was marked by shock, confusion, and a symbolic struggle concerning the Katyn deaths and their circumstances. The key narratives were created in this period, and the clash between a victim discourse, the related counter-discourses, and the attempts at covering up the story all shaped their reception. Already in the 1940s, the name "Katyn" was being openly mentioned along with the symbols of German genocide—Auschwitz and Majdanek (Oseka 2007: 7). The official discourse blaming the Germans subsided in the wake of Stalin's death in 1953, but even in its attenuated form it continued to be one of the key elements legitimating Poland's Communist government. Indeed, there were certainly Poles who actively supported the regime and its claims about the fate of those killed at Katyn. It was not until 1956 that the political climate was changed unequivocally when many of Stalin's crimes were revealed by the Soviet government itself. This revelation provided a new context for the evaluation of what was by that time commonly known as the Katyn Massacre. However, official propaganda did not cease to employ the standard Soviet version for its own purposes of political and cultural control. Throughout the 1950s, "Katyn" had its own entry in official encyclopedias, where it was described as a geographical location in Russia and identified as the site of a massacre of Polish citizens by the German military after the territory had been seized in 1941.

The next twenty-five years saw an official silence on the issue from Poland's Communist authorities. The encyclopedia published by Polish Scientific Publishers (PWN) in 1965 makes no mention of Katyn, and this situation did not change in subsequent decades. It is hard today to judge what the exact motivation was behind the change of strategy in approaching Katyn. Yet, it is not the shift itself or the political intricacies that are of the greatest significance, but rather its cultural consequences. In the eyes of the vast majority of those who remembered the deaths symbolized by Katyn (or found out about the massacre in the wake of the thaw of 1956), the introduction of total censorship on the issue had one fundamental meaning: it was an indirect (and probably "unwitting") acknowledgment of Soviet responsibility (Oseka 2007: 7).

From this moment on, a series of persistent iconic and discursive actions took place. The official silence was countered by repeated unauthorized civil undertakings. The symbolic opening of publicly enacted resistance during this period was marked by the inception of the so-called "Katyn Valley" in the main Warsaw cemetery on All Saints Day in 1959. On this day a commemoration site for the Katyn victims was created through the anonymous placement of a cross and plaque. The site was openly referred to as "the symbolic grave of the Polish officers murdered at Katyn." Perpetrators were not explicitly named, but the plaque stated that the officers "perished on foreign soil at the hands of a cruel enemy" and that "they [i.e., the victims] deserve memory and honor." The tradition of placing candles throughout the area in memory of the departed was carried out in spontaneous acts of public recognition, yet the state militia destroyed the site after only one day in existence. Government officials then announced that "order was reintroduced to the cemetery" (Sawicki 2007: 18), but even with such reestablished order, this public manifestation of mourning and solidarity revealed the existence of an "underground order" that had symbolically destabilized the "state order."

This brief but visible cry for recognition triggered a sense of moral empowerment, first in Warsaw, then in other cities. The "Katyn Valley" became a bottom-up commemorative site in the years that followed. This cry for recognition was a signifier of a secretly lived trauma expressing a deeply suppressed "we," and the response of the authorities clearly showed that they too cared very much about the incident. The government treated the situation seriously, initiating an official investigation and launching a secret police operation that consisted in systematic intelligence efforts to find out who lay behind the "cemetery event." The results, however, were poor, and what might be called "resistance performances" continued to be enacted at this site until the collapse of the regime in 1989. These performances occurred not only on November 1 but also on other symbolic occasions, such as April 13 and September 17. The apogee of this string of actions was reached in the heyday of the Solidarity struggle in 1981 when a four-meter-high monument weighing eight tons was erected on this site. Like all previous material symbols of resistance placed on the site, it was promptly removed by the authorities. In this case, however, the massive monument was much discussed in private circles where it was interpreted as yet another demonstration of civil disobedience and political criticism. In effect, the fame of the Katyn Valley cemetery site had been discursively and iconically cemented within the capital city, particularly for those who were in some way connected to the incident (Sawicki 2007: 19). In the end, the story of these cemetery performances indicates that the dedication with which the authorities sought to erase the memory of Katyn was directly proportional to (1) the cultural potential of this memory as a general signifier of the Soviet-inflicted suffering of the Polish people and (2) the extent of the moral debacle of the Polish Communist regime.

A quarter century after Katyn Valley was created as a symbolic space of anticommunist contestation, there appeared in Poland the first school textbook that described the Katyn Massacre. Its description was vague, but it was nevertheless enough to create precedence in the official discourse. The civil success of Solidarity was preceded by the election of a Pole, Karol Wojtyta, as Pope John Paul II in 1978, which effected a wave of unauthorized discourse about Katyn. No one seemed to be afraid anymore of talking about Soviet responsibility in the Solidarity-inspired time of an unprecedented "festival of freedom" (Materski 2008: 122). Underground materials were circulated throughout the country, and meetings organized by the Catholic Church played an important role in the life of city intelligentsia, the group now most directly attached to the story of Katyn. By then, the Iron Curtain was already porous enough to let in information from the outside. This created a "strange situation" in which the official censorship itself began to be unsure about what exactly was allowed to be published (Abarinow 2007: 11). As a result, there was a plethora of illegal publications created or smuggled into the country from Western Europe, and the probability of encountering information about Katyn increased. The grand international myth of Solidarity was emerging, even if the movement itself was temporarily muffled by the martial law introduced by the communist government in 1981.

Though still relatively arcane, the truth about Katyn became an undeniable fact of life for many representatives of the Polish intelligentsia, a commonly recognizable cachet of increasingly self-confident societal "us" against the discredited governmental "them." Incrementally growing social pressure led to further alteration of the ruling party's stance toward the issue of Katyn, and in the closing years of the 1980s, the Katyn Massacre was sporadically thematized in official media and political institutions. This was also the time when the first large-scale sociological research on Polish collective memory was conducted. Two things about these studies are striking: first, 23% of those surveyed declared that they talked about history "often" and 54% "sometimes"; second, less than 3% declared that they talked with others about such things as Katyn or the Ribbentrop-Molotow Pact, and barely 5% discussed the Stalinist period in Poland or the Martial Law (Szacka 2007: 3). The overall cultural impact of Solidarity and the anticipatory climate of 1980s were obvious, but the research revealed the scale of the damage caused to Polish collective memory by official propaganda. A clear discrepancy between a heightened general historical interest and specific discursive commitments indicated the cultural legacy of four decades of autocratic rule. Even if, as a later study showed, 40% found out about Katyn during the Communist period, that awareness was one among many other tragic incidents, which seemed to indicate that as *trauma*, Katyn was still apparently confined only to those directly connected to its occurrence. In the excitement and then euphoria associated with the end of communism, Katyn appeared to be one of the exhausted memories as far as collective identity was concerned. However, in view of those who cultivated a still circumscribed but now stronger commitment to the issue, the end of the 1980s meant a renewed hope. The demand for proper recognition of Katyn, however slim, seemed unquenchable. In the newly forged climate of broader political change in Eastern Europe, a series of new discourses concerning Katyn had made an indelible impact on the Polish intelligentsia. Thus it came as a profound disappointment when, on July 14, 1988, Mikhail Gorbachev announced at the official meeting with the representatives of Polish intellectuals at Warsaw's Royal Castle that "there exists no secret documentation which would shed a new light on the Katyn crime" (Materski 2008: 124). For a truly radical change in the official presentation of events, Polish citizens had to wait until the revolution of 1989, and specifically until April 13, 1990, when the official news agency of the Soviet Union (i.e., TASS) finally acknowledged, even if somewhat inadvertently, Soviet responsibility for the massacres at Katyn, as well as the existence of other extermination sites at Mednoe and Kharkov.[10] This occurred exactly one-half century after the world first heard the terrible news about Katyn.

Changes in Moscow at the outset of the 1990s seemed to create sufficient symbolic space for a relatively open, long-term dialogue with what was by then a completely altered Warsaw. The eventual release of the relevant Soviet archives was promised and reconciliation appeared possible. A full disclosure of knowledge and responsibility would mean a clear symbolic closure. However, this potential was never fulfilled in the manner suggested by the collapse of communism in Eastern Europe. Instead, within Polish society an unprecedented era of the Katyn trauma drama began. Wajda has said that this was the time when his cinematographic intervention into the Katyn trauma story should have taken place (Wajda 2007: 5).

The Round Table Talks in the spring of 1989 made possible the first partially democratic elections in Eastern Europe. Lech Walesa became president in 1990 and the Polish Communist Party was officially dissolved. The opening of the last decade of the twentieth century constituted a point of no return in the unfolding Katyn trauma narrative. However painful, new prospects of unfettered inquiry and commemorative catharsis were opened. Still, it took another decade to realize a partial symbolic closure and then nearly another decade to launch the fully-fledged process of official ritualization inside the country. Despite what might be interpreted as a significant delay in the official commemoration of Katyn, the event did emerge as a key signifier of the Second World War tragedy and of Polish trauma stemming from the Soviet occupation. This metamorphosis of formerly subterranean and private tragedy into a central traumatic narrative of the country's history is remarkable. The finally liberated country caused many tragic but previously stifled Polish memories to surface. As Michael Kimmelman wrote in the *New York Times*, "Poles have especially good reason to see themselves as long oppressed, having been fought over and occupied for much of the last century by vicious regimes" (2009: 6). How then has it been possible that this particular incident and its ordeal became a distinctive trauma narrative?

After 1989, the most apparent change in Poland vis-à-vis Katyn was its sudden public visibility. Books, articles, documentaries, discussions, and monuments of various kinds filled the media and public sphere.[11] The now classic accounts of the incident and its circumstances finally found their way into bookstores and libraries. Among these were Czapski's diaries and *Without a Last Chapter* by Wladyslaw Anders along with novels such as *The Silent, the Invincible* by Wlodzimierz Odojewski and *Katyn: Postmortem* by Andrzej Mularczyk. The latter would become the narrative base for Wajda's film, which was originally conceived with that very title. However, perhaps most significant of all was the emergence of a new civic association, the Katyn Families Association (KFA) with members both in Poland and abroad.

Through the KFA, the few relatives of the victims who were still alive could finally speak out and express their anguish in an organized, public fashion. It was this nongovernmental and explicitly apolitical organization that created a symbolic forum and established itself as a key carrier of remembrance and an ineradicable sign of an unhealed Polish war wound. It became the voice for articulating a half-century-long persecuted memory. The priority of the KFA's public mission was to establish officially sanctioned symbolic cemeteries at the three massacre sites revealed by Gorbachev. Finding the other sites where over seven thousand other bodies lie hidden was also deemed crucial. The first goal, understood as the symbolic act of dignified commemoration and of "emphasizing the drama" had been realized, while a second still remained. For this reason, symbolic closure up to that time was still felt to be incomplete. However, the official opening of the Katyn cemetery on July 28, 2000 was a watershed moment in the trauma drama and functioned as a form of symbolic closure. For the families of the victims, the opening of the cemetery definitely had this effect, and this carried over in a similar way to the whole of Polish society. This was because over the years Katyn had essentially become a synonym for all the Soviet atrocities suffered by Polish citizens during the Second World War (Bartmanski interview).[12]

In the immediate aftermath of the catastrophic airplane crash of April 10, 2010 (in which the Polish president and other high-ranking Polish military and civilian leadership were killed), another kind of national "catharsis" occurred. The outpouring of grief following the death of the Polish president and 95 of the nation's elite, including Andrzej Skapski who was to give a speech at the ceremony on behalf of the Katyn families, was tremendous. Indeed, the trope of "catharsis" was used in national and international discourses (Iwinski 2010; Zaremba 2010). But whatever catharsis might have been achieved quickly gave way to yet another protracted drama of suspicion and accusation. Public discourse turned divisive and involved a re-politicization of the symbol of Katyn, all of which caused relatives of the fallen who were members of the KFA to speak out against the "appropriation of the trauma of Katyn for political and personal ambitions" (*Gazeta Wyborcza* 2010). As the Polish Parliament unanimously declared April 13 the National Remembrance Day for the Katyn Victims in 2007, with the first official commemoration the following year, the Katyn trauma was at once reopened and closed. On one hand, it contributed to the emergence and maintenance of cultural trauma. On the other hand, there was the recognition, especially among KFA leaders, that even the most tragic events require self-reflexive representation and specific narratives that connect them with the more universal aspects of life. And finally there was the more general understanding in Polish society that even such deeply tragic events need to be, at least partially, laid to rest.

Beside the efforts to officially commemorate the massacres, more personal stories and accounts of the children of the silenced have emerged in Poland. These kinds of testimonies that Geoffrey Hartman refers to as "little narratives" (Hartman 2009) appear to stem from the conviction that in the absence of important authentic documentation, only literature and private memoirs can fill the lacunae of knowledge, recognition, and empathy.[13] Through these narratives, many published for the first time by the KFA, and other representations based on them, the victims of Katyn were reintroduced to the public sphere as prisoners of an undeclared war, killed without trial or funeral, whose names had been consigned to oblivion. They also showed what this meant and continues to mean to those connected to the victims. For them the feeling persists that the perpetrators of the crime have gone unpunished and that the incident was followed by lies and indifference instead of recognition and compensation. And this feeling is not a mere sense of understandable-but-unwarranted bitterness on the part of the victims' families; it is a historical reality. An authoritative monograph in English on the topic published in 2007 is symptomatically titled *Katyn: A Crime Without Punishment*, and the book opens with the statement that its subject matter is "one of the most heinous yet least known of the Stalinist crimes" (Cienciala et al. 2007: 1). This statement captures the gist of the issue, emphasizing a tragedy caused not only by physical brutality but also by systematic symbolic violence and continued problems associated with the completion of a thorough and unbiased investigation. Moreover, because the victims appear to have been chosen by the perpetrators according to specific military and social criteria, and because they were denied what constitutes human symbolic conduct in boundary situations, they can be seen as emblematic victims of communist control and their families as

Antigonic figures who may potentially allegorize Poland's lot both during and after the Second World War. Even though the relevant novels, memoirs, and diaries remain low-impact media, the murdered members of prewar Poland's elite were finally publicly represented in their own country as humanized family members, not merely soldiers. They were rescued from anonymity through narrative frames that connected them to their daily life-world that was destroyed by the grand conflagration of the Second World War. They also indicated that the victims were viewed both by the families and the perpetrators as one of the carriers of Poland's political and cultural independence.

All these symbolic components and anthropological imperatives have been artistically condensed in Wajda's film *Katyń* (2007), to date the most internationally visible artistic statement about the incident. The film explicitly thematizes the Antigonic element. It depicts the incident itself realistically (even if at times too theatrically), and links it to the contemporaneous crimes of Nazi Germany. Most importantly, however, it focuses primarily on what the massacre meant to families, particularly to the wives and sisters of the victims. In the first set of memoirs published under the title *Written with Love*, one finds reference to the "terrible silence" that shrouded longing and despair. Wajda, whose father was among those murdered in Kharkov, visualizes this aspect and through it reveals the cold-blooded destruction of a particular life-world. By shifting the attention from the soldiers themselves to those who loved them and whose loss was publicly unrecognized, he makes the extension of sentiments and identification possible, and thereby reveals the existential depth of the Katyn trauma. Staging the women as so many Antigones can be seen as an instance of intertextuality that renders the story potentially generalizable.[14] The film has garnered broad international recognition and was initially received as a shocking story from Berlin to Los Angeles. However, the difficulties with global distribution of the film,[15] the reluctance of certain audiences to be confronted with it,[16] and what some viewed as a problem of an occasionally "too arcane" contextualization of the film (Applebaum 2008) have combined to temper the film's anticipated international impact. The director was apparently aware of the predicament created by *Katyn*'s obscure historical references, something that for the uninitiated renders parts of the film politically illegible (Wajda 2009: 16). But as a part of the legacy of great silence concerning various aspects of Soviet history, this very predicament renders the movie a kind of invitation to unpack East

European mysteries. Understandably, this problem was reversed with Polish audiences. The Katyn trauma narrative appeared so symbolically and politically charged that the film has been susceptible to political instrumentalization, not unlike the official remembrance of the massacre mentioned above. Referring to this danger, Wajda has stated that he is more afraid of the film's allies than its enemies (Wajda 2007: 5), and his effort to avoid political traps was noticed and lauded by many within Poland (Sobolewski 2007).

Regardless of the specific problems of immediate reception, the widespread visibility of a film by the country's most famous director created a significant intervention that may serve as a pattern to follow, as Wajda himself suggested in one of his interviews. The critic cited previously opened his evaluation of the movie by emphasizing that "this cinematographic image of Katyn will enter the collective imagination in Poland" (Sobolewski 2007). As such, it has made any lack of knowledge of the incident at least much more shameful than before, if not impossible. Certainly few in Poland could fail to notice the film upon its release in the fall of 2007. Before the first screening, 95% of Poles surveyed declared they knew the name "Katyn," yet as many as 40% claimed not to know who exactly was to be blamed for the deaths, while as many as 10% believed that the perpetrators were the Germans (*Gazeta Wyborcza* 2007).[17] Upon its release in September 2007, the film was viewed by 1,021,881 people in Poland during its first two weeks, 265,000 of which viewed the film over the first weekend of its screening (*Wprost* 2009). By October 20, 2007, the number of people who had seen the film had already reached two million (*Wirtualna Polska* 2009). By the end of 2008, the number of viewers had reached 2.7 million (Money.pl 2009). Such attendance could not fail to alter the survey figures mentioned before. Above all, the film represented and recalled Katyn as a grand symbol of individual despondency vis-à-vis totalitarian power and reinscribed this recollection within a personally and concretely grounded narrative. Due to such construction, the film vividly depicts a group experience and, thanks to this portrayal, makes decisive strides toward confirming the collective nature of the event, and hence Poland as a cultural community with particular history. To paraphrase the words of Tomas Venclova, Wajda's film is one of the more important representations that have attached anew the meaning of human suffering to the sign of Katyn and aided in overcoming the victims' silence (Venclova 1999: 133).

Conclusion

The theory of cultural trauma points in several fruitful directions in our understanding of the Katyn Massacre and its social impact. It can call our attention to a "tear in the social fabric," as well as to a narrative structure and public discourse that emerges in response to such a tear. In this chapter we have traced the history of Katyn as a trauma narrative. That is to say, we have examined the attempts by various actors and carrier groups to bring to light and establish the mass murder of members of Poland's elite as a cultural trauma affecting a wider collective than the individual victims and their families. In an insightful discussion of the difference between psychological and cultural trauma, Smelser finds one essential difference in the fact that cultural traumas are made, not born. He goes on to define a cultural trauma as "an invasive and overwhelming event that is believed to undermine or overwhelm one or several essential ingredients of a culture or the culture as a whole" (Smelser 2004: 38). What we have traced in this chapter are the attempts by individuals and groups to firmly establish Katyn as such an event. One may metaphorically understand this process as opening a very heavy door to a large, unlit room; though quickly overwhelmed by the darkness, we come to see and fully understand all there is inside only gradually, never instantly.

As we have seen, the case of Katyn qua cultural trauma starts with the fundamental problem of knowledge regarding the event's facts, something usually taken for granted in trauma discourses. In the case of Katyn, the very awareness of the occurrence was for a long time partial, and what was known was either suppressed or framed in a way that made the story controversial. The specificity of this particular case forces us to ask new general questions about the relation between such categories as knowledge, awareness, memory, commemoration, representation, and mass media. The sociological definitions of these terms are often taken for granted and their epistemological status hardly explored. One of the values of this study is that it contributes to a better understanding of what we really mean when we employ these concepts in sociological practice and how complex that task of reconstruction really is.

Beyond "power/knowledge" there seems to exist the complex notion of "memory/knowledge." Both definitional elements of the latter are mutually constitutive and fundamental. Yet they are also largely passive phenomena. Memorizing something constitutes a necessary, but not a sufficient condition of *using it* (that is, of making it consequential for one's biography and the environment). There is, of course, no memory without knowledge; memory needs its objects (thus one can speak of memorialization as sites of memory, as well as of commemoration and the accompanying ritual practices). At the same time, we cannot really know anything if we do not have memory. In actual practice, these categories largely overlap and thus exist as culturally shaped networks of meanings, not isolated cognitive entities. Therefore, the issue of cultural trauma is less a matter of traditionally conceived memory and more a matter of determining (a) what structures memory, (b) what "activates" it, and (c) and how this activation occurs. The memory/knowledge compound requires symbolically unpacking and articulation through social performances in order to be turned into active remembrance and acts of empathy. Memory/knowledge appears often as something essentially "dormant." To be become "active," and thus culturally consequential, memory/knowledge requires the emotional commitments of various groups, ritualization of its core messages, and recurrent presence in different public media, especially visual ones. Above all, it needs to be experienced affectively and represented artistically within channels of broadly conceived popular culture if it is to matter for a modern collective sense of belonging and continuity, identification, and empathy.

We have also suggested that the denial of representation and lack of symbolic closure only deepens cultural trauma. The Soviet-imposed communist regime of Poland sought to silence the relatives and children and thus erase the traces of the past because it knew that as long as the memory of the crimes symbolized by Katyn lived on, its legitimacy remained tenuous. Similar mechanisms of domination took place later elsewhere, for example in Pol Pot's Cambodia, where, as Ben Kiernan observes, "the Khmer Rouge hoped to use children as the basis of a new society without memory" (Kiernan 1997: xvii). As for symbolic closure, we have tried to show that "the very fact that the story of Katyn was suppressed only made the mystique stronger" (Osiatynski 2010), thus making the imposed silence the story's "worst" aspect. Symbolic closure is also necessary for launching the processes of reconciliation. Here we can distinguish specific aspects: overcoming anonymity and disclosing all information; overcoming the silence of the victimized; the open acknowledgment of guilt by the perpetrators; the establishment of ritualized commemoration; and establishing a reconciliation dialogue between representatives of perpetrators and victims. These elements of civil repair between Poland and Russia have only slowly and imperfectly emerged since 1989. The remarkable and immediate response on all sides to the plane crash on April 10, 2010, suggested that the case could finally cross the positive point of no return, making the requirements of full reconciliation clearer. Referring to the unprecedented openness of Vladimir Putin and Russian authorities, Polish Minister of Foreign Affairs Radoslaw Sikorski said, "I believe that Putin's reaction stems from the fact that he understood what Soviet Russia did to Poland, felt our pain, when another tragedy took place in Katyn" (Sikorski 2010). These words touched upon one of the social dynamics we have discussed in this article, namely that in order for cultural trauma to emerge, a confluence of contingent and symbolic elements that construct a clear and accessible context for empathy and understanding is needed. If this condition is fulfilled, even unlikely identifications are possible, and even the most oppressive silence can be overcome. Artistic representations like Wajda's *Katyn* are poignant stories that may function as "intellectual shock" (Hartman 2009) condensing many meanings of human tragedy under a single name; "Katyn" has become such a name.

Notes

1. This would include Lithuanians and Ukrainians, for example (Snyder 2002), as well as those Poles who fought in the Soviet army and those Polish Communists who remained true to communist ideology.
2. There were also about 7000 civilians killed at other unidentified locations. According to Paul, "for unknown reasons, the NKVD decided to spare 448 men from a total of 14,500 … of those spared, 245 came from Kozelsk, 79 from Starobelsk, and 124 from Ostashkov" (1991: 105); (see Cienciala et al. [2007] for the definitive numbers).
3. According to Paul, "the German and Soviet governments collaborated closely in their efforts to eliminate the Polish intelligentsia" (1991: 65). He and others suggest that the two governments may also have colluded in the Katyn Massacre, making later claims and counter-claims of guilt and responsibility even more complicated.
4. Only one eyewitness lived to describe the moment and method of execution, Stanislaw Swianiewicz, now a professor of economics and author of *In the Shadow of Katyn* (*Wcieniu Katynia*) in 1976.
5. Saloman Slowes, who survived the massacre, published an account of his experiences in 1992 and in it discusses the fate of many Jews in the camp.
6. One survivor, Father Zdzislaw Peszkowski, recounts, "At Kozelsk, I discovered Poland." Paul, who interviewed Peszkowski in 1989, explains,

"What he meant was that, at Kozelsk, he met the best that Poland could offer. At 21, he had been thrown together with men from all parts of the country, a cross-section of the nation's professional elite" (1991: 70–71). Peszkowski was not a priest at the time, but after receiving a PhD in Polish literature from Oxford after the war, he was ordained in the U.S. in 1954.

7. Paul puts it this way, "The Germans recognized from the outset that their discovery presented a golden opportunity to split the Western Allies. They were keenly aware of the serious rift between the Soviets and the Polish government-in-exile over-disputed territory in the western Ukraine and western Belorussia. The Germans knew also that more than ten thousand Polish officers captured by the Soviets in 1939 were still missing when General Anders and his army-in-exile left the U.S.S.R. in 1942" (1991: 207).
8. The advancing Red Army was also the precipitating cause of a very dramatic attempt to preserve some of the incriminating documents that would help establish Soviet guilt. The documents found on the bodies of the victims at Katyn (e.g., newspaper clippings and other dated material) that would have importance in establishing the date of the executions were hurriedly collected by the Germans and shipped to occupied Poland for safekeeping. The Germans feared that if these papers fell into the hands of the NKVD, who was keenly aware of both their existence and importance, they would be suppressed. These documents were later packed into fourteen shipping crates as the Russian army approached Krakow (where the documents were kept) and sent to Germany. Further advances by the Soviet army and the pursuit of the NKVD pushed the documents farther and farther westward, until they ended up in the private home of the elderly father of Dr. Werner Beck, one of the forensic experts enlisted by the Germans to carry out the exhumations at Katyn. Beck had himself seen to it that the documents arrived there as the Soviets were in hot pursuit. Finally, the crates were burned at his request before they could fall into Soviet hands. All this came to light during the American House hearings in 1952, where Beck gave his testimony (see Paul 1991: 269 ff. for the full account).
9. Poland now issues a commemorative stamp for each ten-year anniversary. The first one issued to mark the 50th anniversary in 1990 shows a simple cross, while the 60th anniversary was marked with a more elaborate picture of a Catholic priest and a commemorative cross.
10. As a matter of fact, the Soviet government under Gorbachev appeared to be forced to officially admit its guilt only after a few Russian historians, such as Natalia Lebedeva, obtained a rather unwittingly issued permission to examine NKVD archives that indirectly proved Soviet responsibility

(Materski 2008: 125–126). The text of the TASS announcement itself was cautious, but it was still powerful enough to launch an avalanche of irreversible changes to the Katyn narrative.

11. By 2010 there were so many commemoration sites that when another was proposed, the head of the Katyn Families Association, Andrzej Shapski, was ready to say, "that's enough" and that the money collected for the monument could be put to better social use (January 30, 2010, www.gazeta.pl).
12. Two other official cemeteries were opened in the same year: one in Kharkov, Ukraine and the other in Mednoe, Russia.
13. To this day the Russian government has not delivered to the Polish side the 21,857 personal NKVD folders of the deceased. It claims that the folders have been destroyed. However, there is no confirmation that this is the case (Materski 2008: 131).
14. In an interview Wajda explains that he had to choose between making a film about his father, the murdered officer, or his mother, the distraught and waiting relative. This, he says, is why the film took so long to make. In the end, he has tried to combine both stories (see the "special features" section of the film's DVD). The portrayal of the movie's protagonist as an "Antigenic gesture," however, was obvious to Polish critics (see Sobolewski 2007).
15. The director complained about the problems caused largely by the indolence of Polish National TV, the organ responsible for the movie as a commercial product. Wajda described their treatment as the "murdering of the film" (Wajda 2009: 16).
16. *Katyn* has so far been largely omitted as an "inconvenient" picture. In Italy this fact may be linked to the influence of Italian leftist circles (*Gazeta Wyborcza*, April 23, 2009). Even one of the biggest Italian cinema networks—one that belongs to the family of Silvio Berlusconi—launched only a DVD distribution of the movie. And while this may have come as an unexpected disappointment for some, it should not be surprising that Russian distribution of the movie is almost nonexistent.
17. There is here, of course, a methodological problem at stake, namely, How can researchers be sure that the statement "Yes, I have heard about Katyn" is not distorted by a more general framework that stigmatizes ignorance? It would perhaps be better to formulate questionnaires that indirectly illicit pertinent knowledge or lack thereof. Still, even if the figure of 95% regarding those who declared they knew of Katyn were exaggerated, it is not unrealistic to assume that the vast majority of society had indeed heard about it by 2007, and thus could identify and respond to the issue. It is also interesting that the legacy of communist propaganda is still visible. Even in the European countries not exposed to it in

history, associating Katyn with Nazi German apparently exists. For example, in Sweden, where the daily *Dagens Nyheter* confused historical facts in this way while introducing Wajda's movie (see http://wiadomosci.onet.pl/1698369,12,item.html).

References

Abarinow, W. 2007. *Oprawcy z Katynia* (The Perpetrators of Katyn). Krakow: Znak.

Applebaum, A. 2008. A Movie That Matters. *New York Review of Books* 55 (2): February 14.

Cienciala, A. M., N. Lebedeva, and W. Materski. 2007. *Katyn: A Crime Without Punishment*. New Haven and London: Yale University Press.

Czapski, Józef. 2001 [1951]. *Na nieludzkiej ziemi* (Inhuman Land). Krakow: Znak.

Hartman, Geoffrey. 2009. Foreword. In *Remembering the Holocaust: A Debate*, ed. Jeffrey Alexander. Oxford: Oxford University Press.

Iwinski, T. 2010. Available at http://www.tokfm.pl/Tokfm/1,103454,7761693,Tadeusz_IwinskiWierzeze_to_bedzie_trwale_katharsis.html. Accessed April 12, 2010.

Kaczorowska, T. 2006. *Children of the Katyn Massacre*. Jefferson, NC: McFarland.

Kiernan, Ben. 1997. Introduction. In *Children of Cambodia's Killing Fields: Memoirs by Survivors*, ed. D. Pran. New Haven and London: Yale University Press.

Kimmelman, M. 2009. Poland's Complicated Past Sparks Soul-Searching. *New York Times*, April 20.

Ksiazek-Czerminska, M. 1999. *Wstep* (Introduction). In *Pisane milościa - losy wdów katyńskich* (Written with Love—Lives of the Katyn Widows). Gdynia: Stowarzyszenie Rodzina Katynska.

Materski, W. 2008. *Katyń, nasz ból powszedni* (Katyn, Our Daily Pain). Warszawa: Ryttn.

Nim, N. 2008. Dziekujemy Wajdzie za Katyn (We Thank Wajda for 'Katyn'). *Gazeta Wyborcza*, March 20.

Oseka, P. 2007. *Klamstwo specjalnego znaczenia* (A Special Lie). *Gazeta Wyborcza*, September 15–16.

Osiatynski, W. 2010. Polish Heroes, Polish Victims. Available at http://www.nytimes.com/2010/04/16/opinion/16osiatynski.html?emc=eta. Accessed April 16, 2010.

Paul, M. Allen. 1991. *Katyn*. New York: Scribner's.

Sanford, George. 2005. *Katyn and the Soviet Massacre of 1940: Truth, Justice, and Memory*. London: Routledge.

Sariusz-Skapska, I. (2002). *Polscy świadkowie GULagu* (Polish Witnesses to Gulag). Krakow: Universitas.

Sawicki, J. 2007. *Zanim powstala Dolinka Katyńska. Pamieć o Katyniu w pierwszych dekadach istnienia PRL* (Before the Katyn Valley Was Created: The Memory of Katyn in the First Decades of the People's Republic of Poland). *Tygodnik Powszechny*, September 23.

Sikorski, R. 2010. Available at http://www.tokfm.pl/Tokfm/1,103087,7761052,Sikorski_dzwonil_do_Jaroslawa_Kaczynskiego_Mam_straszna.html. Accessed April 12, 2010.

Slowes, S. 1992. *The Road to Katyn.* Oxford: Blackwell.

Smelser, Neil. 2004. Psychological Trauma and Cultural Trauma. In *Cultural Trauma and Collective Identity*, Jeffrey Alexander, Ronald Eyerman, Bernhard Giesen, Neil Smelser, and Piotr Sztompka. Berkeley: University of California Press.

Snyder, Timothy. 2002. Memory of Sovereignty and Sovereignty Over Memory: Poland, Lithuania and Ukraine, 1939–1999. In *Memory and Power in Postwar Europe*, ed. John-Werner Muller. Cambridge: Cambridge University Press.

Sobolewski, T. 2007. Gest Antygony (Antigone's Gesture). *Gazeta Wyborcza*, September 17. Available at http://film.gazeta.pl/film/l,22535,4497644.html.

Suleiman, Susan Rubin. 2006. *Crises of Memory and the Second World War.* Cambridge, MA: Harvard University Press.

Szacka, B. 2007. Tylko elita pamieta? (Does Only the Social Elite Remember?). *Gazeta Wyborcza*, September 15–16.

Venclova, Tomas. 1999. *Forms of Hope: Essays.* Riverdale-on-Hudson, NY: The Sheep Meadow Press.

Wajda, A. 2007. Przeszlość nieopowiedziana- z Andrzejem Wajda rozmawiaja Joanna Olczak-Ronikier I Tomasz Fialkowski (An Untold Past—An Interview with Andrzej Wajda). *Tygodnik Powszechny*, September 23.

Wajda, A. 2008. Pokazalem światu Katynń (I Have Showed Katyn to the World). *Gazeta Wyborcza*, February 26.

Wajda, A. 2009. TVP blokuje 'Katyn' (Polish TV blocks 'Katyn'). *Gazeta Wyborcza*, January 2.

Walesa, L. 2010. Available at www.nytimes.com/2010/04/11. Accessed April 11, 2010.

Zaremba, M. 2010. Kulturkronikan (Culture Chronicle). *Dagens Nyheter*, April 13.

CHAPTER 7

Cultural Trauma, Collective Memory, and the Vietnam War

(with Todd Madigan and Magnus Ring)

Introduction

There were many sides to what Americans call the Vietnam War. In a wider project, we look at this conflict through the lens of cultural trauma and its narrative representation on the part of the three chief belligerents: (1) the Vietnamese communists; (2) the "South" Vietnamese from the former Republic of Vietnam who fled the country and now live in the U.S.; and (3) the broader, non-Vietnamese American society. In this article we will concentrate attention on the latter social group, calling upon the two others primarily to illustrate by way of contrast how Americans remember the war. We are aware that identifying these three collectivities is a simplification as it overshadows differences in ideology, religion, ethnicity, generation, class, etc. We use them reluctantly and tentatively because they have become common parlance, at least for the English speaking audience. Even using the term "Vietnam" can be problematic for some, as it stems from a colonial vocabulary, but this too has become the established term. The "Vietnam War" is no different, as the war as understood from the point of view of the Vietnamese communists had a different set of names, including the American War and the War of Resistance Against the American Imperialists. With this in mind, we will try to remain consistent in terminology while referring to the general violent confrontation between opposing forces that began in earnest

R. Eyerman, *Memory, Trauma, and Identity*, Cultural Sociology,
https://doi.org/10.1007/978-3-030-13507-2_7

at the end of the Second World War, and in certain respects—for some—still continues even to this day (Nguyen 2016b).

This is a study of how this violent conflict and the suffering it entailed is understood and remembered collectively in American society. It is thus a study in trauma and collective memory and the social processes through which such memory is created, constructed, and maintained. As with all memory, collective memory is represented and reproduced in narrative form through various means including oral telling, literature, music, drama, film, the graphic arts, monuments, memorials, museum installations, and commemorative events such as anniversaries and holidays. Through such media and related ritual practices, the stories and myths that congeal as collective memory serve as a foundation upon which collective identity rests. In the case of nations, there is no single collective memory; rather, there are many voices that over time achieve some cohesive clarity. In this regard, one can distinguish *official collective memory* from *popular memory* (the latter is sometimes called "cultural memory"); often these two different interpretations of the past that coexist within the same society confront one another (Misztal 2003). This is the primary level of analysis in this article. Individual memory and the collective memory of various groups are important of course, as they contribute to collective memory, and in some cases, they offer a narrative that runs counter to official versions. For example, individually and collectively Vietnamese Americans have made various attempts to be included in official American commemorative ceremonies (for example, to participate in Veterans Day and Memorial Day parades), especially in local communities where they are a dominant presence. The published memoirs of former military officers and ordinary soldiers of the Republic of Vietnam have also been an important resource in keeping contested memories vibrant in both the U.S. and Vietnam. Antiwar activist and politician Tom Hayden, who infamously traveled to Hanoi in the midst of the war, has sought in a recently written memoir to counter the downplaying of the antiwar movement in official memorials. As these examples reveal, when publicly expressed, individual memories can be important vehicles in both supporting and countering official collective memory.

While this chapter is not a historical account of the war, it does build upon what is a very impressive historiography (e.g., Fitzgerald 1972; Herring 1993, 2001; Karnow 1983; Moyar 2006; Young 1991). In order to provide a coherent account of how the War in Vietnam is remembered, we distinguish several *arenas of memory*, the social spaces where the various narratives that form collective memory interact. The broad academic sphere that includes historiography is but one of these arenas. In addition we designate three other arenas where the discourses around the War in Vietnam influence the understanding of the war and how it is remembered: the political arena, the popular culture arena (including mass media and the arts), and the community arena, where individual biography and generational experience are important factors. As with all such heuristic differentiations, there is no definitive boundary between them and some overlap occurs (e.g., between the academic debate and political/policy discussions of the war). It is also the case that these arenas are differently composed and significant with reference to our three protagonists. For example, exiled Vietnamese have participated in some of the wider-American society's commemorative events, but the former's ability to influence the way mainstream Americans remember the war has been very limited. We will begin with a discussion of our theoretical frame and key concepts and then offer a brief summary of the war before turning to the arenas within which the collective memory of the war is articulated and transmitted.

Cultural Trauma, Collective Memory, and Collective Identity

Cultural trauma provides the guiding interpretative framework for our analysis. A cultural trauma is a discursive response to a tear in the social fabric, a massive disruption that occurs when the foundations of established collective identity are shaken by one or a series of seemingly interrelated occurrences (Eyerman 2001, 2011). The resulting discursive process can be understood as a struggle over meaning, where individual and collective actors attempt to define a situation and impose a particular meaning to it. Within this meaning struggle, various individuals and groups construct narratives in which trauma is an organizing notion. Central aspects of the cultural trauma process include the collective attempt to locate the causes of suffering, to place blame, and to point to remedies.

Cultural trauma should be distinguished from the classical and popular notions of trauma, which have in common the naturalistic assumption that trauma is the direct result of either a wound inflicted on the body or one visited on the mind through an overwhelming experience

(Alexander 2004). This naturalistic conception roots trauma in a direct individual experience, one that leaves an indelible mark and causes otherwise inexplicable behavior. By contrast, cultural trauma is more contingent and involves discursive practices, collectivities, collective memory, and collective identity in a struggle to define what is experienced as traumatic (Eyerman 2011, 2015). There can be no doubt that the War in Vietnam was traumatic in the classical and popular meanings of the term. The Vietnamese countryside was torn apart by violence and death: more than 2 million civilians died and millions more were displaced. In addition, about 1.1 million North Vietnamese and Viet Cong were killed, and many more were injured, while 58,000 Americans also died along with thousands more who were wounded (Young 1991). The War in Vietnam was both individually and collectively traumatic in the physical and psychological senses of the term (Smelser 2004).

The term *collective memory* refers to the selective and cumulative process through which collectivities, from small groups to nations, make use and meaningful sense of the past. In this understanding we draw upon a tradition in social theory stemming from Emile Durkheim and Maurice Halbwachs. While Durkheim (1995) describes how the past is inscribed in the present through traditions and ritual practices, Halbwachs (1992) explains how the recollected past is filtered through present needs, most particularly the need for group cohesion and social solidarity. As we use the term, collective memory is intimately bound up with identity formation, specifically as it relates to national or collective identity. We assert that nations develop and depend upon core narratives, the mythic accounts of how the nation came to be. In constructing the political community that is the nation, including those who are aligned or unaligned with the official state apparatus, "agents of memory" selectively draw from a reservoir of images and stories in a process of remembering and forgetting. This sometimes occurs with specific aims in view, such as the conscious attempt to project a noble image of the collective. Other times it might not be so intentional, yet still have the same result. Collective memory is an active process of meaning making in which various social forces compete, and as such, it can be distinguished from history—the professionalized reconstruction of the past that aims at factual truth. Since it is so tied to identity formation and to mobilization, maintaining a living collective memory is a distinctly political process, where "collective memory operates as a constraint: by proscription (through taboos and prohibition) and by proscription (through duties and requirements)" (Olick and Levy 1997: 923). As a professionalized discourse, history writing has other kinds of constraints, most notably connected to "its methods and through the rules by means of which it leads to verifiable results" (Koselleck 2004: 94). Of course collective memory and professional history can intersect, as when academic discussions become politicized when faced with traumatic memory and difficult pasts.

Following Benedict Anderson (1983), Anthony Smith (1991), and Paul Connerton (1989), we conceive of nations as imagined communities, where the construction and maintenance of collective identity is a necessary and ongoing process. The existence of core narratives that regulate and inform collective memory implies a notion of the past that is non-objective and fluid. Following the traditions of Durkheim and Halbwachs, we understand collective memory as an integral part of a more general collective consciousness (Durkheim 1995; Halbwachs 1992). Every society requires a sense of continuity in order to maintain social cohesion over time, and a narrated collective memory that is reinforced through everyday rituals and collective events is crucial to that (Connerton 1989; Misztal 2003). However, as Nora (1996) and Olick (1999) point out, collective memory is a sphere of both consensus and conflict. Memories are contested as specific events might be represented and recollected differently by individuals and groups (Tota 2003; Jordan 2005). This is certainly the case regarding the War in Vietnam. In the contemporary Socialist Republic of Vietnam for example, one finds conflicting representations in local individual/biographical narratives. In the U.S., former activists in the antiwar movement, as well as dissenting veterans, represent and thus remember the War in Vietnam differently from those found in official representations. And matters within the Vietnamese–American community are no different, with numerous conflicting narratives of the war continue to struggle for preeminence.

Core national narratives and related ritual practices like holidays and commemorations are meant to cement collective identification as they distinguish "us" from "them," those inside and outside of the collective. The ultimate aim is to secure loyalty to the abstract collectivity we call a nation. The core narratives of national mythology are transmitted in many ways—in modern societies this is done in part through formal means such as school textbooks, as well as through mundane practices like pledges of allegiance and the singing of national anthems at sporting events. Identification is referenced and reinforced through national days of remembrance, with ceremonies arranged at sacred sites on specified dates to enhance their significance. National museums are another central mediator of national narratives; this is especially the case in postwar Vietnam where there has been an organized attempt by the communist leadership to establish a narrative aimed at unifying the recently unified nation around a shared past that is both divisive and traumatic. In this capacity, it is those once part of the South Vietnamese regime that lack major institutional mediators and influential carriers to establish their memory of the war in official discourse. This is especially true for those still in Vietnam where their presence as a distinctive oppositional group is all but erased from public discourse in the government's effort to represent national unity, but it is also true in the U.S. where the traumatic memory of the conflict also tends to render them invisible. For example, the process of designing, erecting, and dedicating the Vietnam Veterans Memorial in Washington, DC was a long and contested process whose initial impetus came from the bottom-up and not the top-down. Its very name calls attention to those who served the nation, rather than the cause for which they fought. Those Vietnamese allies, who fought and died alongside the American service personnel, are not mentioned at all.

A shared mass culture helps orchestrate and disperse these ritual practices over the social, political, and geographic boundaries that define the collective. This mass culture and the media that dispense it create a national frame of reference at the same time as linking widely dispersed individuals in common conversation. Anderson (1983) highlights the daily newspapers that construct and then supply national "news" to an audience that intuitively grasps its meaning; to this one could add television and social media. Most especially in the U.S., the mass media helped make the War in Vietnam meaningful for the American public, and the role of the mass media in that process remains controversial, as will be discussed below. During the war, electronic mass media did not play the same role within Vietnam itself, where older, more traditional forms of representation and dispersion were relied upon. This was especially true in the North, and slightly less so in the South where television and radio did have a more significant impact. As opposed to the U.S., where the existence of a relatively autonomous, commercially driven, mass media is considered the centerpiece of a democratic way of life, popular culture is much more centrally controlled in the Socialist Republic of Vietnam. This too has impacted the way the War in Vietnam is represented and remembered.

The War

For the sake of convenience, we locate the origin of the American involvement in the War in Vietnam at the end of the Second World War, when the French colonial empire in South East Asia crumbled, impelling the French to fight in order to restore their sovereignty. This marks the beginning of what the Vietnamese sometimes call the First Indochina War. This war was understood as an anti-colonialist struggle by all parties, part of yet another attempt to form an independent nation on the part of the Vietnamese and of national prestige and economic gain on the part of the French. On the Vietnamese side, various ethnic, religious, and ideological strands competed to determine what exactly independence would imply. Thus, from the perspective of the factions within the Vietnamese communist leadership, the war against the Americans was but another stage in a long struggle against colonial and imperial efforts. The Americans and their European allies viewed the matter differently.

As part of America's war in Asia, the end of Second World War brought about the removal of Japanese forces from Vietnam and a concentration of resistance forces against the returning French military. France emerged from the European war greatly weakened; its military forces had been defeated and half its country occupied by the Germans. The attempt to regain some of its colonies in Asia was part of a project of national restoration. French weakness provided an opportunity for Vietnamese nationalist groups, among them the Viet Minh (League for the Independence of Vietnam), formed in China in 1941 under the leadership of Ho Chi Minh. Ho, a Vietnamese patriot, was also a member of the Communist International and had founded the Communist Party of Vietnam in 1930. The Viet Minh was affiliated with resistance forces operating in all regions of the country during the Second World War. The U.S. supported them in this struggle; in fact, there exists a photograph of Ho standing amidst a group of smiling, uniformed American OSS officers in a rural campground somewhere in Indochina (the OSS, or Office of Strategic Services, was the precursor of the Central Intelligence Agency [CIA]). The Americans and Vietnamese guerrillas had a common enemy in the Japanese who at that time occupied Vietnam. At this point, the distinction between northern and southern Vietnamese was primarily geographical, though it did reflect old feudal divisions and cultural differences. Resistance forces comprised various groups and ideological factions from all regions of the territory.

Under President Franklin Roosevelt, the U.S. was committed to aiding anti-colonial struggles, as was the Soviet Union. When Roosevelt died unexpectedly in April 1945, the Soviet Union and the U.S. were allies sharing this anti-colonial stance. However, by the time Roosevelt's successor, his Vice President Harry Truman, won reelection in 1948, the situation had changed dramatically, with former allies becoming increasingly at odds. When China came under Communist control in 1949, what came to be known as the Cold War had escalated in confrontation. Truman and his aides abandoned Roosevelt's anti-colonial stance and redefined the struggle in Indochina and Asia generally as part of a conflict between Communism and the "Free World." This was made clear in the so-called Truman Doctrine of 1947, where a more interventionist policy was put forward. In this new worldview, the French were no longer colonialists, but rather an important European ally in defending democracy, not colonialism, across the globe. This division of the world contributed to—and then intensified—the Korean War (1950–1953), which pitted the "Free World" against a monolithic and aggressive Communism. The U.S. claimed its actions were purely defensive, aimed at containing Communist expansion, along with the defense of the Republic of Vietnam, a legitimate "democratic" nation-state. This was how American intervention in Indochina was understood and legitimated when it was more formally initiated in 1950, the same year the Korean War began. This intervention began as financial and military aid to the French, and through them, to their Vietnamese allies. When the French were defeated in 1954, American military "advisors" arrived in increasing numbers during the Eisenhower (1953–1961) and Kennedy administrations (1961–1963).

Formally speaking (from the American perspective), there never was a U.S. "war" in Vietnam. As with the Korean "police action," no American president asked Congress for a declaration of war as required by the Constitution. Three presidents held office before Lyndon Johnson told the American public their country was engaged in a "real war." This was pronounced in 1964, as Johnson addressed the nation to justify sending in more ground troops. American forces had been there in increasing numbers, but purportedly in an "advisory" and "defensive" role. When Johnson left office in 1968, there were 495,000 American soldiers in Vietnam, a number that would soon peak at 543,400. The South Vietnamese Army (ARVN), created and trained by the French, wore American-made uniforms and fired American-made weapons, whereas the military forces of North Vietnam were trained and supplied by China and the Soviet Union; in turn, North Vietnam provided arms and supplies to the Southern communists fighting in the NLF. From the perspective of the Vietnamese communist forces fighting against the South Vietnamese military, the latter was a "puppet" army with no real standing apart from its colonial patrons. What's more, relationship between the Republic of Vietnam's military and American forces was also problematic. This relationship mirrored that between the government in Saigon and the American representatives stationed there; mistrust and misunderstanding was the general rule. The reliability of the South Vietnamese forces and the responsiveness of the government to the needs of the Vietnamese population remains to this day a matter of controversy, coloring the way the War in Vietnam is remembered in the Vietnamese diasporas and in the U.S. by historians and politicians.

The year 1967 was a pivotal one, with Northern strategy becoming more aggressive under the leadership of Le Duan, the General Secretary of the Central Committee, while there was growing frustration and dissent on the American side. There was internal conflict within the Johnson administration between escalating the war and seeking an immediate diplomatic solution (Herring 2001). This was also a presidential election year with the war as its central focus. In a bitterly fought campaign in which leading Democratic candidate Robert Kennedy was assassinated and the country gripped by violence and revolt, Richard Nixon won the presidency on the promise of bringing law and order to the country and "Peace with Honor" in Vietnam. He took office as the North Vietnamese launched their Tet Offensive, attacking all the major cities in the South in a massive, coordinated strike. For the U.S., this proved to be a turning point in the war politically, if not militarily; the war was at its most violent, antiwar protest movements covered the globe, and there was no clear strategy for victory. In response, Nixon and his advisor Henry Kissinger put forward a policy of "Vietnamization," which included gradually withdrawing American forces from the country and leaving the ground war to the South Vietnamese. After the final American withdrawal of combat forces in early 1973, the American government promised continued air support, arms, and ammunition to the South. In April 1973, South Vietnamese President Thieu visited the U.S., where President Nixon reiterated his commitment to providing this large-scale military support. However, in June of that year the American Congress, bolstered by increasingly vocal public opposition to the war and a still powerful antiwar movement, passed a bill prohibiting any further American involvement in Indochina in a veto-proof vote. This, combined with the ongoing Watergate scandal, greatly weakened the Nixon presidency to the point where it became impossible to provide more than minimal backing to Saigon.

Keenly aware of the situation between the U.S. and its Vietnamese allies, the North Vietnamese planned their response. Heavy fighting resumed between their forces and South Vietnamese forces, the latter using American-supplied weapons but without much in the way of ammunition and fuel reserves. In August 1974, Richard Nixon resigned in disgrace and Gerald Ford assumed the presidency. The next month the U.S. Congress drastically cut allocations to South Vietnam, creating a severe crisis within the South Vietnamese military. In this context, the North Vietnamese leadership decided to launch a full invasion. This began in January 1975. Responding to this onslaught, President Ford formally announced that the U.S. would not reenter the conflict. Under the pressure of the communists' monumental attack, a weakened and dispirited South Vietnamese armed forces lost major battles in the central region of South Vietnam. Following these defeats, President Thieu decided to withdraw a large proportion of the remaining forces to defend Saigon. Panic and chaos ensued. The South's military disarray encouraged and emboldened the North Vietnamese, who then decided to continue their push southward all the way to Saigon. Da Nang, South Vietnam's second largest city, fell in March, and over 100,000 troops surrendered as their commanders fled. On April 21, Thieu resigned after a tearful televised speech; shortly thereafter he fled the country. On April 30, 1975, Saigon fell, with the last Americans and some of their Vietnamese allies escaping by helicopter in a chaotic exit that was captured on film and transmitted around the world. These images remain some of the most powerful resources shaping the memory of the war.

War and Collective Memory: Mobilizing and Commemorating

More than an imagined community, the nation-state is a collective actor, gathering its members—the nation—in collective projects such as wars, which typically are legitimated as the defense of the nation and its interests. The imagined past encased in the narratives congealed as collective memory is called upon to mobilize and legitimate such projects.

The Vietnam War was a project where the past, most especially the heroics of the Second World War, was mobilized to support present needs by all sides. In the U.S., major social and political institutions, such as the Congress, schools, and religious organizations, helped to mobilize the population for war. They were supported by various media in popular culture, from Hollywood and television to comic books and mass circulation magazines. American youth were recruited not only through the selective service administration, popularly experienced by 18-year-olds and their families as the draft board, but also through films and literature that glorified war and patriotic sacrifice. Infused with a Cold War view of the world and anxious about a communist threat, politicians, schoolteachers, and religious leaders prepared the populace for war against an evil aggressor. The Vietnamese needed no such preparation; their struggle had been ongoing for many years, centuries even. Vietnamese youth were drafted in both the north and south and mobilized through long-established military traditions.

The memory of previous wars framed the understanding and guided the actions of those who planned and participated in the Vietnam conflict. This was especially the case in Hanoi and Washington, as well as throughout the military organizations on all sides. The "North" Vietnamese leaders, with Ho Chi Minh as the head, saw the war against the Americans as a continuation of the struggle against not only the French but more broadly, against China and Japan, as a war of national independence. The Americans were yet another foreign power seeking to conquer and colonize them and Vietnamese collective memory contained many accounts of victory against more powerful enemies. The strategies and tactics of insurgent warfare learned from previous struggles guided their efforts, as did the idea of national liberation. For them, the "South" Vietnamese were mere puppets, strung along by their colonial masters. The South Vietnamese, at least as articulated by intellectuals who lived in urban areas like Saigon and for whom the war was largely distant, saw themselves as above all "lovers of freedom" and sought to defend themselves from what they saw as the brutal dictatorship of communism. Most were as opposed to the French colonialism as the communists in the North, but they were equally ill-disposed toward colonization by communists. They saw their relationship with the U.S. as wholly different from that of the French (and Chinese and Japanese); the Americans were allies supporting them in their gambit for freedom and independence. But even so, the South was at the same time wary of the

Americans—especially as the conflict dragged on and the American presence in the South grew—and often felt the need to assert itself against its powerful ally. For the Americans, on the other hand, the Vietnam conflict was a stage in the global struggle against Communist aggression, part of a Cold War in which the Vietnamese were pawns to larger forces. Vietnam was merely a place to draw a line. The heroic struggles of the Second World War, against foreign occupation for the Vietnamese, and against the evil of Nazism and Fascism for the Americans, was a key factor in the mobilization of collective memory on all sides.

While it might have been a shared goal in initiating the conflict, the creation of national consciousness and identification was carried out differently in Vietnam by forces in the "North" and "South." State-building and the related issues of loyalty and identification were an important project on both sides in what many considered a civil war. For authorities in Hanoi, the central aim of the struggle was a unified state and a national consciousness that stretched beyond the boundary created in Geneva in 1954 following the defeat of the French. A mythical Vietnamese past was a prime force in this project; it had been transmitted over centuries through oral traditions and represented in traditional literary and visual art forms, such as poetry and graphic arts. The boundaries of the collective to whom this was addressed were always fluid, as the idea of "Vietnamese" nation was always abstract and imagined. This finally achieved more clarity under colonial rule with the existence of a visible common enemy.

Vietnamese nationalism emerged with full force after the Second World War, spurred on by the return of the French and then by American intervention. Throughout this period, the question of the loyalty and identification of those who lived in the now divided country, especially in the rural areas of the "South," was hotly contested. Were South Vietnam, its government, and its military merely a French and American creation, or was there something more basic and vital at stake? How strong and foundational was identification with South Vietnam and its Saigon-based government? Through what means and mechanisms was that imagined community realized? The answer to these questions is still contested among historians and in exile communities. During the war, contention over the South Vietnamese government and society became the source of great tension between the Saigon-centered leadership and the Americans at crucial moments. At first portrayed as the lone bearer of democracy in the region, the autocratic regime of Ngo Dinh Diem

(which jailed opposition leaders, both political and religious) became increasingly problematic after his downfall in 1963, after which no stable, non-military government could be established. With the ideological veil of establishing freedom and democracy removed, what then were the goals of the American engagement in the conflict? The Americans had promoted a massive effort of state-building in South Vietnam, employing social scientists and civil engineers to build political institutions, as well as roads and waterways to integrate and govern various parts of the region (Carter 2008). This project of creating community occurred alongside the bombing that destroyed it, but its ideological justification, the creation of a democratic society, was important to the legitimacy of the project.

Commemorating: Official and Popular Memory

In both American academic historiography and official discourse, the War in Vietnam is now considered "an avoidable mistake" (Dumbrell 2012). It took close to forty years to achieve this degree of consensus in what was from the beginning a contentious debate. Conversely, no such consensus has been reached in the political arena. Politicians and policy makers still debate the "lessons" of Vietnam and struggle to overcome the "Vietnam syndrome." The memory of the War in Vietnam overshadows ongoing wars in Afghanistan and Iraq and other engagements in the Middle East where American leaders debate the consequences of putting "boots on the ground" and argue over reliable "exit strategies." There is also the more general post-Vietnam reluctance to engage in warfare because of "the cost to families and to public life of the casualties we suffered and inflicted," which must now be taken into account in policy decisions despite the new professional army that replaced the drafting of soldiers from the general population (Sapolsky and Shapiro 1996: 122). All this can be traced to the ignoble exit from Vietnam, a ghost that continues to haunt the corridors of the American government, especially its military and strategic policy organizations. This has carried over into official commemorations of the war, where the only real consensus concerns celebrating those who served. It is perhaps important to point out that from the official point of view, such ceremonies are always conditioned by the desire to project an honorable image of the nation.

This consensus around silence about the causes and consequences of the War in Vietnam was reflected in the decision to construct a national memorial on the Mall in Washington, DC, some of the most hallowed ground in the nation. It is not by chance this memorial is called the Vietnam Veterans Memorial (as opposed to something that names the war explicitly) and is in fact a memorial, rather than a monument. On this commemorative site it is not a war that is commemorated, but rather those who died in national service. Although wars have served throughout history to unify nations, the War in Vietnam had the opposite effect. When wars end victoriously, nations build monuments to commemorate the occurrence and memorials to remember those who died (even when those who died did so in service to a lost cause). What monuments and memorials have in common is that they offer official recognition, creating sites of memory and commemoration. As Arthur Danto (1985: 152) famously observed, "we erect monuments so that we shall always remember, and build memorials so that we shall never forget." The initiative to erect the Vietnam Veterans Memorial, now one of the most visited sites in Washington, DC, came from the bottom-up, from popular memory and the efforts of those who served, not from U.S. officialdom. This too marks the War in Vietnam as highly unusual (see Scruggs and Swerdlow (1985) for a personal history, Wagner-Pacifici and Schwartz (1991) for a sociological analysis, and Sturken (1997) for a humanities approach).

The story of the Vietnam Veterans Memorial's emphasizes its origins among the populace. A former soldier, stirred by a viewing of *The Deer Hunter*, a popular Vietnam War film produced in 1979, set the process in motion. The film evoked strong personal memories and a stubborn desire for collective recognition. If nothing else, this reveals the interplay between personal memory, popular culture, and official memory. This impulse eventually led to an organization of veterans who, against all odds, were successful in their dogged attempts to convince government officials to allow a memorial to be erected. The account is movingly told in *To Heal A Nation* by two of the project's instigators (Scruggs and Swerdlow 1985). The Memorial site on the Washington Mall has become a common place of memory for official commemoration, as well as popular recollection.

Like the contested meaning and uses of the Vietnam Veterans Memorial, the War in Vietnam still rages in American popular culture and popular imagination. Wars, as Nguyen (2016b: 4) points out, are always fought twice: once in the real world and then again as fantasy. In liberal societies like the U.S., popular culture is relatively autonomous from political, religious, and commercial attempts to control what is represented. The word "relatively" is of course important, for, as in all wars, the American government and military sought to manage the flow of information about the war through the mass media to the greatest degree possible. Given that American popular culture is largely commercially driven, control and influence were also exerted through corporate ownership. This arena is one of the most important in the debate over the meaning and memory of the American war in Vietnam. Here one can uncover a meaning struggle framed through coded binaries like perpetrator/victim, along with attempts to resurrect a heroic narrative of American exceptionalism, where its wars are fought to spread freedom and democracy and not for material or personal gain. In this, one can find an overlap with official commemoration and political discourse, more generally. At the same time, it is largely through the medium of popular culture that postwar generations access the War in Vietnam, particularly through film and literature.

Within the community arena, biographical and generational factors are significant in terms of what is remembered about the War in Vietnam. For as long as they remain alive, the personal recollections of what has come to be called the "1960s generation," those who lived through those years, will keep their lived experience of the War in Vietnam War from fading from public view. This generation—most particularly those who fought in and for or against the war—is the bearer of a distinctive collective memory, but it is one that is filled with tension stemming from the opposing views of the war itself. Formed largely by the war, the 1960s generation continues its struggle to include its biographical experience within the national story, making corrective claims rooted in lived experience against official and popular representations of the war. This includes many war veterans, like Tim O'Brien and Oliver Stone, whose novels and films continue to shape how new generations remember the war.

The memory and representation of the American War is less contested in Vietnam than in the U.S., as least publicly, where dissention is most often posed in terms of the price paid for victory. Putting aside the enormous cost in terms of suffering, the war is commemorated as a heroic struggle of national liberation and a glorious victory of resilient people against the massive forces of world powers. This is an image that those in authority would like to project and protect. This is reflected in the official sites of memory, most particularly state-sponsored museums and the reconstructed battlegrounds that have become popular tourist sites throughout Vietnam, particularly for American visitors. There is some deep-seated irony to be uncovered here. For the Vietnamese diaspora, the loss of a homeland and the creation of a new collective identity guides the attempts at constructing a collective memory, one that includes the refugee/immigrant hope for recognition, of having their story included into the national narrative of their new homeland. This construction of collective memory is not without guiding interests as various factions and multiple generations struggle to define the collective in particular ways. With this in mind we can say that each of our protagonists remembers this violent conflict differently through similar means and modes of representation. Each has different names for the conflict, as well as different points of departure and outcomes in its retelling. While April 30, 1975, marked the symbolic end of the American War in Vietnam ("symbolic" because the American combat forces had actually all departed by March 29, 1973), it is the point of origin in the South Vietnamese exiles' narrative of the war. The day is commemorated as Black April with ceremonies attended by Vietnamese Americans spread throughout the U.S. It became an official celebration in Canada in 2015, but with the name changed to "Journey to Freedom Day." The collapse of its military forces and the fall of Saigon led to a mass exodus of those who had allied themselves with the U.S. Thousands left immediately with the last Americans and hundreds of thousands more exited in the following years, often in secret by boats that were unseaworthy. They fled to various ports in the region, including destinations in Thailand, Malaysia, and Singapore. More than 280,000 ended up in the U.S. in the postwar period, and by 2014 some 1.3 million Vietnamese had immigrated to the U.S. The early refugees became popularly known as the "boat people," and their collective story is only now becoming more generally known (Nguyen 2016a, b). The fall of Saigon and the exodus by sea has become the primal scene in the formation of a new collective identity born of trauma. Key agents in the articulation of this trauma narrative are the new generations of American-based and educated Vietnamese. This began with the so-called "1.5 generation" who arrived in the U.S. in their early youth and assimilated into American culture in tension with their parents who typically remained more tied to the country they left behind (Lam 2005, 2010). While their parents transmit tales of hardship and resilience, tinged with a longing for what was lost, new generations look through the past into an American future (Lieu 2011).

In many ways this is a typical immigrant story, but one intensified by the trauma that conditioned it. Arriving on American shores as waves of unwanted refugees, the Vietnamese were placed in refugee camps in military bases and were not permitted to leave without private sponsorship. It was a humiliating experience piled on top of great hardship and loss. Many felt twice betrayed, first as an abandoned ally and second as an unwanted guest. As symbolic bearers of a lost cause, Vietnamese refugees were as unwelcome as returning American soldiers. Out of this beginning, separated from extended family and homeland, they were expected to carve out a new identity and way of life. Reading the novels and memoirs written by first and second generation Vietnamese Americans is a moving experience, something that now more than forty years later is finally coming to light in the broader American society, though it has long been known by Vietnamese Americans (Nguyen 2016a, b, 2017).

Conclusion: Memory and Cultural Trauma

In this chapter we have discussed how the traumatic memory generated in response to the War in Vietnam has impacted the U.S., but with an eye to the Socialist Republic of Vietnam and the exiled community of South Vietnamese who fled to the U.S. Our claim is that the War in Vietnam became a cultural trauma in the U.S. as it became a central component of that period of protest and social change known as "the Sixties." Debate, deception, and dissent about that war fractured faith in American institutions and raised the issue of what it meant to be a patriotic citizen in a country that no longer seemed exceptional. As it progressed the war radically polarized the nation, contributing to a broad public debate not only about the aims and claims of the war but also more fundamentally about what it means to be an American. This fracturing of collective identity is not the case in the Democratic Republic of Vietnam, where the war is understood as a war of national liberation and thus a continuation of a longer struggle against several imperialist enemies. Their project was one of nation-building against the will of foreign interests, and while unquestionably traumatic on many levels, the struggle resulted in the strengthening of collective identity rather than its fracturing, even as it is a collective memory that consciously excludes those who stood in opposition. This type of trauma might better be described as "collective" rather than "cultural" in our sense of these terms. In terms of collective memory, the war was traumatic, given its longevity and long-lasting impact. Yet, when measured in terms of collective identity and social cohesion, it was not traumatic—for the victors at least—though it did and still does raise difficult questions of a foundational nature, which linger on in terms of internal conflict regarding former enemies. The South Vietnamese (and some Americans) on the other hand who defined the situation as a civil war, could also make claims of nation-building, but nation-building of quite a different sort. Their individual and collective trauma erupted as cultural trauma after their war was lost and they entered a forced and, for many, unwelcoming diasporic existence.

The experience of trauma was thus different for each of our three protagonists. For the victorious Vietnamese communists, it was part of the continuing violent struggle for liberation from foreign domination; at the same time it helped ground a new collective identity rooted in old (Vietnamese) and new (Communist) traditions. This process is ongoing, as it has currently been modified to include reconciliation with the U.S. and inclusion into the "Western" orbit. For those aligned with the South Vietnamese, trauma was intensified with the loss of a homeland and the necessity to forge a new identity on foreign soil. This process, too, is ongoing. Along with much else, it involves an intense generational confrontation, as those born in Vietnam struggle to maintain a sense of the "old country" and its traditions, while their children look forward to establishing themselves in their new surroundings. This struggle for identification is entwined with a struggle for acceptance and recognition, something that might equally apply to the new unified (at least formally) Vietnamese nation on a more global scale.

As a discursive process, cultural trauma requires articulation and carrier groups that bear the burden of its representation. One can identify such groups for each of our three protagonists. Those who actually fought the war, as well as military, policy, and administrative officials, are central in all three. They and their generation carry the trauma most personally and are the most active in its representation, particularly in the political arena and popular culture, where many have objectified their biographical experiences in published memoirs, novels, paintings, and films. This is especially the case for Americans and for the first and second generations of Vietnamese Americans for whom popular culture is an important medium of individual and collective expression. They are becoming an increasingly visible voice of the war to an American public that has for the most part only known one side. The situation in Vietnam is different because popular culture is more tightly regulated. This has been changing since the 1980s, however, through the impact of the nation's slow movement toward liberalization, as well as the many individual-level interactions with the exile community, including an emergent group of artists and intellectuals, some of whom move regularly between Vietnam and the U.S. and who in some cases offer counter-narratives of the war and its meaning.

A central aspect of the cultural trauma process is the collective attempt to locate the causes of suffering, to place blame, and to point to remedies. These take a narrative form and are constructed by carrier groups using different media and frames of reference to address diverse audiences in various arenas. One can find significant differences in form and content across our three protagonists. In the U.S. where organized protest and political opposition is an inherent part of what Americans mean by democracy, social movements played a central role in constructing arguments against the war. Antiwar protesters "sat in" on college campuses and were joined by their professors and other professionals, including religious leaders, in denouncing the strategies and tactics of the war. Through representative figures like Martin Luther King, Jr. there was interplay between the vibrant Civil Rights movement and this antiwar movement, bringing Vietnam to the attention of a wide range of Americans and exerting great pressure on political leaders and policy makers. Especially after the Tet Offensive of 1968, journalists used the mass media to report on the negative sides of the war in a way that might not have been possible elsewhere. There was also widespread opposition to the war among artists, playwrights, authors, musicians, and other intellectuals who made use of their various media—and popular culture generally—to protest the war and to name and confront those they deemed responsible for it. Other American institutions, the courts, and the Congress became vehicles for protest and challenge, as well.

The situation is different in Vietnam, where the cause of pain and suffering is indisputable and its source easy to identify: the foreign enemy of colonialists and their surrogates. Whether or not the American soldiers and their allies fell into the latter category was a matter of dispute, but they clearly were foreign. How this could be remedied was less clear. Without the long-established democratic traditions of the U.S., many Vietnamese rallied around Ho Chi Minh and the organized opposition his leadership provided against foreign occupation, including the Chinese, Japanese, and of course, the French. When the Americans entered the picture, there was little difficulty in painting them with the same brush. This narrative was diffused through oral and visual means during the war and put in practice through field indoctrination by cadres working among the peasantry. Vietnamese artists, poets, and songwriters were active agents in this process, as they were recruited into the armed struggle. The viewpoint of those aligned with the South Vietnamese was more ambiguous. Some viewed Ho as both a nationalist and a communist, or supported other nationalist movements or groups and thus viewed the American "advisors" with suspicion, if not outright animosity. Others were more strongly in favor of the American presence, though perhaps with the idea that this was something less permanent and dominating than colonial occupation. Such views were formulated by urban elites and expressed through tightly controlled mass media and reinforced through the military and political parties whose interplay and relative power varied over the course of the conflict. In the end there was little distinction between the military and political institutions in South Vietnam. The views of the rural population—the great majority in all regions of Vietnam—are less clear as they had scant access to media and little organization beyond their local communities.

Postwar Vietnam is quite different, especially with the current liberalizing trends gaining ground and their strategy of becoming a regional power by becoming more closely allied with the West. The current population, though still largely rural and poor, is greatly weighted toward youth, and there is a strong incentive to look forward rather than back. Literacy rates are exceptionally high, 94% for adults over 24 years of age, though lower for minorities and women. More than 80% of urban households own a television, and the several government-run channels are available even in remote areas. Newspapers of various shades of opinion are available and the internet, though censored, has also introduced a range of viewpoints and services to the country. The Vietnamese seem to have put the American War behind them, especially since other, more regionally based wars have intervened. With the flow of tourists and the return of significant portions of the diasporic Vietnamese, there is a vibrant urban and urbane popular culture emerging that is outside the direct control of the state. The U.S. is no longer an enemy, but a trading partner and potential ally. The memory of the American War is fixed in museums and memorials and carries on in the living memory for an older generation. However, this memory has become increasingly remote to the majority of the population. That trauma has largely passed into history, even as it lives on in natural landscape where the effects of chemical and other forms of warfare are present. These are the scars of collective memory, rather than the open wound of cultural trauma.

Our analysis has shown that collective memory is a living force in the life of the individuals and societies in which it is embedded. Collective memory shapes the way individuals and groups understand themselves, affecting their understanding of who they are and why they act as they do. It is also the case that groups attempt to control how they are collectively remembered (De Keizer 1996). This is especially the case with regard to those who experience at first hand traumatic events like war, where an entire generation may be shaped by such experience. The War in Vietnam was formative to generational consciousness, which in part explains why it remains alive and contested. But this conflict had a wider impact than that of a generation, at least in the U.S., where the war is still a point of emotional contestation. This is especially true for those Vietnamese who fled their former country and now live in the U.S. The memory of the War in Vietnam significantly shapes the thoughts and actions beyond those who personally experienced it. How long this will remain the case is an open question that is contingent upon the forces of assimilation and relations between Vietnam and the U.S. The memory of war remains a forceful presence in several major American institutions, most prominently those related to the military and foreign policy affairs where institutional memory has a longer lifespan than in popular culture. However, even in the latter, interest in the War in Vietnam is continually revived through new wars and new voices, such as those of Vietnamese Americans who until now had little presence in the broader American discourse. The desire to "put Vietnam behind us," to relegate it to history as a "tragic event," to "move on," is strongly felt by large swaths of American society, but this desire has not yet been satisfied. The War in Vietnam is a war Americans would like to forget, but cannot.

References

Alexander, Jeffrey. 2004. Toward a Theory of Cultural Trauma. In *Cultural Trauma and Collective Identity*, ed. Jeffrey Alexander, Ronald Eyerman, Bernhard Giesen, Neil Smelser, and Piotr Sztompka. Berkeley: University of California Press.

Anderson, Benedict. 1983. *Imagined Communities*. London: Verso.

Carter, James. 2008. *Inventing Vietnam*. Cambridge: Cambridge University Press.
Connerton, Paul. 1989. *How Societies Remember*. Cambridge: Cambridge University Press.
Danto, Arthur. 1985. *Narration and Knowledge: Including the Integral Text of Analytical Philosophy of History*. New York: Columbia University Press.
De Keizer, Madelon. 1996. Memory as *Rite de Passage*: Towards a Postmoralistic Historiography of the Second World War. *Itinerario* 20 (2): 118–127.
Dumbrell, John. 2012. *Rethinking the Vietnam War*. New York: Palgrave Macmillan.
Durkheim, Emile. 1995. *The Elementary Forms of Religious Life*. New York: Free Press.
Eyerman, Ronald. 2001. *Cultural Trauma: Slavery and the Formation of African American Identity*. Cambridge: Cambridge University Press.
Eyerman, Ronald. 2011. *The Cultural Sociology of Political Assassination*. New York: Palgrave Macmillan.
Eyerman, Ronald. 2015. *Is This America? Katrina as Cultural Trauma*. Austin: University of Texas Press.
Fitzgerald, Frances. 1972. *Fire in the Lake*. New York: Back Bay Books.
Halbwachs, Maurice. 1992. *On Collective Memory*. Chicago: University of Chicago Press.
Herring, George (ed.). 1993. *The Pentagon Papers*. New York: McGraw Hill.
Herring, George. 2001. *America's Longest War: The United States and Vietnam, 1950–1975*. New York: McGraw Hill.
Jordan, Jennifer A. 2005. A Matter of Time: Examining Collective Memory in Historical Perspective in Postwar Berlin. *Journal of Historical Sociology* 18 (1–2): 37–71.
Karnow, Stanley. 1983. *Vietnam, A History*. New York: Viking.
Koselleck, Reinhart. 2004. *Future's Past*. New York: Columbia University Press.
Lam, Andrew. 2005. *Perfume Dreams*. Berkeley: Heyday.
Lam, Andrew. 2010. *East Eats West*. Berkeley: Heyday.
Lieu, Nhi. 2011. *The American Dream in Vietnamese*. Minneapolis: University of Minnesota Press.
Misztal, Barbara. 2003. *Theories of Social Remembering*. Maidenhead: Open University Press.
Moyar, Mark. 2006. *Triumph Forsaken*. Cambridge: Cambridge University Press.
Nguyen, Viet Thanh. 2016a. *The Sympathizer*. New York: Grove Press.
Nguyen, Viet Thanh. 2016b. *Nothing Ever Dies*. Cambridge: Harvard University Press.
Nguyen, Viet Thanh. 2017. *The Refugees*. New York: Grove Press.
Nora, Pierre. 1996. *Realms of Memory*. New York: Columbia University Press.

Olick, Jeffrey. 1999. Collective Memory: The Two Cultures. *Sociological Theory* 17 (3): 333–348.
Olick, Jeffrey, and David Levy. 1997. Collective Memory and Cultural Constraint: Holocaust Myth and Rationality in German Politics. *American Sociological Review* 62 (6): 921–936.
Sapolsky, Harvey M., and Jeremy Shapiro. 1996. Casualties, Technology, and America's Future Wars. *Parameters* 26 (2): 119–127.
Scruggs, C. Jan, and Joel L. Swerdlow. 1985. *To Heal a Nation: The Vietnam Veterans Memorial*. New York: Harper & Row.
Smelser, Neil. 2004. Psychological Trauma and Cultural Trauma. In *Cultural Trauma and Collective Identity*, ed. Jeffrey Alexander, Ronald Eyerman, Bernhard Giesen, Neil Smelser, and Piotr Sztompka. Berkeley: University of California Press.
Smith, Anthony. 1991. *Nationalism: Theory, Ideology, History*. Cambridge: Polity Press.
Sturken, Marita. 1997. *Tangled Memories*. Berkeley: University of California Press.
Tota, Anna Lisa. 2003. Collective Memories At Work. *Comparative Social Research Book Series* 21: 63–86.
Wagner-Pacifici, Robin, and Barry Schwartz. 1991. The Vietnam Veterans Memorial: Commemorating a Difficult Past. *American Journal of Sociology* 97 (2): 376–420.
Young, Marilyn. 1991. *The Vietnam Wars (1945–1990)*. New York: Harper Perennial.

CHAPTER 8

Perpetrator Trauma and Collective Guilt: The My Lai Massacre

Introduction

> At times now, I lie awake, I think of Mylai and say, My God. Whatever inspired me to do it? But truthfully: there was no other way. America's motto there in Vietnam is "Win in Vietnam," and in Mylai there was no other way to do it. America had to kill everyone there. (Oliver 2006: 117)

These are the words of Lieutenant William Calley, the only U.S. soldier convicted of a war crime during the War in Vietnam. They were recorded in 1971, soon after his military trial. While Calley was the only individual convicted, there were many others involved in the systematic killing in 1968 of more than five hundred Vietnamese non-combatants in the hamlet of My Lai. The question of guilt and responsibility loomed large at Calley's trial and in the public discourse surrounding it. Was Calley alone guilty? or Was he merely a cog in a military machine, charged by the American people with winning the war at any cost?

This chapter is about trauma, guilt, and responsibility. While most studies on these topics focus on individual perpetrators and their victims, my primary concern here is with collective perpetrators. I will first introduce the idea of perpetrator trauma and then relate it to collective guilt. I will then suggest that while both concepts are contested and problematic, they are nevertheless useful and important in the study of collective violence and its aftermath. Perpetrator trauma occurs when individuals and collectives feel they have acted in ways that are contrary to their own

R. Eyerman, *Memory, Trauma, and Identity*, Cultural Sociology,
https://doi.org/10.1007/978-3-030-13507-2_8

deeply held moral beliefs. These beliefs are so foundational that when one contravenes them, one's identity and self-esteem can feel as though they have been shattered, a sense that gives rise to a strong emotional response including feelings of guilt and remorse. In some cases, pathological symptoms can occur. With regard to individuals, perpetrator trauma is currently couched under the umbrella concept post-traumatic stress disorder (PTSD), a diagnosis that has exploded and expanded in recent years. PTSD has been applied to both victims and perpetrators, though the focus has been primarily on the former. Though I make use of this notion and its psychological purview, my central concern here is with collective responses and responsibility rather than individual trauma and guilt. I will thus—when the focus is on an individual—move the discussion from the psychological to the social realm by relating individual emotional responses to social and collective processes.

In order to concretize these issues, I will use the example of the My Lai Massacre and of Lieutenant Calley and the soldiers of Charlie Company under his command. I will begin by noting that a foundational belief that is constitutive of individual identity in American culture is the Judeo-Christian commandment, "Thou Shalt Not Kill." Given the pervasive nature of religious sentiment in the U.S., American soldiers must be taught that such moral principles—which they are assumed to possess upon entering the military—are situational, not universal, and that any transgression required by their profession is not only permissible, but also right and just under specifiable conditions. Being a good soldier, in other words, does not always imply being a good human being. Military culture rewards skillful killing; guilt feelings within this context are often suppressed and, should they ever rise to consciousness, are more likely to do so upon return to civilian life and another moral order.

Once the killings at My Lai were revealed publically (after having escaped the control of military censorship), the occurrence became cause for great public debate in the U.S., raising issues not only of individual culpability, but also more broadly about the War in Vietnam and American national identity, itself. Though it began as a discussion about the appropriate conduct of soldiers in battle, My Lai quickly invoked probing questions of guilt and responsibility at all levels, from the soldiers who actually pulled the triggers to the military and civilian political hierarchy that put them in that situation in the first place. But the questioning didn't stop there. It continued until finally the entire American public—whose taxes, votes, and opinions ultimately legitimated the soldiers' actions—was called to account (Oliver 2006).

Central to notions of guilt and responsibility is a distinction between perpetrator and victim, positions that emerge when an illegal or immoral act is committed by the former against the latter. The term trauma has been used to describe the affect related to such acts. Victim trauma is well theorized and researched, while perpetrator trauma is less so (indeed, the very concept remains controversial: see Giesen 2004; Heins and Langenohl 2013; Morag 2013). While a perpetrator is by definition guilty of acting in a harmful way toward his or her victim, one can speak of "perpetrator trauma" when such an action injures the doer, as well as the victim, an injury that can be moral and psychological, if not physical. A sense of guilt arising from taking responsibility for the untoward action is often entailed in the trauma that is experienced by individuals, and establishing this sort of individual guilt is the aim and justification of modern legal systems. In the case of collective guilt, the difficulty lies in identifying, and identifying with, perpetrators, those individuals deemed responsible for the act or actions, and in establishing such identification within a wider collectivity. Giessen, for example, suggests that the German public avoided taking responsibility for the Holocaust by placing blame on a fervent group within the Nazi party. In doing so, the German public eschewed identification with those who were deemed the perpetrators of that genocidal crime. As we will see, public response to the My Lai Massacre reversed this reaction, as many Americans (perhaps the majority) identified so closely with the perpetrators that they could not conceive of their guilt. It was not collective guilt that motivated such identification, but a sense that they, too, could have been perpetrators. In fact, many of the perpetrators within Charlie Company (like Calley, himself), far from acknowledging their position as perpetrators, actually felt themselves to be victims. For both Germans confronting the Holocaust and Americans confronting the My Lai Massacre, the roles of perpetrator, victim, and bystander were made relatively fluid as the trauma of war was worked through.

As a contested notion, collective guilt must be narrated, assigned, and accepted by a collectivity that is itself reconstituted in the process. I identify this discursive process as cultural trauma (Alexander et al. 2004; Eyerman et al. 2013) where the foundations of individual and collective identity are brought up for public reflection. In order to move from individual to collective responsibility, a coherent and compelling case must be put forward declaring that members of a collectivity (whose identity and boundaries are established in the process) bear responsibility for the actions of its members. For example, if this collective guilt process were successful, it would imply that "Germans" accept responsibility for the mass killings known as the Holocaust and that "Americans" feel responsible (and perhaps guilty) for what was done "in their name" in Vietnam. Such an argument does not require that all Germans or Americans agree, but that the possibility of collective guilt has been articulated, assessed, assigned, and accepted either by a significant number and/or by authoritative representatives who act in society's name. Such representative figures may, for example, issue an official apology, even though not all members of the collective agree or accept responsibility.

The Incident

In March 1968, in response to the Tet Offensive begun a few weeks earlier in which all major cities and military installations in South Vietnam came under attack by communist forces, American soldiers engaged in a "search and destroy" mission. In the process, the Americans moved through a series of small hamlets in the coastal area of central Vietnam killing hundreds of unarmed Vietnamese, most of them women, children, and elderly. It was a planned and sanctioned operation that aimed at killing combatants in an area known to be sympathetic to the enemy. The entire region had for this reason been designated a "free-fire zone," meaning that every living being, including livestock was to be treated as suspect and a target. The soldiers were told to expect heavy resistance and that local villagers would have gone to market and thus not be present when their helicopters set down. This intelligence proved to be false on both counts, yet the soldiers began firing at everything and everyone in sight as soon as they hit the ground. There was no return fire. The "killing began without warning"; the first victims were a woman and a baby who fled in panic over a rice paddy as the helicopters arrived (Hersh 1970: 48). Once begun, indiscriminate killing went on for nearly four hours. In the end more than 500 Vietnamese lay dead, many of them piled into mass graves. The commemorative museum at the site lists 504 victims, where "twenty-four families were obliterated—three generations murdered, with no survivors. Among the dead were 182 women, 17 of them pregnant. One hundred seventy three children were executed, including 56 infants" (Hersh 2015: 57).

The "post-action" report filed by the field commander listed the action as a major success and commendation was awarded from the highest command downward. However, because of an official complaint lodged by a helicopter pilot who claimed to have observed the killing of unarmed civilians and had attempted to stop it, as well as the great disparity between the large number of enemy claimed killed and the small number of weapons captured, an internal investigation was opened. But the investigation found no evidence of wrongdoing and the matter was dropped. This inquiry would later be called a "cover-up" by a more independent military investigation.

My Lai is now generally accepted as an atrocity and a war crime by all sides in the conflict. Perpetrators and victims have been identified and a military tribunal has established guilt and assigned responsibility. The trial, which occurred as the war was ongoing, was closely followed in the U.S. and around the world and the guilty verdict of Lieutenant Calley raised great public outcry. So great was that outcry (and the political possibilities this entailed) that the sitting president, Richard Nixon, eventually pardoned the guilty officer. For some, the massacre and the resulting trial became symbolic of the war itself; one recent book on the topic bears the title *The Vietnam War on Trial* (Belknap 2002). At issue, among other things, was how an individual soldier could be punished for performing the duty assigned him by his organizational superiors and, ultimately, by the nation itself. In the process, questions were raised about the morality of the war, as well as about the strategies and tactics employed. In the ongoing debate those who carried out the killings, the perpetrators, would be transformed into victims.

The Aftermath: Articulating and Establishing Responsibility

As I will elaborate in the following sections, two primary narrative frameworks about the War in Vietnam were operative during the struggle to understand what happened at My Lai and to identify who was responsible. Whereas both narratives can be characterized as simultaneously tragic and redemptive, one is framed as heroic while the other is framed as ironic. Both these narrative frames derive from long established American political and cultural traditions. The first, which was dominant and hegemonic at least up to the Tet Offensive, is commonly known as American exceptionalism. In this frame the American nation is depicted as having been founded upon the universal principles of freedom and justice and the God-given mission to rid the world of evil. American wars—unlike the wars waged by other powerful nations—are never self-interested or aggressive, but always guided by the goal of helping others in their desire for freedom and justice. From this perspective, the U.S. was in Vietnam to help the "South" Vietnamese in their struggle against an evil Communist aggressor, not only from the "North" Vietnamese, but also from the Soviets and China. Though never officially declared, this war was believed to be righteous and just, one that had to be fought and won. The recently stalemated Korean War provided the prism through which Americans at that time viewed the War in Vietnam, along with the fear of other nations in the region "falling like dominoes" to communism. This narrative is heroic because the U.S. is seen as a righteous protagonist engaged in an endless struggle against evil. It became tragic because, regardless of the reason, this American crusade against evil ended in defeat. For some, the defeat was only temporary, as the fall of the Soviet Union and the post-1989 "end of Communism" eventually revealed the righteousness of American intervention. In the most extreme version of this perspective, the American military was never a perpetrator in the War in Vietnam (though some "bad apples" are admitted to have existed).

The second narrative frame is also tragic, not because the war was lost, but because American soldiers were asked to fight an unjust war in an immoral way, turning "good boys into murderers." From this perspective, although these soldiers had excellent training and the best intentions they had nevertheless been lied to from the very beginning about the real purposes of the war and placed into "an atrocity-producing situation" (Lifton 2005). Several variations exist concerning the purported basis for such lies. In the most radical versions, such as those formulated by Noam Chomsky and others on the political left, the lies stemmed from the imperialistic motives of conquest; other lies stemmed from wrong-headed beliefs about the nature of Communism and/or about the allegedly unified interests of China and the Soviet Union. Finally, and more simply, the lies were seen to have stemmed from an application of the wrong tactics in the "right" situation (Halberstam 1965).

In the case of the War in Vietnam, the mass-media was a central medium for articulating the issue of individual and collective responsibility, and the same held true for Calley's trial and the political processes and opportunities it set in motion. The main agents in this discursive process on both sides were intellectuals in the broadest sense of that term, those who make use of various media and social forums, including newspapers, television, novels, films, theater, and artwork to impact and mold public opinion. Various social movements provided stimulus and became vehicles in this process of argumentation and meaning making, and the worldwide antiwar movement was a powerful stimulus and vehicle for this articulation.

There were two emotionally compelling mass-mediated interventions that helped propel My Lai into a major event after the initial attempt at containment failed. The first was a televised interview with one of the perpetrators, Paul Meadlo, who tearfully confessed to murder to an astonished interviewer. During a nationally televised evening news broadcast in November 1969, reporter Mike Wallace asked Meadlo how many people he had killed at My Lai. The former soldier replied, "Well, I fired on automatic, so you can't—you just spray the area, on them and so you can't know how many you killed 'cause they were going fast. So, I might have killed ten or fifteen of them." Wallace then asked, "Men, women, and children? ... and babies?" To which Meadlo replied "And babies" (transcript published in the *New York Times*, November 25, 1969). The second was the publication in *Life* magazine of color photographs from the day of the mass killings. These were taken by a Ronald Haeberle, a U.S. Army photographer who, along with a soldier/reporter from a military newspaper had been assigned to record the search and destroy operation and the progress of the American response to the Tet Offensive. As public interest in the case was growing, Haeberle decided to sell the photographs he had secretly taken of the murderous events to *Life* magazine. The piles of dead Vietnamese and the terrified women and children huddled together just before being shot have now become iconic images of the war, many emblazoned with Wallace's question, "And babies, too?" Haeberle was complicit in the original cover up as he helped author the false official account that appeared in the military press. However, he was never formally charged because he, like so many of the others involved, was no longer in the military when this was all revealed. The issue of whether Haeberle and others involved either as bystanders or in the cover-up had a moral as well as legal responsibility to speak out is important to consider. Haeberle, who later returned to My Lai to once again photograph the villagers, spoke out only when there was something to be gained.

Even as the story of what actually happened emerged, the American public was divided about its meaning and who might bear responsibility. It was now obvious that hundreds of unarmed women, children, and elderly had been killed and that the act of killing was systematic and cold-blooded. But was this a massacre and a war crime or merely a "tragic wartime occurrence," as the Secretary of the Army preferred to call it? And if it was a war crime, Who was responsible? After a long investigation by a military commission, which included the pros and cons of group or individual trials, it was decided that only one person could, with some certainty, be proven responsible: Lieutenant William Calley. From a strict legal point of view, a murder conviction required that the prosecution show that the perpetrator had "the capacity to form the intent to kill" in addition to actually carrying out the act; also, because this was a military court, only those still in service could be tried. Calley's immediate superior officer, Captain Medina, who was also present on the ground during the operation, claimed to have drawn the line at killing civilians in his pre-operation pep talk. There were conflicting accounts as to the truth of this statement, and Calley claimed to be following orders in his murderous acts. Those more superior officers circling above in helicopters and responsible for overseeing the operation were never brought to trial. They were, however, investigated and charged in relation to the cover-up, and some received career-damaging reprimands. In a thorough study of the trial, its mass media coverage, and the political response, Kendrick Oliver (2006) convincingly reveals the significant pressure to individualize the killings and to convict those deemed guilty. It was, he argues, in the interest of the American military and those holding political power to identify guilty individuals in order to fend off any claims to organizational or collective responsibility. The aim was to ensure that it was not military or political policy that led to the mass killing of civilians, but rather deviant individuals.

In legal matters, responsibility and guilt are adjudicated through the courts; in the case of My Lai, it was a military court that ultimately decided the fate of Calley and those under his command. In this case, individuals were the objects of judgment. The situation is different with regard to collective guilt. Ashenden suggests that the "very notion of political community implies the possibility of collective guilt" (2014: 58). Political community, however, is an abstract concept that must be actualized and made real through public discourse, as well as practices such as political campaigns. Collective guilt must be articulated and attributed through various means; the collective must be named and made aware of itself. Trials can be useful in this process, as they can act as a catalyst to public reflection where notions of guilt and responsibility can be debated and attributed in ways that transcend the limits of the legal system. This, for example, was the point of the Vietnam War Crimes Tribunal led by Bertrand Russell and modeled after the Nuremberg Trials that followed the Second World War. Social movements can play a similar role. In the case of the My Lai trial, the American pro- and antiwar movements and associated intellectuals articulated the idea of collective guilt and named those deemed guilty. Groups of veterans, such as those organized through the Vietnam Veterans Against the War and the "rap groups" that Robert Lifton (2005) helped construct, also provided means of transferring guilt from the individual to the collective level. In these group sessions and the public demonstrations that occurred at the same time, veterans might discover that the things they did and felt guilty about were actually widespread and rooted in military policy. The ongoing antiwar movement was important in providing a context for opposition and the articulation of collective guilt. All this helped lift guilt beyond the individual to the institutional level, which the wider antiwar movement then pushed even higher to include the American government and its policies.

The mass media, and popular culture in general, had their own ways of attributing responsibility, with journalists such as Seymour Hersh (1970, 2015), David Halberstam (1965, 1993), and Neil Sheehan (1971, 1989) writing books and articles about the chain of command in decision-making. The publication of the "Pentagon Papers" by the *New York Times* and the *Washington Post* had an even more powerful impact as it revealed a long history of deception by American politicians and policy makers as the war was still ongoing. On the other side, the pro-war movement received new life after the Calley verdict as protesters took to the streets in support of the convicted murderer. In similar fashion to their ideological opponents, they blamed the government for placing American soldiers in what was described as a morally impossible situation. Initial mass media coverage in the U.S. contributed to this by portraying Calley as a "typical American boy," making it easier for Americans to identify with him (Oliver 2006). All this complicated the attribution of guilt and responsibility.

The Perpetrator as Victim

Basic to the issue of establishing responsibility at My Lai was determining how the massacre could have happened in the first place. The first and most obvious factor is that these were trained soldiers; killing was their profession and part of warfare. However, the deliberate killing of unarmed and unresisting people is forbidden by military protocol, even if they are known to be combatants. Those killed at My Lai were neither armed, resisting, nor combatants. Their killing was illegal by the principles of the Geneva Convention and the rules of engagement printed on a card that all American soldiers in Vietnam were required to carry. These rules of engagement placed responsibility on the individual soldier to refuse an illegal order. The officer giving such an order would also be subject to punishment, but the onus was on the soldier to refuse to obey and also to report an illegal order. While some American soldiers at My Lai did refuse to obey the order to kill, only one reported the incident; the majority neither refused nor reported the illegal order.

Group pressure and group dynamics have been used to explain the killing at My Lai (Grossman 2009; Collins 2009). Those present described a "killing frenzy" that began once the first victim was murdered. The soldiers had been prepared for killing. Prior to the operation, their unit had been subject to several days of frustrating combat operations and had sustained many casualties, most involving land mines and booby traps, circumstances where no enemy was present to be held accountable. Under these conditions, it seemed that nothing could be trusted in Vietnam, not even the ground one walked on. Before heading off to My Lai, there had been a memorial service for those who had been recently killed, and Captain Media gave an emotionally rousing pep talk in which he told the group, "now is the time for revenge." The operation began early in the morning and the soldiers arrived on site fearful and anxious, huddling tightly together in their helicopters. They expected heavy resistance and streamed out firing blindly and at will. Few noticed that there was no return fire. Once the first unarmed Vietnamese was killed, there seemed to be no stopping what followed. Nearly everyone got involved in the rampage that included systematic rape and murder. The order, both explicit and implied, had been to "kill everything that moves" (Turse 2013). And they did.

Grossman (2009: 226 ff.) explains atrocities, which he defines as the "close range murder of the innocent and helpless" with the aid of three factors: peer pressure, the presence of a commanding authority, and a preservation instinct. All were at play at My Lai. Another process involved in atrocities, as discussed by Bauman (1989) and others, is the dehumanization of the other. In the case of the My Lai Massacre, this process began long before the actual day of the killing. Throughout the war, American soldiers of all ranks routinely referred to the Vietnamese as "gooks," "slants," and "dinks." As interviews with American military personnel reveal, the soldiers had little understanding of—or empathy for—those they killed, their world, and a Vietnamese way of life that was not their own. Regarding the factor of peer or group pressure, I include and differentiate group pressure from group dynamics and cohesion. Once the killing began, nearly everyone joined in, not simply because they felt pressure to conform, but because it was part of what it meant to be a member of this particular group. They were a killing machine, oiled and primed. The presence of an "order-giving authority" in the case of My Lai is undeniable, and many present explained their behavior as following orders. After all, this was a military operation, and the entire company was under orders to succeed; success had been defined as clearing and securing the area through the destruction of everything that might be of use to the enemy.

Imparted military culture, through basic and advanced combat training, focuses on the creation and maintenance of group cohesion, stripping away individuality and instilling group dependence. Soldiers are taught that survival depends upon cooperating with others, as well as following the commands of superiors. There is thus a mixture of horizontal solidarity and vertical obedience inculcated through basic military training and reinforced in combat operations. This was also a masculine culture of a peculiarly American sort, where the norms of conformity blend with individual displays of prowess and bravado and where competition and cohesion are not seen as opposites, but rather as intertwined. In these sorts of conditions, loyalty and morality are also intertwined, and notions of right and wrong are both situational and filtered through the group. At My Lai, more traditional military codes of duty and honor interacted with contemporary American notions of masculinity, where the need to prove oneself—to be a "man"—mix easily with youthful bravado. The military focus on deference to authority, teamwork, and group loyalty builds upon the sporting traditions of American high schools where phrases like "revenge" and "pay back" easily resonated, especially when delivered by an officer, Captain Medina, whom everyone seemed to admire and respect.

In the context of Vietnam combat units, Charlie Company was both usual and unusual. It was usual in that it was made up of a cross section of draftees from all parts of the country and included a range of ethnicities. It was unusual in that most of the men had been together since advanced training on Hawaii and had arrived in Vietnam together by ship. Many of those Americans who served in Vietnam arrived and departed individually by commercial airliner. This training and travel together helped create an experience similar to those who served in the Second World War, where most American soldiers also arrived and left collectively by sea. This common experience reinforced the sense of collective effort and group solidarity in both cases. However, because of the one-year rotation policy in place during the War in Vietnam, the men left individually and thus missed out on what Shay (1994) identifies as the therapeutic potential of working through their "collective trauma" on the long route home. In one sense, then, the men at My Lai were akin to the soldiers who served in the Second World War, whose Hollywood and comic book representations they had absorbed. However, as service was limited to one-year rotations for enlisted personnel (and half that for combat officers in the lower ranks), creating a "Band of Brothers" mentality was a bit more difficult, to say nothing about its impact on the development of the skills and experience necessary for successful combat.

In another contrast to those who fought in the Second World War, those doing the killing at My Lai were not the "ordinary men" described by Browning (1998) in his classic study of Nazi executioners. The men of Charlie Company were ordinary in the sense of being draftees, conscripted rather randomly from an American cohort. The qualifying "rather" is important in that the bias in the selection made by the Selective Service Administration is well known (Spector 1992). Upon turning 18, American males were required by law to register for the draft, but the selection of those who would actually serve (especially in combat units) depended upon a range of exemptions, which for the most part excluded those from the middle class or those with a high school education. It was largely the marginalized, those with few other options, that made up the combat units in the American Army in Vietnam. This applied to the lower ranking officers as well. Both Calley and Medina had been recruited from the enlisted ranks and hustled into Officer Training programs when the supply of more qualified others began to run dry. Calley (whom Hersh rather disparagingly describes as a "junior college drop out" [Hersh 2015]) had been rushed into service with a minimal amount of training, and he was deemed and demeaned as incompetent by those he commanded, including Medina, his immediate superior. The soldiers at My Lai were thus a particular segment of "ordinary" men, those from the lower strata of American society, with very little real understanding of what they were fighting for or who their enemy was. They were also very young, the majority being between the ages of 18 and 21.

A fundamental idea in understanding collective behavior is that an individual might do things in the presence of a group of significant others that he or she might not otherwise do. Researchers point to a "loss of self" in-group dynamics, where in a particular context, a set of emergent, group-related norms might be more determinant than any internalized ideas about right and wrong. This appears to be the case at My Lai, where young American males were thrown into an unknown and terrifying environment, and where newly induced norms of group behavior and an order-giving hierarchy were their main points of reference. As many combat soldiers have repeated, there was no right or wrong in Vietnam, only survival, which was largely group dependent. This led to some bizarre behavior, such as the lunch break in the midst of the killing and the American soldiers who shared cookies with some young survivors who emerged out of hiding as the soldiers ate.

From this perspective, the murderous actions at My Lai are not that surprising. In fact, what is surprising is that such incidents did not happen more often (whether they in fact did happen more often has been argued continuously ever since: see Turse 2013 for a recent example). If group dynamics help explain the killing, group pressure helps us understand the cover-up. Almost no one spoke out about the obvious and illegal killing of unarmed and unresisting villagers. Whether or not one also believed them to be civilians did not matter; this should have been reported according to American military regulations. When the first investigation was carried out soon after the incident, virtually no one spoke up; this, of course, includes those who refused to kill. Two factors help explain this. The first is the fact that all were implicated, whether or not they had killed. Speaking out would have been self-incriminating at the very least. Second, there was real pressure to be silent. Anyone speaking out would be subject not only to negative reactions, but also to the direct threat of violence. Death by "friendly-fire" was not uncommon during the War in Vietnam.

From Individual to Collective Responsibility

While it may be clear who actually pulled the trigger at My Lai, it is less clear who bears full responsibility for what happened. As discussed above, it is possible to describe the men of Charlie Company themselves as victims and to place responsibility for their actions higher up the chain of command. This was a viewpoint articulated not only by the soldiers themselves, but also by activists and intellectuals within the antiwar movement. In fact, after Calley's conviction, this view was taken up by some on the pro-war side of the issue, as well.

With the passing of time, this understanding has become a common theme in contemporary analyses of the incident (Belknap 2002; Hersh 2015). The men of Charlie Company have been described as victims of America's class and racial divide and of the Selective Service Administration, the latter being blamed for actualizing this divide and sending mostly the poor and working classes into combat. I have analyzed how their training and that of those who led them may have been problematic. I have also shown that, as young American men, the soldiers of Charlie Company have been described as victims of an ideology-driven socialization process in which schools, religious institutions, and popular culture instilled heroic notions of war and the warrior, while at the same time demonizing enemies. These men—as well as the rest of the American public—are said to have been led into a war on false premises by politicians and their advisors (Halberstam 1993; Ellsberg 2003). Once at war, heavily armed and licensed to kill, they were given little information regarding those they were fighting beyond ideological indoctrination and dehumanizing stereotypes. The rules of engagement cards, one of the "things they carried," to use Tim O'Brien's (1991) famous phrase, informed them that they were guests in Vietnam and ordered them to act accordingly. Up until the Tet Offensive, this may have made some sense to those in rear areas who interacted in superficial ways with those Vietnamese who cleaned their rooms, washed their clothes, and satisfied their sexual appetites, but after Tet, every Vietnamese became suspect. In the "free fire zones," American soldiers were not guests; they were warriors who determined who was to live and die.

Afterwards, some expressed regret even though they believed they were doing exactly what they had been trained and told to do. Upon returning to civilian life and its moral code, some were remorseful. This included Calley, who in 2009 said, "there is not a day that goes by that I do not feel remorse." Most of those who consented to media interviews, including Calley, pushed blame up the chain of command. Some exhibited perpetrator trauma, such that, as Belknap reports, "In the wake of the My Lai Massacre, what had once been the 'best company in Hawaii' seemed to be falling apart. The men were in bad shape, both mentally and physically. They were often ill" (2002: 210). Such a reaction could of course stem from fear of being found out and of possible punishment. However, it could also stem from the shame and guilt that can arise from doing something obviously wrong. An indication of this can be found in an exchange between Meadlo and Calley the day following the massacre, after Meadlo lost a foot to a land mine. As he was being evacuated by medical helicopter, Meadlo yelled at the lieutenant, "Why did you do it? Why did you do it? This is God's punishment to me, Calley, but you'll get yours! God will punish you, Calley" (Belknap 2002: 88). This was the exception, however; most chose silence.

Only after returning to the U.S. was the silence broken. It began with individual feelings of remorse and the encouragement of the antiwar movement, which then fed then into the wider public discourse about the meaning of the War in Vietnam. Along with the "rap groups" and the Winter Soldier hearings, the antiwar movement provided a context in which individual guilt could be made collective. There were calls to make such unofficial expressions of collective guilt more authoritative, with some in the mass media calling upon the U.S. Congress or some other official body to initiate formal war crimes hearings (Sheehan 1971; Paquet 1972). Chants calling President Nixon and his security advisor Henry Kissinger "war criminals" became a common part of demonstrations. There were even veterans who publicly asked to be arrested for their "war crimes" (Oliver 2006: 127). However, Nixon's program of Vietnamization (which allowed the withdrawal of American combat troops while at the same escalating the bombing and Vietnamese casualties), in conjunction with the Watergate Hearings, turned public attention to other matters, and the momentum toward the recognition of collective guilt and responsibility dissipated. What has not dissipated is the impact of images of My Lai that continue to haunt American collective memory.

Collective Guilt Versus Shame

Rape and warfare have always been coupled. Women were traditionally considered legitimate spoils of war, and raping women that are identified with one's enemy is a common tactic of degradation and humiliation. There have been counterforces, including the introduction of aristocratic moral codes—and later, the professionalism of warfare—which condemn rape as well as the killing of civilians. To the extent that such codes were present on the American side during the War in Vietnam, shifting responsibility from the individual to the collective and up the chain of command would seem less likely with regard to rape than the killing non-combatants. While commanders are ultimately responsibility for the conduct of those under their command, it is expected that individual soldiers know and follow norms of proper behavior with regard to women. Thus, an often-overlooked element of the My Lai Massacre is the number of rapes and sexual assaults that occurred alongside the killings. One of the most well known of Ronald Haeberle's photographs shows a clutch of Vietnamese women and children in agony just before being shot. To the right is a young woman buttoning her blouse as she holds a young child on her arm. From official testimony we know that the woman had just been sexually assaulted, and the anguished face of the older woman next to her comes from the attempt to stop the assault. This woman is being clasped from behind by another young woman, presumably also so threatened. In a few seconds, they will all be dead, executed in cold blood. There is no photograph of the assault, as there is none of the actual killing; there are only traces of agony and fear in the moments prior to execution.

There are other documented incidents like this at My Lai, including gang rape. This aspect of the massacre is also seldom mentioned, and except for recent feminist-inspired interventions (e.g., Weaver 2010), it would presumably remain so. At Calley's trial, the focus was on killing, not rape. Wartime rape cannot easily be legitimated by reference to the fog of war and has never been an accepted part of the American understanding of correct military behavior. Soldiers are trained to kill, but they are not trained to rape. The group dynamics of rape are different from those of murder. For one, there are usually no weapons involved, as they must be put down while bodily contact is made. Rape is very personal, an act of power and domination that is thoroughly gender infused; this is not necessarily the case in mass murder. While group pressure and aggressive displays of masculinity may be an accepted part of male-dominated military culture, public confession of rape seems less acceptable and more stigmatized than killing innocents. Rape is more shameful, harder to talk about and to collectivize. As moral as well as psychological injury, its affect is devastating: "Psychological injuries to the surviving rape victims are often lifelong. Likewise the soldier inflicts lifelong injuries on himself when he makes rape or rape-murder part of his war" (Shay 1994: 134). Shay notes that rape and rape victims have never been counted as civilian war casualties. They are elements of the shame of war, a world apart from the killing. In the case where wartime rape is exposed, shame falls upon both the individual rapist and the collective to which he belongs; both the soldier and the military organization are tainted by the act.

Feelings of shame are bound up with how others see us and thus with self-esteem. Guilt is tied to actions, to what has been done and can be relieved by taking responsibility, acknowledging, and confessing. Shame is harder to relieve and often involves aggressive acting-out. If rape is more shameful than killing, it follows that it would be more difficult to acknowledge, and that its impact on the individual would be deep and long standing. Tied to how others see us, shame is linked with honor and respect (Gilligan 2003). In the context of My Lai and the prevailing military culture, gaining respect was easily connected to displays of masculinity, which in that context could be revealed through aggressive acts in which killing and even rape might be included. As Singer puts it, "In the field, a soldier must live up to the expectations of the men he fights alongside of, even if that means committing atrocities, or he will feel ashamed" (2004: 381). However, rape would be more shameful should it be exposed outside the confines of this culture. Though rape might be formally condemned and punishable by reigning military law, it was condoned—even encouraged—within the group culture at My Lai and during the War in Vietnam more generally. Soldiers egged each other on, and there was great pressure to participate. To the soldiers present, it would have been shameful not to. Such behavior was very situational and restricted, seldom spoken of, certainly not written home about, and of course, never photographed. To do so would have exposed the group to the wider moral eye. Like the murder of civilians, it was condemned by organizational rules, yet silently accepted as part of the nastiness of war. As those who supported Calley demonstrated, it was possible to legitimate the murder of women and children; however, legitimating wartime rape is much more difficult. This means that identification with the perpetrator of rape is not as easily assumed as it is with those who commit murder. For the perpetrator of rape, guilt is almost certain to remain individual, not collective.

The idea that there is a causal link that runs from the actions perpetrated by individual soldiers, on up the organizational chain of command, and all the way to the common citizen depends not only on making such a connection explicit, but also on recognizing the humanity of the victim. It is not only the tendency to individualize that must be countered, but also the tendency to dehumanize the enemy. Taking responsibility, whether individual or collective, means acknowledging the humanity of the victim. This requires countering the tremendous pressure of organizational dehumanization processes, both military and civilian. In the case of My Lai and the War in Vietnam, such responsibility would require seeing the Vietnamese as complicated human beings, as potential victims and bystanders, as well as perpetrators. It would also mean seeing everyone involved on the American side—from the soldiers on up the entire chain of command—in a similar fashion.

Perpetrator trauma results from moral injury, an injury that entails humanizing one's victim and recognizing that one has acted immorally toward another human being. Sherman defines moral injuries as "experiences of serious inner conflict arising from what one takes to be grievous moral transgressions that can overwhelm one's sense of goodness and humanity" (2015: 8). Such feelings can arise from (real or apparent) transgressive commissions (and omissions) perpetrated by oneself or others; they can also arise from "bearing witness to the intense human suffering and detritus that is a part of the grotesquerie of war and its aftermath" (Sherman 2015: 8). Similarly, Weaver speaks of "perpetrator-induced trauma" (2010: xii) in her discussion of rape during the War in Vietnam. Such trauma can be thought of here as cultural in the sense that the foundations upon which identity rest have been shattered. One can speak of perpetrator trauma as individual and collective in the same way as one can speak about guilt and responsibility, where the logic of development follows a similar path. A war may cause moral injury to individual soldiers, to the military institutions that train and deploy them, and to the nation that legitimates the entire process.

The killings at My Lai were of a traditional sort. They were hands-on and the enemy was dehumanized and lumped, literally, into a faceless mass. It was the unintended consequence of Haeberle's photographs to put a face on the victims and, at the same time, transform the soldiers into perpetrators. The photographs, as Oliver insightfully points out, "replicate the gaze of the killers" without disclosing their agency (2006: 133). At the time of their killing, no attempt was made to distinguish non-combatants and no prisoners were taken. Still, there was ambiguity of the sort that insurgent warfare makes possible. Also present was the possibility of shifting responsibility up the ladder, even for those who clearly felt they were doing wrong. For others though, any feelings of wrongdoing would come later, usually after they had left the organizational culture and formal control of the military. This time lapse is not the "latency period" one finds in psychoanalytic notions of trauma; it has more to do with moving from one moral universe to another. Shay speaks of modern warfare as a form of "captivity" that generates "a profound gulf" between the combatants and the community left behind. Accordingly, the veteran carries the "taint of the killer" when re-entering society (2003: 152). Any such stigmatization and feelings of alienation are only intensified by negative reactions to the war itself. As is well documented, returning Vietnam veterans were not hailed as heroes and were often branded "baby-killers," as were those, like President Lyndon Johnson, deemed responsible for their acts. The uniform was not proudly worn upon return, but was more often discarded as soon as possible. The transition from one moral universe to another was thus clear and often dramatic.

Conclusion

Let's return to the quotation from Calley with which I opened this chapter. Although he was willing to accept the guilty verdict, Calley placed ultimate responsibility for what he had done with the American nation. "America," he said, wanted to win in Vietnam and to do so had to "kill everyone there." On the one hand, this is a familiar ploy, shifting responsibility up a chain of command, as was done at his trial. What is uncommon, however, is its abstractness. Accepting it would mean viewing the nation as a protagonist, a collective actor with intentions and, therefore, capable of responsibility. This is exactly the idea proclaimed in the narrative of American exceptionalism, the ideology into which Calley and his generation were indoctrinated. Like many Americans caught up in the War in Vietnam, Calley understood his actions through this narrative frame. America had a mission in Vietnam and sent him there to realize it. He was serving his country as an arm of its collective will.

As opposed to other forms of explanation, such as that offered by Grossman (2009) and Collins (2009), which emphasize group and situation dynamics, I have called attention to the stories we are told and tell ourselves in understanding what happened at My Lai, in particular, and the War in Vietnam War more generally. Such scripted frameworks, or social imaginaries, provide actors with the means to understand a situation, as well as prescriptions regarding how to act with regard to it. This is not to exclude these other accounts, but rather to incorporate them within a wider framework of interpretation.

Taking this into account, we can ask whether Calley and the men of Charlie Company are the only ones responsible for the killings at My Lai. Those of the wider American public who identified with Calley clearly thought not. Responsibility, in their view, was collective, not merely because of the nation's presumed mission, but also because they could imagine themselves in the same position doing the same thing. And given the existence of the draft and the selective service system, they could very well have been. Given such responsibility, was the collective then also guilty? And, if so, In what sense? One could further complicate the matter by asking, Which collective? as there were several to blame, including the military and the elected and other civilian officials who designed and organized the war.

Before considering such claims, we should first of all distinguish juridical guilt, such as that determined by the military court, from both responsibility and emotional guilt. Juridical or legal guilt refers to action and commission, emotional guilt to feelings that may or may not follow from such actions. Responsibility, on the other hand, is a wider concept referring to agents and agencies that can be held accountable for the acts or actions of others (see Baier 1991). With regard to juridical guilt, we should ask: Who is guilty of what? What is the purpose of such judgment? and finally, What are we to do with this determination? A military court found Calley guilty of mass murder, and later he might have felt remorse, but Who bore responsibility?

The aim and purpose of the court's judgment was to establish guilt and punishment for an illegal act, a war crime. Another purpose, clearly unspoken in this judgment, was to exonerate the institution of which Calley was part, namely the American military, of any responsibility. The claim that the military and other state institutions might bear some responsibility was never seriously addressed at the trial, but it was articulated through the antiwar movement and by various commentators in the mass media. As I noted above, this has become a theme in many subsequent accounts. Going even further, Kendrick Oliver says the American people—at least that part of the collectivity that supported the war—could be considered responsible for what occurred at My Lai (2006: 166 ff.). This, of course, was Calley's claim as well.

In order to establish collective guilt, one must determine what precisely the military, political leaders, and the American people are guilty of. For example, the military could potentially be guilty of designing strategies and tactics that set the conditions in which actions such as Calley's would likely be carried out. This is a claim made forcibly by Robert Jay Lifton (2005), Nick Turse (2013), and Ronald Dellums (1972). The same could be attributed to the civilian leaders charged with creating the policies that put the military in motion. Furthermore, one could even argue for the appropriateness of holding accountable those institutions and individuals who created and disseminated the ideologies that motivated these policies in the first place (although here we might actually be speaking of responsibility, rather than guilt: see Arendt 2003; Young 2011). Finally, the American public could be held responsible, *in toto*, for endorsing all of the above, including Calley's actions. Alternatively, the public could be charged with indifference, the shirking of all responsibility, or more willfully, of shifting it up the chain of command. Within these collectivities, the positions of victim, perpetrator, and bystander might be fluid. However, with all the media attention given to the war and Calley's trial, American citizens could hardly claim ignorance. The War in Vietnam polarized American society and the visibility and the omnipresence of opposing sides forced spectators in the U.S. to choose sides.

What would be the arena in which such judgment could be made, and what would its purpose be? Many have asked about the "lessons of Vietnam," and this has become one way to couch the issue. For the military, such questioning led to internal reform and reorganization. The American Army was near collapse as troops were being withdrawn from Vietnam in the early 1970s, with morale and trust in leadership at a dangerous low. This was one "lesson" that the military took onboard, which can be construed as recognition of responsibility, if not guilt. As for political institutions, President Nixon oversaw the replacement of the draft by a presumably more reliable professional army, and his Vietnamization policy, which turned over full responsibility for the conduct of the war to the South Vietnamese, was recognition that the war could no longer be won. Prior to that, the war had taken its toll on Lyndon Johnson, who did not run for re-election in 1968 as he was thought he certainly would, and his Democratic successor, the inheritor of his Vietnam policies, was defeated by a Republican who campaigned on ending the war and reuniting the country around an "honorable peace." More directly, former Secretary of Defense Robert McNamara, one of the chief architects of the war, came close to apologizing for his "mistakes" with regard to its "tragedy." In his memoir, McNamara wrote, "We were wrong, terribly wrong. We owe it to future generations to explain why" (1995: xx) McNamara acknowledged responsibility and felt remorse, if not guilt, for his ill-placed beliefs and policies. Members of Congress, that branch of the American government most responsive to the public, called for war crimes investigations and set budgetary limits on funding the war. In direct response to the actions of the executive branch, Congress passed the War Powers Act of 1973, limiting the ability of any president to send troops into conflict zones without oversight and prior approval. In these responses, one can detect the trauma of the perpetrator, with stages of denial (from soldiers who wondered how we could win every battle and still call it defeat) to the shifting of blame and responsibility (from military and political leaders who claimed it was the media and the politicians who lost the war) to hurtful retribution (from political leaders and the general public who denied recognition and refuge to those Vietnamese who were allies). All this, more than the so-called Vietnam Syndrome, is an indication of the American trauma regarding the War in Vietnam.

The individuals who perpetrated the My Lai atrocity could claim victimhood with regard to the military and political forces that placed them in that "atrocity producing" situation. This position was not an easily available stance for the public. While deception and manipulation were clearly involved in convincing Americans of the war's necessity, the public bore ultimate responsibility for the war. The claim to public accountability and responsibility is fundamental to the American idea of democracy. As the basis upon which legitimate political action rests, the American people, or at least that segment that votes and pays taxes, bear responsibility for what is done in their name. As Young puts it "the imperative of political responsibility consists in watching these institutions, monitoring their effects to make sure that they are not grossly harmful, and maintaining organized public spaces where such watching and monitoring can occur and citizens can speak publicly and support one another in their efforts to prevent suffering" (2011: 88). For the American public, claiming to be a victim—or merely a bystander—would be hard to sustain given the recorded surveys of support for the war. A vast majority of Americans expressed strong support for the war until the 1968 Tet Offensive, after which that support increasingly turned into open criticism. Recognizing the notion of collective responsibility and guilt as something more than empty rhetoric, the conservative political scientist Guenter Lewy was moved to ask in 1979, four years after the war had ended, "Is American Guilt Justified?" (1989). While Lewy's answer would be "No," the pervasive sense of guilt was, to him, apparent: "The impact of the war on American society was highly damaging ... it has left the country with a tremendous sense of guilt, not only because, in the eyes of many, the entire enterprise was flawed, the war was criminal and immoral" (Lewy 1989: 257). That such questions could even be raised in a public forum, especially by someone supportive of the war, is indicative of the depth of the moral issues the war raised in the American consciousness.

Defeat may have been the key factor in opening the possibility for such questioning beyond the bounds of the antiwar movement and its supporters. The humiliation of defeat, represented so spectacularly in the images of the last days of Saigon and the hasty withdrawal of the last Americans and some of their Vietnamese allies in late April of 1975, brought the issue of guilt and responsibility into everyone's home. Defeat not only affected political and military organizations; it also forced its way into the collective conscience as it threatened the myth of American exceptionalism. A deep sense of betrayal permeated the country, one that emerged from the loss of war after all the rhetoric about its importance and the repeated promises of easy victory. What's more, these feelings were intensified by the ongoing Watergate hearings. The growing distrust in government and in American institutions generally resonated for a time with narratives of collective guilt. Those Vietnamese who allied themselves with the U.S. and who came to identify with the fledgling nation of South Vietnam felt betrayed by the American government—and Richard Nixon in particular. Many Americans, including some of those who fought the war, felt betrayed by their military and political leaders. Some military leaders, such as General Westmoreland, felt betrayed by politicians and policy makers, by the mass media, and the antiwar movement. Such feelings encouraged the shifting of responsibility from oneself and one's group or organization to more abstract others; with no settled center, collective responsibility became difficult to establish. In the end no one knew whom to blame, so those who fought the war became easy targets; by and large, responsibility was eventually attributed to this collectivity, and the public's individually experienced feelings of guilt were thereby largely alleviated.

Coda

The 1968 Tet Offensive changed the way the American press and then the American public viewed the war (Oliver 2006: 26 ff.). As the possibility of defeat became clearer, death and destruction were suddenly visible in a way that they had not been prior to that moment. Despite attempts by the military command, most especially by William Westmoreland, to counter this new awareness by rhetorically propounding the idea of American victory. However, this sea change away from cheerful military optimism was already underway in media reporting and—more importantly—in public opinion. When Westmoreland and Johnson lost control of the discourse, "negotiated settlement" and "honorable withdrawal" became the bywords in official circles, with the once-unthinkable defeat looming at the edges of consciousness. This shift in the public discourse helped create the possibility of My Lai as a traumatic event for American society and intensified its impact. What had been occurring all along—the potentially meaningless death of American soldiers and their part in the killing of Vietnamese civilians—was now suddenly within the public's consciousness. The shift in discourse also impacted what Oliver identifies as the "moral coordinates" of the war (2006: 26). Could the death of American soldiers and Vietnamese civilians so easily be justified with the stakes so drastically changed? Could the ultimate sacrifice be justified in the absence of victory? Who was willing to die to ensure an honorable withdrawal? The effect was to make soldiers more reluctant and at the same time more brutal. The idea of helping others and of being an invited guest aiding an ally evaporated; for the individual combat soldier, it was now more than ever a question of sheer survival. This added to the soldiers' anger and frustration and their sense of being captive in an impossible and morally ambiguous situation.

Could "My Lai" as media event have happened (i.e., Could it have been reported?) pre-Tet? Would it have been visible within the discourse of victory? Probably not. As we now know, numerous other similar incidents, though on a lesser scale, had taken place before Tet and had been passed over in silence within the public sphere (Turse 2013). My Lai was seen only because it had been photographed, and these images were released when the public was more or less ready to view them. My Lai occurred because the perpetrators were out of the military and its culture of silence and group solidarity. It entered public consciousness because American citizens had been prepared by the growing antiwar movement that helped shatter the hegemony of the victory discourse. Tet created My Lai and raised the specter of defeat. With the war's altered "moral coordinates," My Lai became visible and along with it, the understanding that American soldiers could be perpetrators. And all of this added force to claims of collective guilt.

References

Alexander, Jeffrey, Ronald Eyerman, Bernhard Giesen, Neil Smelser, and Piotr Sztompka (eds.). 2004. *Cultural Trauma and Collective Identity*. Berkeley: University of California Press.

Arendt, Hannah. 1963. *Eichmann in Jerusalem*. New York: Viking.

Arendt, Hannah. 2003. *Responsibility and Judgment*. New York: Schocken Books.

Ashenden, Samantha. 2014. The Persistence of Collective Guilt. *Economy and Society* 43 (1): 55–82.

Assmann, Aleida. 2016. *Shadows of Trauma*. New York: Fordham University Press.

Baier, Kurt. 1991. Guilt and Responsibility. In *Collective Responsibility*, ed. Larry May and Stacey Hoffman. Lanham, MD: Rowan & Littlefield.

Bartmanski, Dominik, and Ronald Eyerman. 2013. The Worst Was the Silence: The Unfinished Drama of the Katyn Massacre. In *Narrating Trauma on the Impact of Collective Suffering*, ed. Ronald Eyerman, Jeffrey Alexander, and Elizabeth Breese. Boulder: Paradigm Publishers.

Bauman, Zygmunt. 1989. *Modernity and the Holocaust*. Ithica, NY: Cornell University Press.

Belknap, Michal. 2002. *The Vietnam War on Trial*. Lawrence, KS: Kansas University Press.

Browning, Christopher R. 1998. *Ordinary Men: Reserve Police Battalion 101 and the Final Solution in Poland*. New York: HarperCollins.

Brownmiller, Susan. 1975. *Against Our Will*. New York: Fawcett.

Clark, Janine. 2008. Collective Guilt, Collective Responsibility, and the Serbs. *East European Politics and Societies* 22 (3): 668–692.

Collins, Randall. 2009. *Violence: A Micro Sociological Theory*. Princeton, NJ: Princeton University Press.
Crawford, Neta. 2013. *Accountability for Killing*. Oxford: Oxford University Press.
Dellums, Ronald. 1972. *The Dellums Committee Hearings on War Crimes in Vietnam*. New York: Vintage.
Derwin, Susan. 2016. Moral Injury: Two Perspectives. In *Traumatic Memories of the Second World War and After*, ed. Peter Leese and Jason Crouthamel. New York: Palgrave Macmillan.
Dine, Philip. 1994. *Images of the Algerian War*. Oxford: Oxford University Press.
Ellsberg, Daniel. 2003. *Secrets: A Memoir of Vietnam and the Pentagon Papers*. New York: Penguin.
Eyerman, Ronald, Jeffrey Alexander, and Elizabeth Breese (eds.). 2013. *Narrating Trauma on the Impact of Collective Suffering*. Boulder: Paradigm Publishers.
Falk, Richard. 1989. An Interview with Richard Falk on Vietnam. In *The American Experience in Vietnam: A Reader*, ed. Grace Sevy. Norman, OK: University of Oklahoma Press.
Gibson, James William. 2000. *The Perfect War: Technowar in Vietnam*. New York: Atlantic Monthly Press.
Giesen, Bernhard. 2004. The Trauma of the Perpetrators: The Holocaust as the Traumatic Reference of German National Identity. In *Cultural Trauma and Collective Identity*, ed. Jeffrey Alexander, Ronald Eyerman, Bernhard Giesen, Neil Smelser, and Piotr Sztompka. Berkeley: University of California Press.
Gilligan, James. 2003. Shame, Guilt, and Violence. *Social Research* 70 (4) (Winter): 1149–1180.
Grossman, Dave. 2009. *On Killing*. New York: Back Bay Books.
Halberstram, David. 1965. *The Making of a Quagmire*. New York: Knopf.
Halberstram, David. 1993. *The Best and the Brightest*. New York: Fawcett.
Hashimoto, Akiko. 2013. The Cultural Trauma of a Fallen Nation: Japan 1945. In *Narrating Trauma on the Impact of Collective Suffering*, ed. Ronald Eyerman, Jeffrey Alexander, and Elizabeth Breese. Boulder: Paradigm Publishers.
Heins, Volker, and Andreas Langenohl. 2013. A Fire That Doesn't Burn? The Allied Bombing of Germany and the Cultural Politics of Trauma. In *Narrating Trauma on the Impact of Collective Suffering*, ed. Ronald Eyerman, Jeffrey Alexander, and Elizabeth Breese. Boulder: Paradigm Publishers.
Hersh, Seymour. 1970. *My Lai*. New York: Random House.
Hersh, Seymour. 2015. The Scene of the Crime. *The New Yorker*, March 30: 53–61.
Kolko, Gabriel. 1969. *The Roots of American Foreign Policy*. Boston: Beacon Press.
Kolko, Gabriel. 1994. *Anatomy of a War*. New York: The New Press.

Lewy, Guenter. 1989 [1979]. *The American Experience in Vietnam: A Reader*, ed. Grace Sevy. Norman, OK: University of Oklahoma Press.
Lifton, Robert Jay. 2005. *Home from the War.* New York: Other Press.
Lipstadt, Deborah. 2011. *The Eichmann Trail.* New York: Schocken.
Marlantes, Karl. 2011. *What It Is Like to Go to War.* New York: Atlantic Monthly Press.
May, Larry. 2012. *After War Ends.* Cambridge: Cambridge University Press.
McCarthy, Mary. 1972. *Medina.* New York: Harcourt Brace Jovanovich.
McNamara, Robert. 1995. *In Retrospect.* New York: Times Books.
Morag, Raya. 2013. *Waltzing with Bashir: Perpetrator Trauma and Cinema.* New York: I.B. Tauris.
Morris, David. 2015. *The Evil Hours.* Boston: Houghton Mifflin Harcourt.
O'Brian, Tim. 1991. *The Things They Carried.* London: Flamingo.
Oliver, Kendrick. 2006. *The My Lai Massacre in American History and Memory.* Manchester: Manchester University Press.
Olson, James, and Randy Roberts. 1998. *My Lai: A Brief History with Documents.* Boston: Bedford/St. Martin's Press.
Oppenheimer, Joshua. 2013. *The Act of Killing.* Austin, TX: Draft House Films.
Paquet, Benjamin. 1972. Is Anyone Guilty? If So, Who? *New York Review of Books*, September 21.
Ridenhour, Ron. 1993. Perspective on My Lai: 'It Was a Nazi Kind of Thing'. *Los Angeles Times*, March 16.
Ridenhour, Ron. 1994. *Nobody Gets Off the Bus: The Vietnam Generation Big Book*, Vol. 5, Nos. 1–4.
Ridenhour, Ron. 1997. What We Learned in Vietnam. *In These Times* (PBS Radio), March 3.
Savelsberg, Joachim, and Ryan King. 2011. *American Memories.* New York: Russell Sage Foundation.
Schalk, David. 2005. *War and the Ivory Tower.* Lincoln, NE: University of Nebraska Press.
Scheff, Thomas. 2006. Aggression, Hypermasculine Emotions and Relations. *Irish Journal of Sociology* 15 (1): 24–39.
Sevy, Grace (ed.). 1989. *The American Experience in Vietnam: A Reader.* Norman, OK: University of Oklahoma Press.
Shatan, Chaim. 1973. The Grief of Soldiers: Vietnam Combat Veterans' Self-Help Movement. *American Journal of Orthopsychiatry* 43 (4): 640–652.
Shay, Jonathan. 1994. *Achilles in Vietnam.* New York: Scribner.
Shay, Jonathan. 2003. *Odysseus in America.* New York: Scribner.
Sheehan, Neil. 1971. Should We Have War Crimes Trials? *New York Times Book Review*, March 28.
Sheehan, Neil. 1989. *A Bright Shining Lie.* New York: Vintage.
Sherman, Nancy. 2015. *Afterwar.* New York: Oxford University Press.

Singer, Mel. 2004. Shame, Guilt, Self-Hatred, and Remorse in the Psychotherapy of Vietnam Combat Veterans Who Committed Atrocities. *American Journal of Psychotherapy* 58 (4): 377–385.
Spector, Ronald. 1992. *After Tet: The Bloodiest Year in Vietnam*. New York: Free Press.
Stacewicz, Richard. 1997. *Winter Soldier: An Oral History*. Chicago: Twayne.
Taylor, Telford. 1970. *Nuremburg and Vietnam*. Chicago: Quadrangle Books.
Turse, Nick. 2013. *Kill Anything That Moves*. New York: Picador.
Walzer, Michael. 1977. *Just and Unjust Wars*. New York: Basic Books.
Weaver, Gina. 2010. *Ideologies of Forgetting Rape in the Vietnam War*. Albany, NY: SUNY Press.
Young, Iris Marion. 2011. *Responsibility for Justice*. Oxford: Oxford University Press.

CHAPTER 9

Conclusion: Ron Eyerman and the Study of Cultural Trauma

Eric Taylor Woods

Ron Eyerman observes in the introduction to this book that the study of cultural trauma has now reached the status of a research paradigm. The speed at which this has occurred is remarkable. As Eyerman notes, it was only in 1999 that he and his collaborators (Alexander, Giesen, Smelser, and Sztompka) first embarked on research into cultural trauma. Nearly twenty years on, it is timely to reflect upon the findings and achievements of this new research paradigm. Eyerman's *oeuvre* is a good place to start. As his prolific output attests, he has remained an important driver of research on cultural trauma. Through close reading of his works, we can therefore gain valuable insights about his development, as well as the field more generally. In this short essay I review Eyerman's contribution to the study of cultural trauma, paying particular attention to his approach and methodology. To do so I refer especially to the works collected in this book.

Looking across Eyerman's body of work on cultural trauma, one thing that immediately stands out is his willingness to adapt, to let theory evolve in relation to research. This is especially evident in the evolution of his approach. In the landmark 2004 book that Eyerman

Adapted from "Cultural Trauma: Ron Eyerman and the Construction of a New Research Paradigm," forthcoming in *American Journal of Cultural Sociology*.

The original version of this chapter was revised: Chapter author information have been corrected. The correction to this chapter is available at
https://doi.org/10.1007/978-3-030-13507-2_10

R. Eyerman, *Memory, Trauma, and Identity*, Cultural Sociology,
https://doi.org/10.1007/978-3-030-13507-2_9

(see Alexander et al. 2004) jointly published, his co-authors Jeffrey Alexander and Neil Smelser put forward a program of research emphasizing above all that cultural traumas are socially constructed. In contrast with conventional realist approaches, such as Arthur Neal's (1998) analysis of the impact of several traumatic events in American history, they suggested that analyses should focus on how certain events become *represented* as traumatic, rather than assume that they are by their very nature inherently traumatic. To uncover how this process occurs, Alexander argues that researchers should focus on the ontological "gap between event and representation" (2004: 11). It is within this gap that the process of cultural trauma can be found, typically expressed as an agonistic struggle over the meaning of an event, in which key social actors performatively seek to convey their intended meanings. Interestingly, although Eyerman has remained broadly committed to this proposition, his work nevertheless belies an increasing acknowledgment that, depending on the contexts in which they occur, certain events are inherently so shocking or upsetting that they should also be seen to play a part in how they are represented.

Eyerman's approach has taken shape over the course of his research. In his study of slavery and African American identity in Chapter 2, Eyerman focuses on the collective memory of slavery rather than slavery as such, thereby adhering relatively closely to a strong constructionist approach. However, in Eyerman's subsequent works on political assassination (Chapter 4; see also Eyerman 2008, 2011), the event itself takes on more importance. Here Eyerman finds that the way in which assassinations are performed have bearing on how they are represented. Later, in an analysis of the Katyn Massacre in Chapter 6, Eyerman and Bartmanski suggest even more strongly that the inherent nature of an event can have bearing on its representation. Despite a decades-long attempt by Soviet authorities to control the meaning of the mass killings of thousands of Polish officers and citizens in 1940, Eyerman and Bartmanski show how families and friends privately held on to their own interpretations, such that once Soviet power began to weaken, demands for a public airing of the truth arose, and the Katyn Massacre subsequently became represented as a national trauma. Reading this essay, it seems unlikely that the massacre would have continued to exert such enduring power in the face of state repression if it had not been such a terrible event in and of itself. The nature of the event also looms large in Eyerman's essay on collective responsibility and the Vietnam War in Chapter 8. Here again, the act of mass killing—in this case, the massacre perpetrated by American soldiers at My Lai in 1968—is so horrific that when it becomes known, certain meanings seem to be unavoidably associated with it. In Eyerman's analysis, the process of cultural trauma therefore does not result from a confrontation over the meaning of My Lai per se, but rather it results from a confrontation over who is responsible. In all these recent studies, there is a sense that for Eyerman, processes of social construction are clearly important, but the reality of certain events matter, too. In turn, this suggests that only certain kinds of events can trigger a cultural trauma. If there is a continuum between Alexander's constructionism and Neal's realism, Eyerman's current approach can be found somewhere near the midpoint.

Another significant development in Eyerman's approach to cultural trauma is the growing significance of emotion. In Eyerman's analyses, social actors involved in a cultural trauma process are often shown to have been deeply affected by the potentially traumatic event. They are not distant "cultural entrepreneurs," coolly seeking to ensure that the meaning of the event is constructed in a way that best suits their interests. Rather, according to Eyerman, it is their emotional response to the event that drives them to act. Thus, in Chapter 4, Eyerman shows how Harvey Milk became embedded in American collective memory in large part because of the outpouring of grief that his assassination unleashed within the San Francisco gay community, thousands of whom marched in his memory. Later, after Milk's killer Dan White was perceived to have been treated too leniently by the criminal justice system, thousands took the streets once again, this time acting out of anger and dismay, in what is known as the "white night riots." Eyerman finds that even efforts to have Milk memorialized were driven by individuals who *felt* that his death must not be forgotten. According to Eyerman, they were motivated by a deep sense of injustice, not just on Milk's behalf, but also on behalf of the gay community as a whole.

The increasing significance in Eyerman's work of the particular types of events that are involved in a cultural trauma, and the emotions that these events unleash, has helped to flesh out what is distinctive about a cultural trauma in relation to other kinds of processes of social construction. In a recent definition, Eyerman writes that a cultural trauma is a

> discursive process, resulting from extreme violence and exposing the deep emotional base that grounds individual and collective identity, cultural trauma is both an articulation/representation of this emotional grounding and at the same time a working-through, a searching attempt at collective repair. (2012)

It is notable that Eyerman specifies in this definition that cultural traumas result from "extreme violence" and that they seem to be driven primarily by emotions. In addition to helping to specify what a cultural trauma is, these key points point to a potentially fruitful new direction in its study.

But perhaps Eyerman's most important contribution to the study of cultural trauma is his effort to situate it within the broader field of collective memory. By extension, this has shed light on the relationship between cultural trauma and collective identity. To return to his study of African American identity (Chapter 2), Eyerman demonstrates how slavery was embedded in the collective memory black Americans and became an indelible, unavoidable point of reference in expressions of collective identity. Despite the passage of time, Eyerman observes that each new generation of black intellectuals who sought to articulate a novel sense of collective identity was made to confront the meaning of slavery. The fact that slavery constitutes a cultural trauma for African Americans is therefore evidenced by its indelibility, by the seeming impossibility of reconstructing a "post-slavery" collective identity. Interestingly, Eyerman's arguments in this regard imply that cultural traumas are not only agonistic, but also a source of solidarity. Thus, even though Eyerman finds deep divisions among intellectuals over the meaning of slavery, the fact that it is embedded in collective memory more broadly helps to ensure that African American identity endures. In other words, the memory of slavery both divides *and* unifies. Although this point about the dual nature of cultural trauma is implied rather than expressly argued by Eyerman, it is a critical insight emerging from his work, one that demands more study.

Eyerman's subsequent works on political assassination uncover further insights on the relationship between cultural trauma and collective memory. In this regard, Eyerman shows that cultural traumas rarely occur *ex nihilo*. Rather, they more likely occur in a social order that has been periodically riven by cultural traumas throughout its history. According to Eyerman, the ways in which these past cultural traumas were incorporated into collective memory will have bearing on subsequent cultural traumas. Thus, Eyerman (2008) shows how the cultural trauma that was triggered by the assassination of van Gogh was partly structured by memories of the treatment of Jews during German occupation, the loss of Dutch colonies, and even the Dutch military's ineffectual response to the murder of Muslims in Srebrenica in 1995. Dutch collective identity in this analysis thus appears as a patchwork of past cultural traumas, many of which remain highly divisive.

Moving now from approach to method, Eyerman's case studies increasingly reflect his call (2008: 23) for the importance of "thick explanation." This can be understood as a call to incorporate as many relevant perspectives into analysis as possible. In this regard, Eyerman's analyses of cultural trauma are remarkably multidimensional. His studies of the impact of political assassination exemplify thick explanation (see Chapter 4). Through a careful biographical reconstruction, Eyerman begins by seeking to understand the meanings that were intended by the perpetrators of the assassinations, which he connects to the social, economic, and political contexts in which the assassinations were performed. Eyerman then moves outward to include the often-contradictory responses of various social actors who make use of their relative access to social power and resources to partake in public debates over the meaning of the event. Following Alexander (2004), Eyerman refers to these social actors as "carrier groups." For Eyerman, carrier groups can include a broad range of professions, such as academics, artists, authors, journalists, photographers, filmmakers, and many others. Among these groups, the most important in Eyerman's analysis is the mass media, and he therefore pays particular attention to how various segments of the media report upon the event. Finally, Eyerman adds a historical perspective by investigating how the responses of these various groups are structured by past cultural traumas, which might have been partially resolved, but which remain sources of potential conflict.

In order to interpret all these perspectives, Eyerman integrates narrative analysis into his methodology. In Eyerman's hands, the process of cultural trauma is cast as a struggle over how an event should be narrated—it is, in other words, a struggle over competing stories about an event. For example, in his comparative study of how the Vietnam War is remembered by Vietnamese communists, Vietnamese Americans, and the broader American society, Eyerman (along with his co-authors Madigan and Ring) focuses on the different ways in which the war is narrated by each collectivity (see Chapter 7). The use of narrative analysis also enables Eyerman to connect seemingly disparate individual narratives about an event to more established narratives. This, in turn, helps Eyerman to identify patterns of potentially competing narratives. For example, in his study of African American identity in Chapter 2, Eyerman suggests that individual representations of identity tend to align with either a progressive or tragic narrative of the meaning of slavery, and the struggle over the meaning of slavery is thus framed as a binary between these two narratives. Eyerman also makes use of narrative analysis to demonstrate how broad societal divisions can structure the emergence of conflicting narratives regarding the meaning of a potentially traumatic event. In his analysis of the struggle over collective responsibility for the My Lai Massacre in Chapter 8, Eyerman demonstrates how the responses of various social actors, include the military, and Lieutenant Calley (who stood trial for the massacre), were connected to societal divisions in the U.S. about how the Vietnam War should be narrated.

A key theme of this review has been Eyerman's openness to change. We have seen how a succession of new projects has led to an evolution in his approach and methodology. This process looks set to continue. For example, Eyerman's essay on the role of intellectuals in a cultural trauma in Chapter 3 hints at two new directions he might take next. First, Eyerman comments on the significance of trials in a cultural trauma. He observes that not only do meaning struggles associated with a cultural trauma occur within a courtroom, but that the decisions made during and at the conclusion of a trial can have bearing on the trajectory of the wider cultural trauma process. This is an important insight and it is surprising that there has not yet been a study of cultural trauma that specifically focuses on trials, given that cultural traumas almost always involve questions of justice. It seems that there is a glaring research gap vis-à-vis the relationship between the formal institution of the courts and cultural trauma processes. Second, Eyerman includes in the same chapter a discussion of the implications of the rise of the internet, a phenomenon that has enabled many more people to participate in public life than previously. As Eyerman observes, anyone with a blog could potentially be labeled a "public intellectual." This suggests that analyses of cultural trauma should move beyond conventional carrier groups to include ordinary people who come to the fore in a cultural trauma process through the use of new media. Eyerman also points out that new media technologies blur the distinction between producer and consumer. Much research on cultural trauma has taken a "top-down" approach, focusing on meaning struggles among traditional cultural producers, such as the mass media. However, if ordinary people can also now be conceived as cultural producers, it is surely possible that a cultural trauma could emerge from a bottom-up process through online networks of small-scale producers.

In "Social Theory and Cultural Trauma" (Chapter 5), Eyerman undertakes an aesthetic analysis of several important texts in social theory. Much like analyses of fiction, Eyerman seeks to uncover meanings associated with these texts, rather than engage with their arguments. It seems fitting to conclude this review of Eyerman's work with a similar exercise. What kind of narratives underlie Eyerman's analyses of cultural trauma? As I noted earlier in this essay, in his essay on African American identity, Eyerman uncovers two leading narratives of slavery among intellectuals: a progressive narrative and a tragic narrative. The former looks to a better future; it is a story achieving redemption by overcoming suffering. The latter denies the possibility of a better future; it suggests that suffering will not be overcome. Eyerman's analyses of cultural trauma do not convey a progressive narrative. Rather, they conform more closely to a tragic narrative. In Eyerman's works, there is ultimately no escape from a cultural trauma, no progression to a better place. The searing emotions associated with a cultural trauma might lessen, but they do not completely disappear. Eyerman often uses metaphors borrowed from physical trauma, likening a cultural trauma to an open wound within a community. According to Eyerman, even if the wound heals, the community will remain scarred. And for Eyerman, there is always a chance that those scars can become enflamed and torn open again. A community might be transformed by a cultural trauma, but it does not progress.

References

Alexander, Jeffrey. 2004. Toward a Theory of Cultural Trauma. In *Cultural Trauma and Collective Identity*, ed. Jeffrey Alexander, Ronald Eyerman, Bernhard Giesen, Neil Smelser, and Piotr Sztompka. Berkeley: University of California Press.

Alexander, Jeffrey, Ronald Eyerman, Bernhard Giesen, Neil Smelser, and Piotr Sztompka (eds.). 2004. *Cultural Trauma and Collective Identity*. Berkeley: University of California Press.

Eyerman, Ronald. 2008. *The Assassination of Theo van Gogh: From Social Drama to Cultural Trauma*. Durham, NC: Duke University Press.

Eyerman, Ronald. 2011. *The Cultural Sociology of Political Assassination*. New York: Palgrave Macmillan.

Eyerman, Ronald. 2012. Cultural Trauma: Emotion and Narration. In *The Oxford Handbook of Cultural Sociology*, ed. Jeffrey Alexander, Ronald Jacobs, and Philip Smith. New York: Oxford University Press.

Neal, Arthur G. 1998. *National Trauma and Collective Memory: Major Events in the American Century*. Armonk, NY: M.E. Sharpe.

Correction to: Conclusion: Ron Eyerman and the Study of Cultural Trauma

Correction to:
Chapter 9 in R. Eyerman, *Memory, Trauma, and Identity*, Cultural Sociology, https://doi.org/10.1007/978-3-030-13507-2_9

The original version of the chapter has been revised with the following corrections:

Conclusion for this book was contributed by another author "Eric Taylor Woods", but it shows as authored by Ron Eyerman (the book's author). So the author information in the Chapter 9 has been changed to "Eric Taylor Woods" with email id "e.t.woods@uel.ac.uk" and affiliation "University of East London, UK".

The final corrections have been incorporated.

The updated version of this chapter can be found at
https://doi.org/10.1007/978-3-030-13507-2_9

R. Eyerman, *Memory, Trauma, and Identity*, Cultural Sociology,
https://doi.org/10.1007/978-3-030-13507-2_10

Index

R. Eyerman, *Memory, Trauma, and Identity*, Cultural Sociology,
https://doi.org/10.1007/978-3-030-13507-2

The manufacturer's authorised representative in the EU is Springer Nature Customer Service Centre GmbH, Europaplatz 3, 69115 Heidelberg, Germany. If you have any concerns regarding our products, please contact ProductSafety@springernature.com

Printed and bound by CPI Group (UK) Ltd, Croydon, CR0 4YY
30/09/2026
02225442-0003